THE UTAH UFO DISPLAY

A Scientist Brings Reason and
Logic to Over 400 UFO Sightings
in Utah's Uintah Basin

FRANK B. SALISBURY, PhD

In collaboration with and based upon the
files of Joseph Junior Hicks

A Scientist Brings Reason and
Logic to Over 400 UFO Sightings
in Utah's Uintah Basin

FRANK B. SALISBURY, PhD

In collaboration with and based upon the
files of Joseph Junior Hicks

Bonneville
Springville, Utah

© 2010 Frank B. Salisbury
First published © 1974 Frank B. Salisbury by Devin-Adair Publishing Company

ISBN 13: 978-1-59955-405-1

Published by Bonneville Books, an imprint of Cedar Fort, Inc., 2373 W. 700 S., Springville, UT 84663
Distributed by Cedar Fort, Inc., www.cedarfort.com

LIBRARY OF CONGRESS CATALOGING-IN-PUBLICATION DATA

Salisbury, Frank B.
     The Utah UFO display : a scientist's report / Frank B. Salisbury ; with Joseph Junior Hicks. -- [2nd ed.].
        p. cm.
     Includes bibliographical references.
     ISBN 978-1-59955-405-1 (alk. paper)
     1. Unidentified flying objects--Sightings and encounters--Utah. I. Hicks, Joseph Junior. II. Title.

TL789.8.U5S25 2010
001.942--dc22

                                      2010005456

Cover design by Megan Whittier
Cover design © 2010 by Lyle Mortimer
Edited and typeset by Heidi Doxey

10 9 8 7 6 5 4 3 2

Dedicated to

The Uintah Basin UFO Watchers

Contents

Foreword to the
First Edition

It is both refreshing and rewarding to find a treatment of the tremendously fascinating subject of Unidentified Flying Objects (UFOs) by one who has a keen understanding of the scientific method. "One doesn't believe in UFOs," the author writes, "one simply seeks the truth about UFOs, forming tentative conclusions as one goes along."

In my long experience with the UFO phenomenon, the question, "Do you believe in UFOs?" has never ceased to irritate me. UFOs should neither be a matter of our blind faith (which the word "believe" implies) nor of our blind skepticism. Like any other entrant to the "playing field of science," the UFO phenomenon should be asked to show its credentials. What are the facts? Can they be tested, intercompared?

A growing number of established scientists—particularly those associated with the newly created Center for UFO Studies—feel that the subject of UFOs is eminently worthy of scientific study. Frank Salisbury is one of these. First off, in the true spirit of science, he does not "take sides." He avoids becoming emotionally entangled with the subject and thus losing objectivity. He approaches the subject of UFOs in the same manner he would approach interesting phenomena in his own field of biology. He is aware that the UFO phenomenon—whatever its causes—is far more complex than is generally felt. It appears to have both physical and psychic components and it is with this awareness that Dr. Salisbury engages the problem.

In a relatively remote region in Utah—the Uintah Basin—there occurred, mostly in 1966–67, a remarkable series of UFO sightings. They represent a sort of microcosm of sightings in the total universe of UFO sightings from countries all over the world. By and large, they are representative of the UFO phenomenon, exhibiting many of the patterns of UFO sightings familiar to students of the subject. Dr. Salisbury, a native of Utah and long interested in the UFO phenomenon, chose to study and examine the Utah sightings as a definite body of data, much as a biologist might select for study the flora and fauna of a given geographical region.

So, first we have in this book a well-documented account of UFO data which fully deserve to be put into the record and which might otherwise have been lost. But this book is far more than a telling of Utah UFO stories, as exciting as they are in themselves. Dr. Salisbury goes beyond the mere telling of "incredible tales told by credible persons" and is concerned with the paradoxes presented by the UFO phenomenon: the apparent intelligent control exhibited (certainly the reported motions are not random, for example) contrasted with the unintelligibility (to our minds at least) of the recorded actions of UFOs. He wonders, "Is it some sort of camouflage?" "Is there method in their madness?"

The author objectively examines the UFO data in the context of modern science and is not afraid to come to grips with various UFO hypotheses. The hypothesis of extraterrestrial intelligence is, of course, one of these. But he does not feel that, just because the truly puzzling UFO cases do not fit in our present scientific picture, this must mean that UFOs are the product of some very remote, highly developed intragalactic intelligence. His unbiased handling of the pros and cons of the UFO enigma is admirable.

I would suggest to the reader if the presentation of raw data in the first section of the book becomes too mind-boggling or intoxicating—as a barrage of one seemingly incredible tale after another often will—that he temporarily skip to the discussion sections and then come back to further consider the raw data. One or two repetitions of this process will prove rewarding as it keeps both the data and the speculation about the data in perspective.

Should the reader be only newly acquainted with the UFO subject, let me assure him on two points: first, that the reported happenings in the Uintah Basin, as incredible as they seem, are no more so than UFO reports from any other parts of the world, and second, that the witnesses to the UFO sightings pass all normal tests of credibility. I had the opportunity in the summer of 1972 to spend some time with Mr. Joseph Junior Hicks and tour with him some of the sites discussed in this book. I interviewed several of the witnesses to the sightings and found them highly credible. I discovered no reason to indicate that, on the whole, their statements would not indeed represent the facts of the Uintah Basin UFO sightings. Like so very many witnesses I have interviewed in the past two decades, they are people whose testimony in any other circumstances would surely be accepted in a court of law.

Dr. Salisbury's comprehensive grasp of the complexities of the subject keeps him from incautiously "buying" any theory—even the popular but perhaps too simple hypothesis of visitors from distant solar systems. Though the UFO phenomenon itself exhibits seemingly intelligent behavior, one can still say, "Intelligence—yes, but whose?"

Whether new to the subject or long familiar with it, the reader will, I believe, welcome this book as a positive addition to the authoritative literature on UFOs.

[The Late] Dr. J. Allen Hynek
Chairman, Astronomy Department
Northwestern University

1974

Preface

    This book is about strange goings-on, mostly related to UFO activity, in the northeastern part of Utah called the Uintah Basin. What are we to make of such far-out happenings? Most mainstream scientists today reject them out of hand. They assume that these apparitions are something to do with stars or planets or maybe weather balloons, which a witness sees but cannot explain—or maybe they are tricks of the mind, if not out-and-out lies. These scientists even quote, as evidence for the abominable state of science-understanding in our country, polls that show that over half of the population "believes in" UFOs. How stupid people must be, they imply! But these scientists and other skeptics who dismiss the UFO phenomenon usually have no idea just how complex and extensive the phenomenon is.

    True, a few confirmed skeptics have studied the UFO data in detail but still reject the UFOs. Most scientists, however—those who do not know much about what is going on as well as those who do—hang up right at the phrase: believe in UFOs. In today's world, that phrase has connotations first of blind faith and second of humanoid beings visiting Earth in spaceships from other solar systems and studying us and our planet by taking samples of soil, plants, and so forth. After all, interstellar distances are simply too great to allow space travel in anything like reasonable times, the skeptic says.

    But visitors in spaceships flying here from other worlds (the "Extra-Terrestrial" or ET hypothesis) is only one theory to account for the UFO phenomenon, and by now I have pretty much rejected it, as I'll hint at throughout this edition and explain as best I can in the Epilogue. When I wrote the first edition of this book, I was already leaning toward rejecting the ET hypothesis, and now that is where I firmly stand. But I don't have a truly comprehensive theory to replace it, and that is the challenge to science. Let's be clear, however; in my mind there is no longer room for doubt about the reality of the UFOs—it's just that we are not sure what they are. As seems obvious, some might be machines with highly advanced technology, but others might not be quite that simple.

As we'll see, the ideas upon which most skeptics reject the UFO phenomenon just don't get the job done. Instead, their rejection depends heavily upon "just-suppose stories," a phrase that I'll overuse in this edition because I think it describes the situation so well. The skeptics' total rejection of the phenomenon depends to a very great extent upon suggestions about what might have happened: "You think you saw a spaceship, but just suppose that what you really saw was a weather balloon with the sun reflecting on it." Robert Frost said it nicely: "We dance round in a ring and suppose, but the Secret sits in the middle and knows . . . ." Any understanding of the phenomenon in all its richness requires much more than supposing, which is again the challenge to science. First, a scientist needs to become aware of the whole story: the UFO evidence. Then, if many millions of sightings and interactions with the UFOs can be explained in conventional terms, this scientist must explain them in a way that really fits our modern understanding of the universe! Pure guesses, regardless of how well contrived, just won't cut it. Or if that proves impossible, the scientist should admit that he has no explanation.

The UFO phenomenon challenges more than contemporary science—in many cases, it seems to challenge our sanity. We wonder if someone who gives a report that goes well beyond what seems logical must be crazy, or if we are crazy for even considering that it might be true. In many cases, the witness and the report have all the credentials of an account of a real event. Even the skeptic will admit that the witness truly believes what he is reporting (except for a few deliberate hoaxes). And in virtually all of the reports in this book the event was experienced while the witness was wide awake and perfectly conscious of his surroundings—not in some kind of hypnotic trance (which is indeed an important part of modern ufology—but of which I am almost as skeptical as the skeptic, as we'll see in Chapter 6). Yet the accounts, even those given as solid memories formed while the witness was conscious of what was going on, typically contain elements that truly challenge our current understanding of how the universe works.

Shouldn't that be of great interest to science, which exists to find understanding of how our universe works? Things are going on that simply do not fit the understanding of educated people, including scientists. Shouldn't that catch the attention of a truly curious person, especially a scientist? In many cases, the explanations, if found, could give us startling new insights into this strange universe. Why should a scientist or other skeptic think that, first and foremost, all such things should be debunked?

There are two aspects to the challenge to science: First, can we understand UFOs within the bounds of our understanding of the physical universe—and, second, if not, how can we understand them? In Chapters 1 and 2, I will present a body of data: the Uintah Basin interviews that were published in the first edition of this book. These were based on the files of Joseph Junior Hicks, a retired science teacher who lives in Roosevelt, right in the center of the Basin. Other interviews were obtained in 2009, and I'll summarize them at the end of Chapter 1. Most of the new interviews are included in later chapters, however, because they illustrate some point I'm trying to make. Chapter 2 examines the characteristics of the interviews, mostly the old ones but with some reference to the new ones. Chapters 3 to 7 address the challenge to science by examining UFO sightings (both in and outside of the Basin) in light of attempts to understand them as natural or man-made phenomena, lies or hoaxes, secret government projects, psychological manifestations, or vehicles from other planetary systems that have worlds supporting advanced civilizations. You'll see that all these approaches encounter formidable problems; some aspects of UFO activity seem to defy even the most reasonable laws of physics as we understand them.

Throughout this report you'll encounter cases that might make you question your sanity! I'll emphasize some of them in Chapter 7, and in the whole of Chapter 8 I'll discuss an example, taken from a ranch right in the middle of the Uintah Basin, that nicely illustrates both the challenges to science and the challenges to our sanity.

Finally, in the Epilogue, I'll speculate about how future science might open areas that will lead to understanding—but I must admit that such is now only in the realm of speculation. You'll also see that some of the UFO evidence has much in common with religious experiences that go back through history—or, in the case of my own theology, are relatively recent.

In case some readers are unaware of the background of the UFO phenomenon, I will review it in the Prologue. But the majority of this book has been written to report on and speculate about several dozen UFO cases from the Uintah Basin of Utah. But as Dr. Hynek noted in his foreword, written many years ago, it can be a bit mind-boggling to encounter one interview after another for page after page. Furthermore, with the new material added to this edition, the length was getting out of hand. Although I fought with myself to keep the full interviews, it became apparent that I would have to summarize the stories, presenting only significant parts of the interviews. Having done that, it is clear that the book is now much easier to read. But if a true ufologist wants to see the full interviews, I have them and would be happy to furnish them via email. (See my website www.casefordivinedesign.com for more details.)

To assess the current status of Utah UFO watching, I have spent a few days with Joseph Junior Hicks in the Uintah Basin and much time on the telephone. Over the years, his files of cases from the area have grown to include at least 400 sightings, and some of these were very recent. UFO activity on the ranch described in Chapter 8 took place in the second half of the 1990s, continuing at some level to the present. (Apparently, as I'll explain, the owners are studying the phenomena now but not divulging any of their findings to the rest of us!)

Because I want to turn immediately to the Uintah Basin sightings in Chapter 1, I have limited my review of the broad UFO field to the Prologue—which is aimed at readers who are not familiar with the field. UFO buffs might want to just skim the Prologue—except for a few comments about my personal story, which might help in evaluating my many speculations. There is an annotated bibliography at the end of the book. Any book or article referred to in this volume (by author's name and year of publication) is in that list.

Checking Amazon.com, I found that there is still demand for copies of the first edition. Hence, the basic format of this edition is based on the first version, and I have retained what I considered to be the most valuable parts of the original. Speaking of the first edition, I had forgotten how many people read the manuscript of the first edition! These are listed at the end of the following section. Other talented people have helped with this edition: Ted Bonnitt, Ray Alvey, my son Frank Clark Salisbury, Lee Nelson, and Junior Hicks read and commented on the manuscript. Parts were also read by James Carrion, Elaine Douglass, Mary T. Salisbury,

Steven Salisbury, Blake Salisbury, Michael Salisbury, Cynthia Koerner, and Michael Van Wagenen.

F. B. S.
Salt Lake City, Utah
May 2010

Excerpts Modified from the Preface to the First Edition

There seems to be two ways to go about a scientific approach to UFOs. First, one needs to become as intimately acquainted with the available data—the UFO reports—as time and abilities will allow. Then, one must apply scientific thought to the data. Often there is little opportunity to use the details of one's speciality in UFO investigation. Seldom does plant physiology, my own field, have much to offer, for example. But science is a method, not a collection of information. Objective data are assembled (the reports are subjective, but they may be treated objectively), hypotheses are formulated and tested by new observations and by comparison with existing scientific knowledge, and finally the results of this combination of experience and logic are published. This is done in plant physiology as well as in any other science, and it ought to work with UFOs.

A scientist who would study unidentified flying objects must consider several possible consequences. Future historians of science, if they ever happen to worry about his UFO investigations, may well class this scientist with the alchemists or the defenders of phlogiston (a postulated substance to account for oxidation). On the other hand, they may class him with the scientific greats who had the prophetic foresight to realize that some phenomenon, though not fully understood at the time, contained the seeds of discoveries that would profoundly remold the future of mankind. Furthermore, this scientist will not only find it difficult to apply his scientific training to a study of UFOs, but he will probably be surrounded by controversy. Fanatical believers in salvation through our big brothers from space will pester the scientist for not "accepting the obvious," while sarcastic comments in the news media, and even from his fellow scientists, will imply that he must be a little off his rocker to consider the possibility that UFOs might have anything but a perfectly "natural" explanation (whatever that is).

So why bother? Well, to begin with, there just isn't anything in the rules of science that describes what one may or may not study. Science is a way of applying logical procedures to objective data to arrive at true conclusions about how nature works. There are some areas of endeavor (e.g., religion, philosophy) in which this is extremely difficult to do because of the paucity of objective data. Since this is somewhat true in the UFO field, it is the assignment of the UFO scientist (called a ufologist) to decide what are objective data and what is subjective interpretation. This is not an easy task (often it may be impossible), but the potential consequences of the study are so significant, and difficult science can be so challenging, that some of us make the attempt.

Besides, a UFO scientist isn't really in danger of losing his scientific soul (or reputation!). If he is honest and objective in his efforts and approach, there should be no reason to lose the respect of his friends in science. This can happen in any field of science when a person says he knows something to be true, yet presents data that his colleagues feel do not support his conviction. So let the reader be forewarned that any "conclusions" of this book are to be considered as tentative and based upon what currently seems to be the most logical way to look at the available data. I stand ready at any time—as the reader must also—to change any given "conclusion" in light of future data or logic. One doesn't believe in UFOs; one simply seeks for the truth about UFOs, forming tentative conclusions as one goes along.

Actually, the scientific climate for UFO study never was as harsh as one might be led to believe. I have yet to experience real ridicule from my colleagues. Furthermore, the public remains reasonably open-minded in spite of much debunking from official and media sources.

Many people have provided wonderful help with the manuscript: Patricia Hagius [my secretary at Utah State University] did a marvelous job with the original manuscript, not only typing several revisions, but chasing down references and specific information on the telephone and in the library—and often on her own time. Nancy Williams has done the same with this version, and her skill in the finishing of photographs is also especially appreciated. Jan Luque helped during the final manuscript stages. The original or final manuscript was read and criticized by J. R. Allred, Frank Brooks, Jack Carey, Janice Devine, Devin Garrity, Stewart Nixon, Leo Sprinkle, Jacques Vallée, Steven Wolfe, Richard Greenwell, and Coral and James Lorenzen. The last three were kind enough to provide, at my request, numerous bits of information from the files of the

Aerial Phenomena Research Organization in Tucson, Arizona. Virginia Lott and Tricia A. Hawes volunteered much help with last-minute additions and to them, also, I am most grateful.

F. B. S.

Logan and Roosevelt, Utah

April 1974

Prologue
Some History

The modern era of UFOs, in which the extraterrestrial spaceship became the predominant theme of interpretation, began in the United States in 1947. The wave of sightings during that period first came to public attention because of the report of Kenneth Arnold, a fire equipment salesman from Boise, Idaho. On June 24, Arnold was flying his private plane on a business trip when he decided to assist in the search for a downed plane on the slopes of Mt. Rainier in the state of Washington. As he approached the mountain from the west side, his eye was caught by a flash as from a mirror. He looked around for other aircraft and saw to his left, north of Mt. Rainier, a chainlike formation of nine brightly scintillating, disc-shaped objects rapidly approaching the mountain on a roughly southern course. He estimated that the objects were stretched out in a step-down formation about five miles long. They were many miles away from him. He clocked their speed between Mt. Rainier and Mt. Adams as they flew erratically, swerving in and out of the lesser peaks. Occasionally they would slip from side to side in unison, flashing brightly as they did. The fifty-mile distance between the two mountains was covered in one minute and forty-two seconds, indicating a speed of 1,700 miles per hour. Even allowing for miscalculations, he was certain that their speed exceeded 1,000 miles per hour.

Arnold landed in Yakima and told his story, generating considerable interest. The story preceded him to Pendleton, Oregon, where he was met by a platoon of reporters. His reputation, experience as a pilot, and careful calculations changed the highly skeptical attitude of the reporters to one of keen interest. The story appeared in newspapers all over the country. It contained the term "flying saucer," which has been with us ever since, although it is now more common to speak of UFOs—unidentified flying objects (which are not necessarily flying!).

No one was able to provide an explanation for the Arnold sighting, and indeed, none has become apparent in the ensuing years—although several have been presented. (It is suggested, for example, that Arnold saw a mirage in which the tips of the peaks on the horizon appeared, because of a layer of warm air, to be suspended above the mountains. But how could this account for the rapid motion to the south in front of and behind the peaks?)

With the publication of Arnold's story, many similar ones began to appear. A few of these were carried widely in the press, but the majority appeared only in local newspapers. Ted Bloecher (1967) studied the UFO wave of 1947. Most investigators were aware of only one or two dozen sightings for that summer, but Bloecher documents 853. Of these sightings, 546 occurred in the daytime, with 231 at night and 76 unspecified. There were 468 reports of single objects and 363 reports of multiple objects similar to Arnold's (with 22 not specified). Some 3,283 witnesses were involved! Activity reached its peak between July 4 and July 8, with more than 160 on July 7. A few occurred as early as May, but very few occurred after July 13. (And if they were only ploys for attention, why should they stop so suddenly at the peak of public interest?) Undoubtedly, many sightings went unreported. I know of one!

While working on the first edition of this book, I learned from my wife that her uncle Earl Page, his wife, Beaulah, and their then six-year-old son, Ronald, had a sighting during this period. I wrote him for details. His flight log provided the date of July 12, 1947 at 2:30 PM Pacific Standard Time. The three of them were flying a light plane from Las Vegas, Nevada, to Salt Lake City, Utah. Over Utah Lake, a formation of disc-shaped objects approached their plane from the front, passing to the right. Mr. Page felt that they may have been as close as fifty feet, but he was quite aware of the impossibility of estimating distances accurately under such circumstances. He banked the plane sharply in pursuit of the objects only to see them disappear rapidly in the distance. The Pages experienced an overwhelming emotional reaction, including nausea, to this completely strange experience. The Pages made no official report of their sighting, which is typical, and indeed they told no one after experiencing the initial skeptical reaction of a few friends and relatives. Yet, except for the estimates of speed and distance, their sighting was better than that of Arnold—much closer, with more than one witness.

Beginning in early July of 1947, people began reporting UFOs around the town of Roswell, New Mexico. Generally speaking, the sightings were not spectacular and might have involved astronomical phenomena such as bolides (bright meteors that leave a trail in the sky). On July 4, rancher Mac Brazel heard a loud explosive noise, and the next day he found some interesting debris that he was not able to identify. The nearby Roswell Army Air Field was contacted, and intelligence officers visited the crash site. On July 8, the air base actually announced that the remnants of a flying saucer had been found—but the next day, the story was retracted, and it was announced that the debris was from a weather balloon. Many years passed and more information became available. In 1978, ufologist Stanton Friedman, who has credentials as a nuclear physicist and who is an outspoken advocate for the reality of flying saucers from outer space, reopened the case. He found additional witnesses; one of these witnesses told Friedman that he had seen small bodies near the crash site! Other witnesses claimed to have seen an almost intact crashed UFO! In response to all this accumulating information, books were written (Berlitz and Moore, 1981; Randle and Schmitt, 1992; Friedman and Berliner, 1992), TV programs aired, and a movie was made. By now the case may be the most famous UFO case—perhaps because it has grown so complex, with many contradictory details and astounding implications. Believers are adamant that one and more, probably two, UFOs crashed that July, and skeptics have had a field day pointing out inconsistencies and errors in the prevailing stories. My account here is greatly condensed. If you're interested, check the above books and see Friedman (2008), Rutkowski (2008), and the many internet sources available (including Wikipedia, which has a long Roswell article).

Roswell is one of many cases now considered to be classic (cases known to most people who have a fairly strong interest in the UFO phenomenon). I'll mention a few of these classic UFO cases in this Prologue for historical perspective. Several of them are important to a specific aspect of ufology so I'll mention them here but save their stories for a more appropriate chapter later in this book. The cases that I'm outlining in slightly more detail in this Prologue are not presented again, although I may have occasion to refer back to them briefly.

As to sources of information about these sightings, most of the classic sightings can be researched on the Internet; indeed, Wikipedia has good discussions about most of them—and the debunker theories and suggestions are usually presented along with the details reported by the witnesses. A book by Chris A. Rutkowski (2008) is a good recent source of information about the classic cases as well as many cases that are less well known. Clearly, it is impossible to present more than a very few of the thousands of cases now in the ufology files kept by several organizations (such as MUFON: the Mutual UFO Network, with headquarters in Greeley, Colorado) and discussed in many books and other publications. I'm writing this second edition of my book to report and emphasize the Uintah Basin sightings, nearly all of which have only been published in the first edition of this book—except for some cases from a Uintah Basin ranch discussed in Chapter 8 that are also discussed in *Hunt for the Skinwalker* (Kelleher & Knapp, 2005).

Following the wave of sightings in 1947, other waves occurred at intervals (usually about two-year periods, from 1948 to 1957). Many sightings occurred in the United States between 1947 and 1952. The 1952 excitement surrounding the radar and other observations over Washington, D.C. was widely reported in the media. Europe, especially France, had a large number of sightings in the period 1953–60. South America has experienced many sightings since 1954, and waves of activity have also occurred in Japan, Australia, and New Zealand. No area of the earth's surface has been completely exempt. For many years, little was heard from what were then the Iron Curtain countries, but in about 1966 Russian scientists initiated an investigation into the UFO phenomenon. In 1966, for example, I received a letter from a Russian, a fellow plant physiologist, whom I had met on one occasion, requesting UFO information and reprints. I provided this material and asked about Soviet Union sightings—but never received an answer. Since then, however, many reports of sightings and studies have appeared from the former Iron Curtain countries.

UFO activity cannot be judged accurately from the newspaper accounts available to everyone. If the sightings are sensational, and the press is interested, accounts will be circulated by the wire services, and the public gains an impression of high UFO activity. On the other hand, sightings may be equally numerous but less sensational, or the press may be less inclined to be interested, and the reports may then appear only in small local newspapers or in special publications devoted to the circulation of UFO information. The number of sightings in the United States, for example, remained relatively high from 1957 until about 1969 (with a bit of a quiet period in the early '60s), but the press ignored most of this until the spring of 1964. A wave of sightings beginning in 1972 was ignored until the autumn of 1973. Current sightings are also mostly ignored by the media.

In the summer of 1965, there was a wave of sightings that exceeded anything recorded before that time. Thousands of reports came from the United States, South America, and other parts of the world. In the fall of 1965, a particularly interesting series of sightings occurred near Exeter, New Hampshire, and in the spring of 1966 hundreds of people in Michigan observed UFOs. The late Dr. J. Allen Hynek (who wrote the foreword to this book) was director of the Dearborn Observatory and headed the department of astronomy at Northwestern University. He was also the Air Force Scientific Consultant to Project Blue Book, an investigation of UFOs. He provided, among other suggestions, the very tentative proposal that some of these sightings might have been marsh gas (methane), furnishing an almost inexhaustible source of humor for the nation's cartoonists. "Swamp gas" jokes continued for years. (Before presenting it, Hynek had called me about the swamp gas suggestion, but I didn't know what to tell him. I later visited him at Northwestern University, and his walls were papered with swamp gas cartoons!) Sightings remained numerous until the spring of 1968, although press reporting dropped off again so that most of the activity went unobserved by the public, including virtually all of the Utah sightings reported in this book. You'll see that the peak of Utah sightings was the mid-1960s.

The reports of strange objects in the skies naturally caught the attention of many countries' governments. Clearly, UFOs could be a threat—secret weapons being developed or even, as was (and is) being suggested, armed visitors from other worlds. To study the phenomenon, as early as 1947 the United States Army Air Force set up Project Sign at Wright-Patterson Air Force Base in Ohio. After a rather short life, this project was replaced by another one called Project Grudge. That project was suspended in December 1949 but reactivated and named Project Blue Book in 1952. As such, it lasted until 1970, accumulating files on 12,618 UFO reports. For the most part, as long as enemy activities could not be proven, these Air Force projects were attempts to explain the UFOs as natural phenomena, such as hallucinations—although many reports remained unexplained (see Friedman, 2008).

In 1966, the United States Air Force commissioned a study of UFOs that had high public visibility. Edward Condon, a physicist at the University of Colorado, was the leader of the project. The study group examined hundreds of reports from Project Blue Book and also from the Aerial Phenomenon Research Organization (APRO) and from the National Investigations Committee On Aerial Phenomena (NICAP), both private groups devoted to UFO study. The Condon group selected what they considered to be the 56 best cases. A final report, the Scientific Study of Unidentified Flying Objects (commonly called the Condon Report) was published in 1968. The report offered solutions for many but not all of the "good" cases, but it concluded that ufology was not likely to yield major scientific discoveries. A panel (called NAC) of the National Academy of Sciences endorsed the scope, conclusions, and recommendations of the report. That is, the Condon report and the NAC panel reports were basically negative, and that was the impression picked up by the public, although the report contained many excellent unexplained cases.

The Condon report faced much criticism, both from investigators who worked on the project and from others. It was said to have used flawed methods and to have been biased from its start.

In any case, the actual number of sightings began to diminish, and a low point occurred just before publication of the Condon Report. However, the numbers of sightings then increased, producing a heavy wave of sightings (1972–73), but thanks to the belated interest of the press, the public did not become aware of this wave until October 1973, when certain spectacular events simply could not be ignored. (Some are presented in this book.) Again, the wave appeared to be worldwide. This was when I was working on publishing the first edition of this book. After that, for reasons that I'll describe below, I began to withdraw from the scientific study of UFOs, so the remainder of this history is based on some catch-up study since I decided to get back into the field and prepare a second edition. Let's go back to 1955 and take a chronological look at my selection of a few classic cases.

Some Classic Cases

In 1955, a family in Kentucky was terrified for three hours by some very strange beings who surrounded their home. I'll tell that story in Chapter 7, where I emphasize some of the strange features of reported UFO encounters. Speaking of strangeness, much of the more recent interest in UFOs has been generated by people—by now thousands!—who claim to have been abducted, typically from their beds at night, by extraterrestrials. I'll discuss that phenomenon in Chapter 6, which considers psychology in the UFO enigma. There I'll tell you about Antonia Villas Boas, who as early as 1957 claimed to have been abducted and seduced by a space lady! That case comes from Brazil.

In April, 1959, Father William Booth Gill, a missionary in Papua New Guinea, had a most unique experience. Previous to this, there had been sightings of interesting lights, and one evening Father Gill noticed such a light in the sky above the planet Venus, which he had been observing for several evenings. The object began to approach, and Father Gill called his assistants plus more than three dozen villagers. Before long the object was just a few hundred feet away, hovering in the sky. It was a disc-shaped object with "legs" and "portholes." On top were four humanoid figures that appeared to be doing some chore with a blue beam projected into the sky. At one point, one of the figures seemed to take notice of the group on the ground. Father Gill waved, and the figure on the object waved back! Before long, all those who were gathered on the ground were waving, and all four figures on the UFO were waving back! Father Gill watched for almost four hours and finally went inside for dinner. At that time he assumed that he was watching an American "hovercraft" staffed by military personnel (which was impossible for several reasons). The object returned the next night. Debunkers have tried to explain the sightings by postulating that Gill mistook planets for UFOs, that Gill was not wearing his glasses (which he was), and through various other wild ideas, but the sighting is a truly remarkable one with numerous details and many witnesses.

In 1961, Betty and Barney Hill experienced one of the best known stories in ufology. (There was even a movie about the case.) I'll examine their story in Chapter 6. In that same year, Joe Simonton encountered a UFO on his farm in Wisconsin, and the occupants of the UFO offered Joe some pancakes they were eating for breakfast—an event that I'll return to briefly in Chapter 4 on hoaxes. (Whether Joe's story was a hoax or not, it relates to another story I'll be telling in that chapter.)

On April 24, 1964, Police Officer Lonnie Zamora of Socorro, New Mexico, witnessed an egg-shaped object landing on the ground in a ravine not far from town. As he approached in his car, he saw "white coveralls" standing near the object in the distance, which he first thought was a wrecked automobile. When he came over a rise in the landscape and found himself only about one hundred feet away, the object's oval shape became more apparent. It then emitted a blue flame with a roar and took off over the horizon, leaving Zamora in a very frightened state. When his fellow officer, Sam Chavez, arrived a few minutes later, the top of a bush was smoldering where Zamora said the object had landed, and there were four clear imprints in the ground where Zamora had seen the landing gear. J. Allen Hynek was among those who investigated the case in detail. The Zamora case received wide press coverage, initiating a new period of public interest in UFOs within the United States.

In 1972, a family in Delphos, Kansas, reported that a disc-shaped UFO had landed on their farm, leaving a glowing ring of soil. The case was widely investigated, but I'm almost convinced that it was a hoax, so I'll discuss it in more detail in Chapter 4 on hoaxes. In 1975, Travis Walton from Snowflake, Arizona, claimed to have been abducted by a UFO and kept for about four days before being released. The debunkers have claimed that his story was all an elaborate hoax, but I'm not so sure. I'm going to discuss it in Chapter 6 as another abduction case.

Continuing chronologically with classic cases, there are three interesting ones that I won't be mentioning later, so here they are—but condensed a great deal. Books have been written about each of them, but my main source is a book by Rutkowski (2008):

In September, 1976, in response to calls from citizens who were watching strange lights, the Imperial Iranian Air Force (IIAF), headquartered near Tehran, decided to scramble a F-4 fighter jet from Shahrokhi Air Base to pursue one of the lights. The pilot was at first unable to close in on the object, and when he lost communication with the base, he returned, as was standard procedure. Communication was restored, and the pilot reported that the object was closing in on him from behind, missing him narrowly as it passed by. A second pilot, dispatched a few hours later, was chased by two large objects so dazzlingly bright that he could not determine an exact shape. He estimated that one was as big as a large airplane—and from his vantage point, about half the size of the full moon. A third object appeared, seeming to emerge from the first object, before the plane returned to its base. Approaching the runway (which they had trouble seeing because their night vision was apparently impaired by the bright objects), the crew saw a fourth object, this one cigar-shaped. Skeptics have provided guesses to account for these observations, but most of these guesses can be rather easily refuted.

It was just after midnight on December 26, 1980, near Suffolk, England. Skeleton crews at the nearby Woodbridge and Bentwaters air bases were relaxed with no planes scheduled to land or take off. Two airmen at the (back) east gate at Woodbridge noticed some strange lights near the edge of the nearby Rendlesham Forest. They went to investigate and became frightened when a very bright white light appeared to move toward them. Other airmen were dispatched to investigate. They followed a logging road until it became impassable, after which they continued on foot. Eventually, after feeling disoriented and as though an electric field were causing the hair to stand up on their necks and hands, they came upon a cone-shaped object standing in a clearing in the forest.

One of the men got close enough to touch the object, noting that its surface was smooth and hard like glass. The men moved back as the object started to rise silently, moving erratically back and forth. Hovering just above the trees, "literally with the blink of an eye it was gone." The men found marks in the ground where landing gear might have been, along with some other evidence such as scorched leaves on nearby trees. The deputy base commander heard about the encounter the next day, and after various arrangements, went himself to investigate the landing site. Suddenly he and the men with him saw a bizarre object, only about 500 feet away. It looked like a large glowing, red eye with a black pupil in its center. The object, after disappearing and then reappearing, seemed to explode and vanish! There were sightings on a third night, and one airman claimed to have met alien occupants from one of the objects. UFO investigators have uncovered many details during the intervening years (Warren and Robbins, 1997), and recently Air Force documents about the case were released, but the documents did not contain much new information.

As in other cases with high public visibility, skeptics have tried very hard to discredit this case. Some suggested that the sightings were related to a Russian satellite that was re-entering the atmosphere or to a lighthouse that was visible sometimes through the forest. Obviously, such suggestions are so far removed from the reported events that they are ludicrous.

Yet Jacques Vallée (2008 c., see pp. 150–70) does present a fairly convincing argument that the events were not caused by a non-earthly UFO, but rather that the events were staged by some intelligence agency to test the responses of the witnesses. He provides information about how the events could have easily been staged in late 1980, but perhaps most convincing to me is the report of a TV interview with one of the principal organizers, who stated that some forty witnesses were assembled, with all their weapons confiscated, before the UFO appeared. (Note that Vallée is not a UFO debunker; in several books he presents strong evidence that UFOs represent a real phenomenon—even that UFO abductions have occurred.) It is the complexity of such UFO events that seems to test one's sanity!

Rutkowski (2008) tells about the Giant Yukon Saucer of December, 1996. Again, several widely separated witnesses were involved; twenty two of them gave detailed reports. Four people driving near Fox Lake in central Yukon, Canada, reported that they saw a huge object with lights placed in various places and covering sixty to ninety degrees of night sky. A family in Carmacks saw an object from their home at the same time and place, and a lone driver watched the object over the far end of Fox Lake as he drove about ten miles toward Carmacks. Occupants of two other vehicles driving toward Carmacks also reported seeing the object. Some of them provided detailed descriptions of the huge object with its lights and "windows." A trapper in the area described how a huge object with perhaps a hundred lighted "windows" blocked out the stars over a wide angle. Two more witnesses said the object covered an expanse of sky at least as large as the Big Dipper. These sightings are obviously remarkable because of the huge size of the reported object. But the sightings are also notable because of the careful and extensive investigation of ufologist Martin Jasek, who was able to interview the twenty-two witnesses and who later found from secondhand accounts that at least thirty witnesses were involved.

The night of March 13, 1997 was for thousands of witnesses a spectacular night in and around Phoenix, Arizona. There were not only many witnesses, but there are also many photographs and videos as well. Spectators first reported that formations of amber lights passed over the Superstition Mountains east of Phoenix and that they were connected in such a way that they represented a mile-wide aircraft! Then a formation of blue-white lights moved from Nevada into Arizona airspace, eventually reaching Phoenix and continuing on to Tucson. There were reports of a huge circular object about a mile in diameter with yellow lights around the edge and city lights reflecting off its underside. There were other formations and individual lights as well; the situation is complicated because of the many witnesses, whose stories are too complex and detailed to be related here.

Some witnesses reported that Air Force jets were scrambled to check on the objects, but the Air Force denies any such involvement. Hence, what actually happened is, typically, highly controversial. Some said that the lights were ordinary aircraft, but there is no record that such craft were in the air at the particular times and places. Apparently, a visiting Maryland National Guard squadron was in the area dropping flares, but officials have stated that such an exercise would never be conducted over populated areas. Furthermore, it is clear that flares cannot explain the many events of that evening, although they could perhaps account for a few of the sightings.

My Story

With that broad picture of the UFO story as background, I would like to tell my own story, which stands behind the many opinions and personal suggestions that show up in this book. You'll be in a better position to evaluate those ideas if you know where they are coming from; that is, if you know a little about me and my interest in UFOs.

It all started with Mars and an astronomy class at the University of Utah. I enjoyed the class very much (partially because I took it with a girl-friend, and there were long lines in the dark observatory while we waited our turn at the telescope!). I earned an M.A. degree at the University of Utah, working on the Big Rock Candy Mountain in south-central Utah—a kind of ecology/plant physiology/geology study. So when I got to the California Institute of Technology to work on my Ph.D., I chose geochemistry as a minor to plant physiology, my major subject. And when in 1953 Harrison Brown's geochemistry class discussed the solar system as a setting for Earth, I got a chance to return to astronomy. I chose the topic of life on Mars for my term paper. Although Brown only awarded my paper with a B, it was published in various places and even abstracted in a book on Mars by a Caltech astronomer (Richardson, 1954). The most important outcome of that term paper was a hobby that lasted for years. I gave many talks about the possibilities of life on Mars, and almost a decade later, as an assistant professor at Colorado State University, this Mars activity led to a cover story, titled "Martian Biology," in *Science* magazine (Salisbury, 1962). All of which led to even more talks and articles.

Emphasizing the bluish-green (difficult to describe) markings on Mars that darkened with the coming of spring in the Martian southern hemisphere, I argued, along with others, that there might be vegetation on Mars and went on to speculate about how life might exist there. But I went beyond that: Many people were still intrigued by Percival Lowell's descriptions of

Mars and his speculations about intelligent life on that planet. He was a rich business man, author, and mathematician who decided to check out the idea that there were Martian canals, an idea that had been around since the Italian astronomer Giovanni Schiaparelli had reported in 1877 that Mars had straight-line features, which he called canali, meaning channels but mistranslated as canals. In 1894, Lowell chose Flagstaff, Arizona Territory, as the site for his observatory. He and his associates on Mars Hill in Flagstaff continued to report and to map the canals. Lowell wrote three books (in 1895, 1906, and 1908; references not given) in which he speculated that the canals were built to carry water from the polar caps, and that they were wide enough to be seen from Earth because they supported strip farms. At the "nodes" where canals met, cities existed. All this was well known to the public in 1962 when I wrote "Martian Biology."

I cited three evidences for intelligent life on Mars: First were those "canals," which some observers saw but most did not. Second were the satellites, the moons of Mars: Phobos and Deimos. They were thought to be highly atypical satellites. Could they be artificial? The third evidence concerned some very rarely reported flashes of light. Could they be atomic-bomb explosions?

Based on what we knew, it was safe for me to speculate about intelligent life on Mars, even in *Science*, the premier scientific journal, and my paper got considerable publicity. Unfortunately for all my ideas about Mars, as we learned more and more about the planet, beginning with the 1965 probes that returned close photos of Mars (the first being Mariner 4, which sent back pictures on July 14, 1965), none of these three evidences panned out. We see no canals nor cities in high-resolution photos. Apparently, the canals were an optical illusion caused when the brain subconsciously drew lines between dark spots ("oases"—now known to be craters) on Mars. And we now have close photos of both satellites; they are hunks of rock. Flashes of light were marginal evidence all along; now they are never mentioned. The darkening of the markings is said to be caused by dust blowing in spring off of a darker base (but I'm not totally convinced!). Clearly, there are no cities and farms on Mars—but might there be some much less visible form of life with features unknown to us? The question remains, and science continues to consider the possibility.

One life-changing result of the *Science* article for me was a letter from Coral Lorenzen (1962) with a copy of her book about UFOs. Could the UFOs be coming from Mars, she asked? I read her book and was impressed with her approach, which seemed to be quite reasonable. I contacted her and her husband, Jim, in Tucson, Arizona, and before long I had paid my dues to the Aerial Phenomenon Research Organization (APRO), which they had organized. I was spending more and more time learning about the UFO phenomenon, and I started including UFO stories in my talks on Martian biology. Most of those talks were to scientific groups, the ones who might be the most skeptical about UFOs. Somehow, I managed to be positive about them but objective enough so that no one argued with me. My approach then and now was that we are confronted with a real mystery, not easily shrugged off, for which we have no definitive answers.

Some of these talks were before various NASA groups. At Colorado State University, a colleague (Tex Baker) and I landed a NASA contract shortly after NASA was organized (ca. 1960). With continuing NASA grants, I studied life under extreme conditions (justified by the possibility of some form of life on Mars); plant responses to gravity; and finally, before retiring in 1997, growing plants in controlled environments to purify the air and provide food for astronauts. I led a project from 1992 to 1997 that grew wheat in the Russian space station, Mir. (There were also other research projects unrelated to NASA's interests.)

In July of 1966, I moved to Utah State University, and already by October I had given a Mars/UFO talk to a Utah Teachers group. Joseph Junior Hicks, a junior high school science teacher from Roosevelt, Utah, was present. He came up after my talk to tell me about some interesting sightings going on in the Uintah Basin of northeastern Utah. I made a note to check out those stories but put the idea on the back burner.

In Chapter 1, I tell how this contact with Junior Hicks eventually led, twelve years later (1974), to the first edition of this book. I was impressed with how the Uintah Basin UFOs seemed to be showing themselves to witnesses, so I called my book *The Utah UFO Display*.

Even before the book, and through my friendship with Coral and Jim Lorenzen, I ended up on the *National Enquirer* "Blue Ribbon Panel" to evaluate submissions of UFO evidence that would prove UFOs were of intelligent, extraterrestrial origin. The prize for proof was $50,000, but it eventually went up to 1 million dollars. The first meeting, at the *National Enquirer* offices in Florida, was in the spring of 1972. (The last for me was in autumn of 1977.) The panel (Fig. P-1) included Leo Sprinkle (a psychologist at the University of Wyoming), Jim Lorenzen (of APRO), James A. Harder (an engineer at the University of California—Berkeley), Robert

Fig. P-1 *The* National Enquirer *Blue Ribbon Panel. This photo was taken at the first meeting, at the* National Enquirer *offices in Florida, in the spring of 1972. From left to right, the panel included Leo Sprinkle, Jim Lorenzen, James A. Harder, Robert Creegan, me, and J. Allen Hynek.*

Creegan (a philosopher at the State University of New York in Albany), J. Allen Hynek (an astronomer, as noted), and me. We also worked with Bob Pratt from the *Enquirer.* No one ever came close to collecting the big prize, but it gave us much food for thought about what it would take to qualify as proof that UFOs were of intelligent, extraterrestrial origin.

It soon became clear that proof would be very difficult to come by— although the half dozen of us on the panel were at that time all favorable to the possibility of extraterrestrial visitation. In our first meeting, we sat around in a room with boxes containing piles of entries, and it was soon apparent that virtually all were witness accounts with nothing approaching tangible proof. Over a thousand people said they had experienced events—sightings, mostly—that left them confused and amazed. My feeling was that they desperately wanted to tell their stories—just to be heard. That feeling is typical of witnesses to highly strange things. For a mere six of us to wade through those hundreds of letters was truly mind numbing. We were constantly interrupting each other to read from some interesting letter. After that first frustrating experience, we let the *National Enquirer* staff do some preliminary sorting and sifting.

What kind of evidence could be conclusive? This question is at the heart of any kind of scientific evaluation of the UFO phenomenon. The discussion of the question fits better in Chapter 3, where I'll discuss science in general and UFO evidence in particular. For now, it is enough to note that good science usually depends on objective evidence that can be obtained by anyone who uses the proper methods to get the evidence. This won't work with UFOs because in the vast majority of cases, UFO sightings are based only on witness accounts and cannot be repeated. However, a witnesses's testimony should not be ignored just because it can't be checked. We can at least analyze large bodies of testimony for patterns and such.

What happens when this process doesn't quite work? And what if we are dealing with truly strange events, such as close encounters with UFOs? At this point, much depends upon the mind-set of the investigator. A truly scientific mind-set should be objective and let the evidence lead to a conclusion. But there are those "debunkers," as we ufologists call them, whose minds are completely made up that all UFOs can be "explained" as some natural or psychological phenomenon if only we had the data. Since we don't have the data in the vast majority of cases, the debunker must simply make up an explanation that seems (in his mind) to fit what is known. I call such explanations just-suppose stories. That's a term that will show up quite frequently in this book.

Chapter 3 also examines such UFO evidence as photographs, marks on the ground, and pieces of crashed UFOs. It is almost impossible to be sure about such evidence, mostly because it is almost impossible to prove that it is not fraudulent. In any case, the *National Enquirer* panel gave me and my colleagues the opportunity to wonder about these matters.

As the 1970s drew to a close, it became more and more difficult for me to be truly scientific (i.e., objective) about UFOs. Although in one chapter of my 1974 book I more or less argued for the space ships by shooting down the arguments against them, in the next chapter I told about my growing doubts that the nuts and bolts or ET hypothesis really makes any sense. Shortly after my book was published, some of my doubts began to center around religious explanations. As these doubts intensified, I realized that I was no longer being truly scientific.

Then there was the *Playboy* Panel. On February 22, 1976, a group of us assembled at the home of Murray and Barbara Fisher in Los Angeles

(Hollywood), California. The participants included J. Allen Hynek, Leo Sprinkle, Jacques Vallée (a computer scientist and UFO author from California), and me. (Herb Schirmer, who claimed to have been abducted by a UFO, was also there but didn't take part.) We sat around a table all day, talking with each other and to a tape recorder in the middle of the table. It must have been a terrible job to transcribe all that conversation, but *Playboy* managed to do so. The transcript was sent to us to change in any way that we desired. It was also sent to James A. Harder and two UFO skeptics: Philip J. Klass (a senior editor of *Aviation Week & Space Technology* and author of two debunking books) and Ernest H. Taves (a psychoanalyst from New York who had coauthored a debunking book with the late Harvard astronomer, Donald Menzel). The edited transcript was passed around among the participants until it was finally published in January 1978, almost two years after the panel met (see bibliography under *Playboy*). As a reprint, it fills almost sixteen pages, most with three columns of small print.

In rereading this panel discussion, it is interesting to see that virtually all of the arguments discussed now were also discussed then by the panel. And arguments there were! Although neither Harder nor the debunkers were present, the editors had so skillfully put together all the comments that there was always an exchange between Klass or Taves and the rest of us. This was also facilitated by the many times the document circulated among us, allowing us to thrust and counter-thrust.

Near the end of the discussion, I strongly expressed my growing doubts about a nuts and bolts explanation for UFOs and wondered if the phenomenon would someday be accommodated by theological considerations. J. Allen Hynek also raised doubts about extraterrestrial machines while strongly defending the reality of the phenomenon as a whole, as did Jacques Vallée, who kept reminding us that there might even have been reality to fairies and elves in earlier days. Leo Sprinkle emphasized how psychological phenomena should be important in our research. In addition to frequently countering the debunkers' arguments with facts, James Harder emphasized the important (for him) role of hypnosis in UFO studies.

By June 1977 at the International UFO Congress in Chicago, after the *Playboy* panel but before its publication, I was publicly stating some of my doubts about UFOs as hardware or extraterrestrial machines and noting that my views were including religious thoughts—though my thoughts were obviously very tentative (see Fuller, 1980).

My "non-scientific" thoughts developed over that period (about 1980) until finally I simply decided that if I could no longer apply a scientific approach to the study of such phenomena, it was time to pull out of the field and wait to see where it was going. I did.

For one thing, the field went in the direction of more and more abduction stories (though none from the Uintah Basin). I learned this best by writing a foreword to a 1993 book by James L. Thompson, a lawyer who was a Mormon or member of the Church of Jesus Christ of Latter-day Saints (LDS Church). Thompson had looked deeply into abduction accounts and other UFO events up to that point. I read his manuscript and was amazed at the kinds of things people were reporting. For example, he quoted extensively from Budd Hopkins's 1987 book, which documented attempts by the aliens to crossbreed with humans. In his book, Thompson based his explanations mainly on LDS theology. It was a valiant attempt but of course it had to be mostly speculation. I didn't buy into all of his conclusions, but I found them highly interesting. I'll get back to the abduction problem in Chapter 6.

Now that I've decided to reenter the UFO fray with this book, I ask myself where I stand in my own thoughts. I no longer try to apply LDS theology to my understanding of UFOs, although in the Epilogue I will return to some general thoughts about my religious heritage; however I do think such things add supporting data for consideration in my currently favored interpretation of the UFO phenomenon. This conclusion is highly tentative, as any interpretation has always been for me, but I'm saving it for the Epilogue.

As a final point, let's avoid saying we "believe in" UFOs. In the English language, that phrase often infers a blind faith —and today it also implies that we accept the extraterrestrial machine hypothesis. Instead, let me say that the data presently convince me that the phenomenon is real—that the skeptics have failed in their attempts to debunk it. And for me personally, I've come to realize that the data that are most important to me consist of the interviews that Junior Hicks and I had with witnesses in the Uintah Basin of northeastern Utah. Let's get on with those interviews!

PART 1

The Uintah Basin UFO Display

1

Junior's Files

The Reports

The Uintah[1] (you-**in**-taw) Basin sightings turned out to be better than most UFO hunters' dreams. I had seen a small article or two in the Salt Lake City papers and heard a couple of announcements on the radio, indicating that something interesting for the UFO business was going on near Vernal, Utah, the largest town in the Uintah Basin. But such stories were common in 1965–66. Then, as noted in the Prologue, one evening in October 1966 I gave a talk about the possibilities of life on Mars to the Association of Utah Science Teachers. I also tossed in a few comments about UFOs. Following the talk, a man came up and introduced himself as Joseph Junior Hicks, a junior high school science teacher from Roosevelt, Utah, right in the heart of the Uintah Basin. Many people were asking questions, so there wasn't time to say much, but he told me of some exciting sightings in Roosevelt and Vernal. I wrote down Junior's name and decided that this might be the opportunity for which I had been waiting.

How badly I wanted to head for Roosevelt and Vernal to personally interview some of those witnesses! In January of 1967, when "The Scientist and the UFO" appeared in *BioScience*, publisher Devin Garrity asked if I would enlarge it into a book. I remembered the brief stories from Junior Hicks, so I asked Mr. Garrity if he could finance an excursion to the Uintah Basin. He did, but it was over a year before I made the trip.

As it turned out, many good sightings occurred in that year. Junior Hicks was still collecting data regarding sightings until the time I arrived on June 13, 1968—and in 2010 he still is!

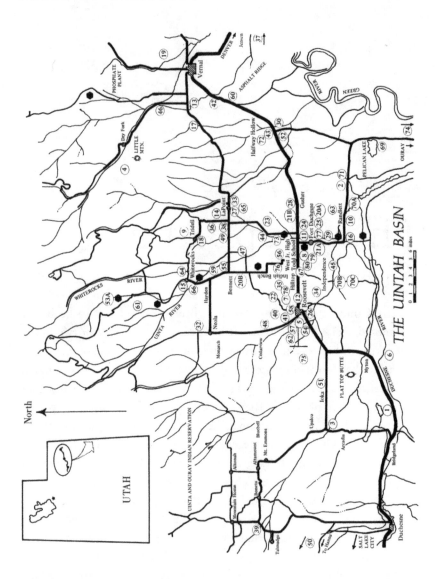

Fig. 1-1 *Map of the Uintah Basin showing highways, principle towns, streams, and location of the Basin in the state of Utah. The heavy line running from Duchesne to Vernal represents Highway 40, an important highway between Salt Lake City and Denver, Colorado. Numbers in circles represent the sightings of Table 1 (Appendix). Locations are reasonably accurate, except for those clustered around Roosevelt and Fort Duchesne, where accurate locations would have required much overlapping. Sightings 31 and 68 could not be located accurately from the descriptions of the witnesses and hence were left out. Sightings 70D and 70E took place at West Junior High School. Black hexagons represent the positions of witnesses to Sighting 53.*

I spent the first Sunday afternoon looking over Junior's files. Here was a microcosm of UFO activity, representing nearly everything I had read, and providing so many sightings that one could begin to think in statistical terms. Before we examine some of these sightings, however, let's diverge for a few paragraphs and examine the Uintah Basin itself.

The Uintah Basin

The Basin is located in eastern Utah at the north end of the Colorado Plateau Province (Fig. 1-1). The Basin is about 75 miles long, measured along an east-west line. It is a high (5,000 to 6,000 foot elevation), dry desert that gets quite cold in winter. On the north are the Uinta Mountains, the only major chain of mountains in North America running east and west. This is wild country, with many peaks above 13,000 feet, and part of the region designated as a national primitive area. Most of the Uintas are penetrated only by dirt roads or trails. The south border of the Basin is the Tavaputs Plateau, also desert country, and there are mountains to the west and the east, forming the huge Basin. The Green River flows through the southeast corner of the region, cutting Desolation Canyon through the Tavaputs Plateau, but the Basin itself is primarily formed by the Duchesne (pronounced dew-shay-ne) River and its tributaries (especially the Uintah River), which flow southward, draining the Uinta Mountains, and then eastward through the Basin and into the Green River. Highway 40 runs east and west, roughly parallel to the Duchesne River. Coming from Salt Lake City, the first town is Duchesne, with a population listed at 770 in 1960 (2000 pop: 1,407). Driving another thirty miles east leads one to Roosevelt (1960 pop. 1,812; 2000: 4,299) in the middle of the Basin, and another thirty miles on east takes one to Vernal (1960 pop. 3,655; 2000: 7,714).

This is a spectacular land. In the summer heat, the desert badlands shimmer in red, yellow, orange, and gray hues, while the Uinta Mountains share some of the most sublime alpine splendor to be found on the North American continent.

The Indians were there first, the Utes and the Ourays, and remained the sole possessors (on the Uintah and Ouray Reservation, which occupies nearly all of the Basin) until about 1900 when the center of the reservation, primarily along Highway 40, was opened to white settlement. Several towns were founded, but most remain small villages, sometimes with only

ten or twenty people. Most of the Caucasians are Mormons (members of
the Church of Jesus Christ of Latter-Day Saints) who came in from other
parts of Utah when the area was opened. Several other religions are represented, however, and their small churches and missions to the Indians are
an important part of the local culture. The Mormon Church, as in the rest
of Utah, with its intricate organization of stakes (comparable to dioceses)
and wards, provides the guiding motivation for the majority of people in
the area.

Most of the agricultural income is from livestock (cattle and sheep),
but Uintah Basin honey is known throughout the Intermountain West for
its high quality. Oil and gas wells have been developed, and this is becoming a major industry. The Uinta Mountains also provide timber and some
mining. Dinosaur National Monument on the eastern border of Utah
brings in many tourists. Yet, in spite of the influx of oil drillers and tourists, the Uintah Basin was and to an extent still is one of the most rural,
isolated frontiers left in the United States.

The people remain rural in their outlook and as conservative and
down-to-earth as New Hampshire Republicans. Native Americans are
omnipresent in the Basin, and many of them have broken away from the
dire poverty, alcoholism, and other problems still faced by others. A few
have intermarried with Caucasians and live in the towns and villages as
stalwart members of the community. Because many Native American children were in Junior's classes, he has made friendships with them and their
parents—and some have had interesting UFO experiences.

So this is the land where the UFOs cavorted, and here are the people
who watched and watched some more and wondered.

Joseph Junior Hicks' Files and Our Interviews

Junior Hicks' laboratory classroom in a then-new modern-style building was a model for such facilities. He was and is an enthusiastic person
(Fig. 1-2) and an excellent teacher. For decades he has been moonlighting
as an electrical contractor and electrical inspector for the town of Roosevelt. Active in the Mormon Church, he has been in constant contact with
the students, farmers, and townspeople of the central Uintah Basin. Early
in 1966 he gained a reputation as the local UFO authority, often speaking
before local groups. As a result, people brought him their reports. Though
far too busy to spend many hours searching out cases, if an interesting

Fig. 1-2 (A) *Frank B. Salisbury (left) and Joseph Junior Hicks (right), taken in 1973.* (B) *The same, taken in 2009, illustrating the aging process!*

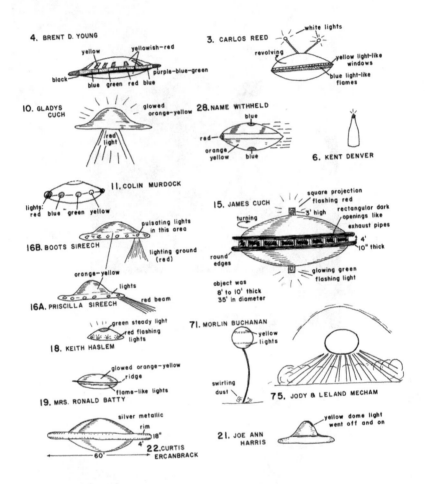

Fig. 1-3 *Fifteen UFO drawings as depicted by witnesses. The originals were done with colored pencils on the bottoms of their reports. These were laid out, overlapping each other, so that they appeared as shown. A photograph was taken, and then a tracing from the photograph. Numbers refer to sightings in Table 1. (Numbers 71 and 75 were drawn by me from my memory of the drawings on the reports, since these sightings occurred after the photo was taken.)*

report turned up, he drove out to interview the witness(es). He always requested drawings from them, and several of these are shown in Figure 1-3.

About three out of four cases, he estimates, appear to be satellites, stars, or perhaps some other natural phenomenon. Yet the number of unexplainable sightings he has accumulated is truly fantastic. In 1968, I first condensed his file into Table 1 (Appendix) so that we could number the sightings and look for correlations in sizes, shapes, sounds, and so forth. In addition, I picked up a few sightings on my own. Junior located all of the sightings in the table on a map (see Fig. 1-1). From about 400 sightings Junior had encountered by about 1973, we finished up with a total of 80 unexplained sightings and about 260 witnesses. Few of the witnesses are duplicated, and considering that the area covered by nearly all of the sightings (eliminating Duchesne and Vernal) contained only about 4,000 people, this was a rather phenomenal number. Since 1973, Junior has accumulated about 400 more sightings, and in 2009 we interviewed witnesses relating to eight of these. Interestingly enough, most of the sightings after 1973 are similar to the ones in Table 1, Junior tells me. However, some of the eight interviews that we conducted concerned rather unusual cases, which Junior chose because they *were* unusual.

Judging by the interviews we've had, the number of good cases in Junior's file could easily be doubled. Nearly everyone knew of someone else with a good story, or had another good story himself. A conservative estimate would indicate that 10 percent of the population of the Uintah Basin had experienced excellent sightings by 1973. A door-to-door survey might have been in order, but that would have been beyond our time and resources.

In the 1960s and 1970s, although I had to pass up many excellent witnesses, I recorded about twenty interviews on tape. As Table 1 indicates, the intense wave of sightings in the Uintah Basin occurred in late 1966 through 1967, but sporadic sightings occurred both before and after that—as they have done and still do all over the world. Table 1 does not include sightings since 1973.

Clearly, the primary data upon which UFO investigations must be based consists of witness accounts. Yes, there are photos, markings on the ground, and other tangible evidence, but such could virtually always be fraudulent. And any witness report could be a misinterpretation of what actually happened—or an out-and-out made-up story! Sadly for science, there is no way to go back in time to see what the witness(es) really experienced.

So the interviews (witness accounts) take on a high level of importance. It is the accounts taken as a body, supporting each other in a certain sense, that have convinced me that there is really something going on that is beyond our present understanding of how our universe works. Thus, the interviews were included in the main text of the first edition of this book.

But for this edition, space was limited, and I have new accounts and new ideas to present. Furthermore, as J. Allen Hynek said in his foreword to the first edition, it can be a bit mind-boggling, even tedious, to read case after case in a very long chapter.

What to do? Our compromise has been to only summarize and quote from the accounts in this chapter. Depending upon your level of interest, I encourage you to read some or all of the interviews, which I would be happy to email to you.

When you do read them, you'll see that many details in the interviews could represent distortions in the telling, exaggerations, interpretations, and other pitfalls. That's the name of the game. Nobody's memory or ability to put memories into language is perfect. Yet I am convinced that the Uintah Basin witness stories, including many that we have insufficient space to report here, as well as many others from around the world, provide a basis for concluding that there is indeed a real and important UFO phenomenon to consider. Read the interviews and see what you think.

The Uintah Basin Sightings

1. Some Sightings around Duchesne

My opportunity to find sightings on my own, independently of Junior's files, was realized as soon as I first entered the Basin on my way to visit Junior. I was stopped for speeding in Duchesne! To dispel the sick feeling that was working its way into the pit of my stomach, I tried to strike up a friendly conversation with Officer Bradford Baum. Sure enough, he had a couple of friends who had sightings to tell about. (Incidentally, the people of the Uintah Basin didn't bother to report their sightings to the authorities. Except for my Duchesne accounts, people reported to Junior Hicks, so sheriffs, town policemen, or other officials didn't know any more stories than did other citizens of the community.)

I returned Tuesday morning and hunted up Kay Stratton, the Justice of the Peace, who was also a local barber. After waiting for his customers to disperse, I paid my fine and then asked him about the UFO. Sure enough, he had a reasonably good story to tell. One evening between ten and eleven in early summer of 1967, during hot, dry weather, he and his wife had seen a red ball "as big as a car" sitting on the crest of a hill near a large TV transmitting antenna south of town. After they had watched a while, the object had gone straight up or toward the south until it was out of sight. He told me it was "as bright as a fire or a neon sign."

Justice of the Peace Stratton in turn referred me to Officer Bernard Hadden, a deputy sheriff, who told me his story in the Courthouse. In the fall of 1966 he had seen a brilliant light in the heavens up at an angle of about forty-five degrees. He watched with binoculars. Although he got the impression of considerable size, it did not exhibit a distinct shape "—more of a glow, you might say." Appearing a mile or so away, it was interesting because of its maneuvers, seeming to come toward him, change direction, disappear, come back into sight, and finally go on a straight line from east to west. "It didn't seem to have any response to gravity at all." This account is quite typical of a "distant-light" sighting—and less impressive than many of the sightings we will discuss in this book.

To illustrate the point about distant lights, here is another example: In the fall of 1967, probably September or October, Mr. Douglas Horrocks and his wife, using binoculars, had watched a brilliant light (like a mercury vapor lamp) hovering to the west over a reservoir near Duchesne. They thought that the object was about three hundred feet above the dam. It was quite stationary, but after five or ten minutes, it had disappeared. The Horrocks were excited about their sighting, but at that time, Venus was the evening star, right in the west. Their description matches Venus perfectly. A moving cloud cover would account for the sudden "disappearance" after ten minutes. Or the planet might have set below the western horizon (just as the earth's rotation causes the sun to set).

The County Attorney had overheard our conversations about UFOs, and he gave me the name of Dean Powell, a man who had had an excellent sighting.

Dean Powell's Silver Craft. Mr. Powell's story turned out to be one of the best of the lot. The planet Venus just won't do for this one. Mr. Powell delivered mail from the main post office in Duchesne to several outlying points in the Basin. He was in his sixties (though he looked younger; Fig. 1-4) and was clearly a good, solid citizen. He wouldn't tell his story until I had identified myself, which is definitely a point in his favor.

Dean Powell was delivering mail to a tiny post office in Hanna, on the North Fork of the Duchesne River. It was June, probably 1966, about

Fig. 1-4 (A) *The view from the Hanna Post Office (white spot shows UFO location, as indicated on the photograph by Mr. Powell);* (B) *Dean Powell standing at the back of his mail truck; and* (C) *a drawing of the object seen by Mr. Powell. (Photographs taken in 1968.)*

10:15 in the morning. He was leaning on his truck, waiting for the post-mistress, Mrs. Cristal Hackett, when he noticed a silver craft hovering in front of a nearby hill across the river. It was perfectly silent. He called Mrs Hackett, and she came out and saw the object but immediately ran to get her children so they could see it. When she returned, the object had moved to the north. Powell could still see it, but he was not sure that the others saw it. He was adamant that it "was [not] a flying saucer . . . but a real flying craft . . . that they're keeping a secret in this country."

I checked with Mrs. Hackett, and she confirmed her part of the story in detail, expressing regret that she had not observed the object more carefully before running to get her children. (There are many other important details in the full text of the interview.)

2. The Early Sightings

Sightings 1 and 2 in Table 1 (Appendix), are very interesting but a bit older and atypical of the remaining sightings. Data for all of the other sightings were collected shortly after the time that they occurred, but these two came to the attention of Junior Hicks after the wave of sightings began in the fall of 1966.

Sighting 2 is particularly fascinating because of the mention of a face in a window. No other account in Table 1 mentions occupants of any kind, although there were several opportunities to see inside (such as with reports of windows). By now (2010), Junior does have some additional accounts that include occupants.

Kent Denver's Rocket/Bowling Pin. Sighting 6 describes an object with a very unique shape, exhibiting a rather interesting motion as well. The witness was Kent Denver (Fig. 1-5).

On August 9, 1965, about midnight, he was driving in the desert with his fiancée (now his wife) and her little brother. Coming around a turn, they saw a very large object that looked like a bowling pin but with windows all around the top. As their headlights swung toward it, it lifted up with a red flame out the bottom—but the flame was there only when the

Fig. 1-5 *Kent Denver (1968).*

object was hovering. It would go out, and the object would move upwards, hovering again when the flame appeared. It finally shot upwards.

3. Autumn, 1966

The sightings during September, October, and November (there were none during December) account for thirty-three of the eighty sightings in Table 1. And some of them are packed with interest and drama. Sighting 10 is important because the object was seen at close range by a number of witnesses. Unfortunately, I didn't have time to talk to this family. The sighting is also special because of the presence of a "red beam." This beam was a sort of pencil of light that came slowly out of the craft, probing around in various directions but ending in midair. Only if it touched the ground did the ground light up. To me such a beam of light is so utterly beyond comprehension that it is very tempting to try to forget the whole thing as a bad dream of the witness. Yet, beginning with this sighting, the beam shows up in Junior's file on several occasions, and so I suppose it must be reckoned with. I wonder if it is some kind of confined plasma rather than a beam of light?

The Massey/Batty Landed Oval Machine in Vernal. The Massey sighting (#13) was an excellent one by virtually any criteria. It was the only one of those discussed in this chapter that received any publicity. A TV crew went to Vernal to interview the witnesses and look for flying saucers themselves. Although they didn't see any, the local joke is that while they were in the lobby of one of the Vernal hotels, a number of witnesses had a rather spectacular sighting northeast of town.

Both Valda Massey and his wife, Donna, were schoolteachers in Vernal. As Donna finished canning tomato juice around eleven-thirty on September 7, 1966, she went to talk to her husband who had just gone to bed. On the way she noticed an odd red light in the west. On the way back, she went into the utility room for a better look. The light was moving slowly (perhaps five miles per hour) just above the treetops about a mile away. It was in front of a range of low hills. Soon it became evident that she was watching a large machine, "as big as a house." She noticed the strange red beam, this time going out in a horizontal direction. The machine was a "round, oval shape, then there was a yellow light that had tinges of blues and greens and what-not in it." The yellow light also acted like the red beam. The machine landed on a knoll about a mile from the Massey's home. "It just came down real soft and just sat there." Garth Batty, a close friend and a local Mormon bishop, arrived in time to watch the object, which remained on the knoll for about an hour. They finally left the house and began to drive toward the object, at which time it moved vertically so rapidly that it "just vanished." About three nights later the machine appeared again, following the same pattern of cruising above the treetops and landing on the knoll. This time the dome light was much brighter, dimming after a few moments to its previous intensity. Bishop Batty had observed the machine through binoculars on the first occasion, but for some reason he had not handed these to the other witnesses. On the second occasion, the object stayed around until everyone finally went to bed. No one saw it leave that time. A few nights after the second visit, a "great, big, huge yellow light" was seen. "It looked like you could take your arm and gather it all in. You could just hold it right in your hands. It didn't shoot out any rays from it, and it was a different type of light from what our lights are." Donna Massey, who gives the above descriptions, ran inside to call Bishop Batty again, but while she was gone, the object left at a high rate of speed. Valda Massey and his daughter were watching. "It was clear over Jensen [fourteen miles away], and the light went out, and the next time they picked it up, it was over Red Wash." There was no sound such as rushing air, even though the light was seen at fairly close range, perhaps only a few hundred feet away, over some trees on the Massey's farm. Several witnesses reported a similar object on the same night (e.g., Clyde Wilkins and others).

The "machine" seen on the first two occasions provided the most interesting details. Donna Massey seemed to think that she could see shadowy figures moving around inside of the windows, but she didn't look through the binoculars. She assumed that Bishop Batty had seen the figures clearly, but in my interview with him, he said that he did not.

Bishop Batty seemed to think that the second sighting was "more vivid" than the first one. He was referring to the intensity of the lights, although the details seen in the first sighting exceeded those seen in the second.

Following the first and second Massey sightings, someone with a Geiger counter was called to check for radioactivity. None was found, nor were any other markings or physical evidence of any kind. During that winter the Masseys and many others in Vernal often observed lights in the sky, maneuvering and traveling at speeds atypical of satellites or airplanes. The Masseys were impressed that these seemed to converge and cross over at a point on "Ute Hill." Donna Massey also had considered that the landings occurred near a spot where a number of beehives were located, and she thought that perhaps the hives had something to do with the landings.

Of course, this is the purest of speculation, as she well knows, but it is quite typical of the reactions of the witnesses. After seeing something so very strange, they can't help but attempt to reconcile or explain it through rational means. Dean Powell's emphasis on government machines is an excellent and typical case in point.

Daytime, Double Convex Prototype: This sighting (#15) included some of the best detail in Junior's file, and so we hoped to talk with the witness, James Cuch. He was a young Native American lad who was a student of Junior's at the time of the sighting. We called on him at his home in White Rocks. Unfortunately, we probably approached him too abruptly. A moment or two after arriving, we simply asked him to tell his story, and his reply was that he had forgotten. He never did tell the story, but after a little conversation with him and with his parents, we were able to confirm certain details recorded in Junior's file. At 2:00 PM on September 15, 1966, he had seen a large (fifty to sixty feet in diameter) silvery, metallic object hovering some five feet off the ground in a clearing in the woods only a few

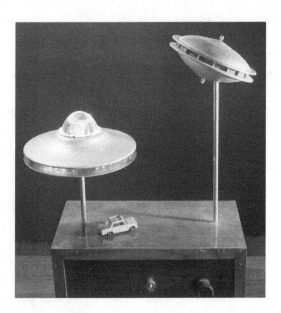

Fig. 1-6 *UFO models made by Junior Hicks. The one on the left is referred to in Table 1 as convex planar; the one on the right as double convex. The model automobile is approximately the same scale as the objects, based on accounts of the witnesses.*

hundred feet behind his house. He had approached within a hundred feet, at which time the object began to rise vertically, spinning slowly and then more rapidly as it rose. James is an excellent artist, and his close observation furnished a fine drawing (Fig. 1-3) from which Junior built one of two models (Fig. 1-6). The double-convex model was one that was described by several witnesses as well as James Cuch. James was able to describe a row of "windows" going around the center of the object, as were a few but not all of the other witnesses.

Bigger than the House it Hovered Over. The event of September 20, 1966 (#16), was spectacular. We interviewed Priscilla Sireech, a young Native American girl in high school, but other participants were not available, although Junior had interviewed them earlier. The children were home at Randlett watching TV in the living room. At about eight-thirty, the room began to light up with a red color, "so bright you could see each other's faces, and the lights were all turned off." They ran outside in time to see a large object, flat on the bottom with a dome on top, (Junior's convex planar model in Fig. 1-6) hovering over the house, almost appearing to balance on top of the house. It was twice as large as the small home. They heard a humming noise, and lights around the bottom edge of the object were blinking on and off, giving a predominantly red impression, but also appearing at times to be green and yellow. "It was too bright. Every time you look at it, it kind of hurts your eyes." No occupants were seen inside the dome. The object moved east from the house rather rapidly for about a quarter of a mile and then came back over the house, finally disappearing over the horizon in the southwest. The "red beam" that only illuminates things that it touches was described. Other witnesses besides the children had also seen the object, but from a distance.

Sighting 19 is interesting in several respects, particularly because the cows were bellowing outside. Such responses in animals have occurred in many sightings all over the world, although this seems to be the only early instance in the Uintah Basin (but see Chapter 8).

Red Ball on Agency Hill. The sightings of September 28, 1966 are among the most interesting of those in Junior's file. Four groups of witnesses came to our attention, and if a search could have been made within a few days after the sightings, more witnesses probably could have been found. The sightings took place east of Roosevelt around Ft. Duchesne. In our records they begin about 9:00 PM with another report (#20A) from Kent Denver (see Fig. 1-5):

Fig. 1-7 *Verl and Leah Haslem with their son Alan (1968).*

Denver was riding bicycles with Chuck Thompson, a buddy from Ft. Duchesne, and his sister Kay. (Charles Thompson was a Native American student of mine at Utah State University, where I had already heard a UFO story from him.) The UFO they saw was a "ball of fire," but the fire would disappear, and then they could see a double-convex shape. They watched it for perhaps half an hour.

The Haslems' Meteor in Reverse. The next three groups of witnesses apparently all saw something within a few minutes. Probably Verl Haslem and his wife and son (Fig. 1-7) were the first of the three groups, and it seems probable that the object they saw, which could conceivably have been the one seen by Kent Denver, was not the one seen by the other two groups of witnesses (#20B). The time of Verl Haslem's sighting coincides almost exactly with that of Joe Ann Harris (10:15 PM), yet their accounts of what happened suggest that they were not watching the same object. Their descriptions of the object also differ.

Verl Haslem was an assistant bank manager in Roosevelt with a small farm a few miles east of town. He and his wife proved to be intelligent and very thoughtful witnesses who were deeply impressed by their experience with a UFO. They were coming home from a bank party with one son, Dan, asleep on the back seat but another son, Alan, awake and watching. As they came up over a hill, there was a bright orange light hovering over their home and rhythmically changing in intensity. They had a strange feeling and were a little worried about their house. Verl floored the gas pedal, but as they got within perhaps a quarter of a mile of their place, the object moved quickly to the south. As their truck slid to a stop by their home, they jumped out, and the light went out. "But it didn't go off just like shutting off a light in your room; this bright light went from bright orange to a yellow to a blue to a gray and nothing left." Then, "the light came on again in the opposite fashion, from a gray to a blue to this bright orange. Just as we jumped out of the car, it went up in the sky. It looked like a meteor in reverse. It left a trail far behind it, and it was a very clear night." Leah Haslem thought that they were making contact with their conversation. When they first saw them, Verl said, " 'Look. There's a flying saucer.' And the light went out, immediately.' " All of this speculation is quite typical of Uintah Basin sightings.

Contrary to Dean Powell's interpretation, the Haslems had no doubt that "it was something beyond anything ever produced by men on this planet. That was entirely some type of extraterrestrial machine, the way it went upward and out of sight. Oh, you just could hardly believe it. When it first started, it didn't just slowly start; it seemed instantly to be going. Not with a jerk but almost without a jerk . . . . In just a second or two it was out of sight."

Terror: Attack on the Road to Randlett. The high point of the evening of September 18, 1966, was the sighting of Joe Ann Harris (later Joe Ann Lube) and her companions (#21A). Joe Ann (Fig. 1-8) and her husband were living in an apartment attached to a small Latter-Day Saint (Mormon) chapel in Randlett, a Native American town about fifteen miles southeast of Ft. Duchesne. Joe Ann had driven some Native American girls to Roosevelt and was taking them home. As they rounded a turn south of Fort Duchesne, they saw a big bright light just below a ridge at about treetop level. It started moving toward them. As it got closer, they could see that there was a large dome, which was flashing a yellow color. When the light was on, the object was stationary; it would go out, and when it came back on, the object was much closer. When the light was out, they could see a flat bottom that extended out on either side (see convex planar model in Fig. 1-6). Joe Ann thought it was a big bomber or something about to crash into them—or an Air Force experiment! She even half expected to see Air Force boys in the dome, grinning at the trick they were playing on her. It approached very closely, and she and the Native American girls, as well as a large Native American woman in the front seat, were terrified. At its closest approach, within 30 to 50 feet, Joe Ann estimated, it filled the windshield of the car. "It was as big as the chapel in Randlett." The girls were trying to get on the floor in the back seat, and the woman was

Fig. 1-8 (A) *Joe Ann Harris and* (B) *the location of her sighting (1968). The UFO first appeared as a flashing light to the right of the picture just below the crest of the butte. At its closest approach, it nearly filled the windshield of their automobile.*

trying to get on the floor in the front. Joe Ann had stopped the car and was trying to back down the highway when a car came around the bend behind her. As she looked back to the front, the object was gone. She followed the car that came from behind, but the driver, Gail Wilkins, had not seen the object. Apparently, it disappeared while Joe Ann had her head turned to the rear. The next day, another woman who had been with the girls in Roosevelt contacted Joe Ann. Shortly after she and Joe Ann had parted, she apparently saw the same object.

Estel's Meteor in Reverse on the Road to Vernal. A few days after talking to Joe Ann, Junior and I drove over to Vernal to talk to Estel Manwaring (later Mrs. Harry Dee Kidd). She is a schoolteacher there and proved to be an exceptionally coherent witness. After requesting my credentials and asking what I was up to, she told us her story (#21B).

Estel and Joe Ann were working together in a Native American mission. They had taken the Native American girls to Roosevelt to play in a ball game. One girl lived in Vernal, so Estel offered to take her home, and they continued east on Highway 40 after Joe Ann turned south at Fort Duchesne, toward Randlett. As Estel came up on a hill east of Fort Duchesne, the girl who was with her noticed a yellow light just above the trees to the south. There was a large house along the otherwise deserted highway, and Estel pulled into the driveway to get a better look at the object. She said, "When I pulled out from the trees, then apparently, it was watching me as we were watching it, and it went up very rapidly, straight up. I never heard any sound at all." While they were driving and before its departure, it looked about the size of "a small house," but with a dome that was lit up and flashing on and off. There were extremely bright lights around the bottom, as in Junior's planar convex model (Fig. 1-6). But the lights were so bright that it was difficult to make out the shape of the bottom. As in so many Uintah Basin sightings, the lights were pulsating in brightness and changing colors. At first the object was cruising along at the same speed as the car, which Estel had slowed for a better look. Judging by a row of trees on the other side of a field, it might have been about 400 feet away. The departure was spectacular: "And when it went up, it went up so fast that our heads just moved back on our necks! Now, my windshield slopes up (I have a Pontiac), and it just went so fast that I could hardly follow it, and the lights changed underneath it with a glowing. It looked like a glowing, burning thing as it went up, sort of a bluish-reddish color." As other witnesses, Estel compared the color with the end of a welding torch—"a different colored light; it wasn't like a car light or a light in a house."

Estel and Joe Ann sat down and compared notes carefully and were quite agreed on what they had seen, especially the dome on top, lighted from inside. If they did see the same object, it had turned on its bottom rim lights after frightening Joe Ann and her fellow travelers. These lights occur in the accounts of several people.

The Ercanbracks' Bumper-Colored, Daylight UFO. One sighting (#22) of September 30, 1966, was particularly interesting since it took place in broad daylight at close range and involved three young teenaged boys as witnesses: twins Keven and Bevin Ercanbrack and an older brother, Curtis (age 15). Because the object hovered above some nearby trees, the witnesses were able to make a rather accurate measurement of its diameter (fifty to sixty feet).

At about four o'clock in the afternoon, the boys were on a tractor, going to bury a dead calf, when they saw the large object hovering directly above some trees. They suggested that it was looking at the calf! They jumped off the tractor and ran toward it, "and it just went kind of slow until it got about forty-five feet away from us." It took off rapidly, but the boys could see it at "long distances away" until it "got up in the clouds and went away." It had the planar-convex shape and "it was shiny like metal or something, like the color of a bumper. It didn't make any noise."

The sounds described in Sighting 23 ("like a busy signal on a telephone") are unusual and interesting. In Sightings 25 and 26, the double convex object appeared, but this time turned on edge. The color green does not go neglected in our accounts, but it is rather unusual, and a brilliant green light, bright enough to light up the bedroom (#39), is indeed of interest. This was also a close sighting, involving maneuvering.

The fall of 1966 was clearly the time of the UFO in the Uintah Basin. It was also the time of close approaches, landings, and near landings. The double-convex and the convex-planar objects were observed repeatedly, as were windows or flashing lights of different colors. Several of the features apparent during the fall of 1966 failed to show up in subsequent sightings, or at least they were infrequent.

Sharon's Big, Glowing, Uncomfortable UFO. Recently, my son Clark read the manuscript for this edition and reminded me of a good sighting his wife had when she was a small girl, probably in the summer of 1966. Not only did her close-encounter UFO head off toward the Uintah Basin, but it left a physical trace, something not seen in Junior's files before the rash of cattle mutilations in the 1970s (which may or may not be con-nected with the UFO phenomenon; see Chapter 3). Here is the story as remembered vividly by Sharon M. Peterson Salisbury:

> I grew up in a rural community [Pleasant Grove, north of Provo, Utah]. I was about 9 years old [in 1966]. One of my favorite pastimes in the summer was sleeping on top of my parent's flat-top roof; this gave me an opportunity to test my knowledge of the constellations . . . . I loved looking up at the night sky, watching the stars change through the night. One night my brothers and I ventured up on the rooftop . . . . My older brothers didn't much [like] that I came along and said I had to sleep far away from them because they didn't want girls around. We slept on the north side of the house—I on the west end and they on the east.
> Some time in the middle of the night, around 2 or 3 AM I'm guess-ing, I woke up because I was cold and had to go to the bathroom. I remember the smell of the cool night country air. When I raised my head I could see over the bricks to the field in back of my parent's prop-erty. There, hovering about 10 feet over the ground, I saw a large disc-shaped object at around 40 feet wide. It had a soft orange glow about it that seemed to change like the coals of a fire. It did not change loca-tion; it just hovered there for at least 15 minutes. There was no sound. I remember I was so scared to move because I was afraid I might be dis-covered, yet my bladder was prompting me to do so. I wondered if my brothers were awake and could see it too. I remembered slowly turning my head, whispering their names. They were sleeping hard. I watched and waited and waited—it seemed like forever. Then suddenly, without any sound, it lifted straight up, and without even slowing down, it turned and went southeast over the mountain, disappearing from view. I remember coming down off the house, trying to find my way in the dark. It was an especially dark night with hardly any moon. The next day I ventured to the back field, which was about 300 feet from the house, and could see the black charred weeds in a large circle.

In a recent conversation, Sharon noted that it was her brothers who found the charred weeds, which she then went out to see. When she told them about the UFO (after they discovered the burned area), they made fun of her, so she told almost no one (not even her parents) about the sight-ing until she married my son and found that his dad had written a book about UFOs! Her parents still live in the same home, so Clark and Sharon have since measured the distance from her parents' roof to the location of the UFO and found it to be almost exactly 500 feet, a little farther than she originally estimated.

4. Winter of 1967

In contrast to the over thirty sightings during the fall of 1966, only about ten got into Junior's file during the winter of 1967. Several are noteworthy, however, and we shall discuss two of them.

The McDonalds' Ouija-Board UFO. Sighting 41A is well calculated to frustrate the careful objective approach of a scientific UFO investigator. The Clyde McDonald family was informed by one of its members, a fourth grader, that a flying saucer was going to appear above the Roosevelt Hospital at eight o'clock on the evening of February 23, 1967. How did the young lady know that the flying saucer was going to appear? Why, some of the students in the other fourth-grade class had been playing with a ouija board, and the ouija board had informed them that this event would take place. Mother and Father chuckled properly and sat down to watch television. They were relaxing in their bare feet when the children began to bundle up and go out to meet their eight o'clock appointment with the UFO. Mother said, "You'd better hurry. It will be gone before you get there." Then, as Mrs. McDonald said,

> Tim looked up, and he hollered, "Oh, run, Tammy. There it is!" and they about broke that door off getting in. So we all ran, the three of us, jumped up and ran to the door, and, of course, then we could see that big light right out there by the Jennings' yard. Boy, they were behind us and they wouldn't go out then. . . . . We just stood out there then and watched, and we about froze—we were barefoot and everything—but we didn't want to come back in and lose it! It was kind of an orange ball, orange to red, kind of in a circle, bigger than an ordinary light.

"How big was it compared to the full moon?" I asked her.

"Well, it wasn't that big. I'd say probably a third, wouldn't it be?"

One of the children ran in to call the neighbors, and Mr. McDonald went to get his rifle scope. By the time he got back, it was gone. They watched out of the windows of the house for a half hour or so but didn't see it again.

This sighting was unusually well documented by Junior Hicks, as is apparent from Table 1. He found at least five other witnesses who described the same object, which they claim to have seen at the same time and in about the same place. Some of them saw it at different times, moving rather than stationary. In the case of Roy Marchant, it flew alongside his car for about a mile and then went straight up in the fashion described by so many witnesses. Of course, the really perplexing thing about this excellent sighting (excellent, not so much because of details, but because of the number of witnesses involved) is the prediction from the ouija board. What can a non-superstitious, modern scientist say about this? I suppose he could suggest that it was purely coincidence, and perhaps it was.

Thyrena's Escort from Vernal to Roosevelt. The outstanding case of a UFO flying along with a moving car, and surely one of the remarkable sightings in the Uintah Basin, took place on the evening of February 27, 1967 (#42). Thyrena Daniels (Fig. 1-9), a registered nurse then in her mid-sixties, told her story straight and without apology, and what a story it is! How I would have liked to have been riding in the front seat with Mrs. Daniels that evening.

She left the hospital in Vernal a little after seven in the evening, driving home alone to Roosevelt. Swinging around a big curve not far out of Vernal, she noticed a light in a rather peculiar place, off to the right of the highway. It kept getting larger and lower, and she wondered if it was a plane about to crash. It was behind a hill for a moment.

> And I kept hoping that I wouldn't see it again! You know the kind of a feeling, because it did give you quite a numbness of a feeling. But as I came right around this little curve, why here it was, just right here. I wouldn't know how to say how close. About as close as that closest house across the street. . . . But it was raising up, and I could see that plainly, and coming sort of in the way I was going. Now it was never out of sight but once from Vernal to Roosevelt. And the one time that it was, it was sort of over me, and I felt worse, a little more frightened then, than when it was out where I could see it, because I was getting sort of control of myself, you know, as I came along. . . . Sometimes it would be almost directly over the highway, and sometimes it would be a little to the right of the highway but not too very high. . . . I don't think that at any time in that almost thirty-mile stretch that it was over three good treetops high. . . . Now it looked like a ball. . . with about a third of the bottom cut off so it was flat.

The drive home took about forty-five minutes with the object in sight virtually all of that time.

> And I was going at a pretty good speed too, but I wasn't trying to

Fig. 1-9 (A) *Thyrena Daniels (taken in 1972) and* **(B)** *the location of her first encounter with the UFO. Mrs. Daniels was driving her automobile along Highway 40 from right to left (east to west). The object was first seen to the right of the highway at about the center of the photograph.*

outrun it or anything! I had controlled myself. It was not going to bother me! It had all kinds of chances, had it been something wanting to block my passage or using me in any way, it could have done that because there were no cars out on the road. In fact, I only encountered one car coming home, and they passed me at a terrific speed [going the same direction], so they had to have seen it. It was a dark maroon colored car, and it was heavily loaded with people. But I don't know . . . .

Now, I tried taking off my glasses. I have to have them to drive. I tried taking them off to see if that would change it, which it didn't. Or the coloring of it. Now, it was as orange as a new risen moon. That color. Not exactly orange like an orange. I mean it looked like a new [full] moon, that wasn't quite up. . . . And then on this bottom part where it was cut across, there were streaks of sometimes a real bright red, sometimes they looked blue, and sometimes a kind of greenish cast. . . . It looked like, you might say, fire.

Thyrena said the "streaks" were like flames, but "They didn't go up. They went out. And sometimes they'd go quite a bit farther than other times." The flames extended to either side to a distance equal to the width of the object—extending sometimes to the fences on both sides of the road. As she came into Roosevelt, a culvert crossed above the highway, and she thought the object might hit it, but it ascended above the culvert and kept ascending until it was almost out of sight. When she pulled into her home, she ran into the house to get her husband, but by then it was only a red/orange light far to the west.

It wasn't imaginary, no how! That was definitely out. I know I saw it, and I know it was something. It wasn't just a dream or just imagination. . . . And this one time it was right up over the car, and I didn't feel too good about that. I liked it out there where I could see it. Then I didn't feel scared of it.

I just couldn't sleep. You can imagine something like that. And I was so against thinking that there were such things, so I sat here just right like I am now. He'd gone to bed, and I couldn't go to sleep, so I was sitting here crocheting, and the moon came up over the neighbor's house, and I thought, "No, no, not again." But that's what it looked like just for a minute, like that moon. And I got almost the same start again, and that was two or three hours later.

(The Moon was full on February 24, 1967, so on the 27th it would have been a little past full and would rise almost three hours later than when it was full. Several Uintah Basin witnesses called the full moon a "new moon"—but went on to describe a full moon. You might say it was "newly full"!)

Thyrena goes on to tell about someone who probably saw the same object, but when I checked with that witness, he said the object was going from west to east—opposite to Thyrena's UFO. She speculates about

Fig. 1-10 *Halfway Hollow. Photo was taken in 2009 from Highway 40, looking south. The road south to Ouray is left of the photo. Sightings 30, 43, 52, and 72 occurred at this location. The pointed butte is where Czar and Orvil Rudy saw their "burning haystack" (Sighting 52).*

government experiments but says that Junior convinced her that couldn't be the case.

I was interested in the little experiment Thyrena had performed: "I'd take off my glasses and no, it looked just the same. Then I ran my windows down and looked out at it . . . and it was the same thing. It still had that bluish-green, what looked to me like flame, coming out from it, but it looked like it was coming out both sides. Sometimes it got more red, but most of the time it had this greenish-blue cast. Sometimes it looked quite blue, and sometimes it looked quite green."

5. Spring of 1967

Tony Zufelt's Train Windows. Halfway Hollow is a dry desert gully halfway between Vernal and Roosevelt (Fig. 1-10). Several sightings in the Uintah Basin have occurred there, typically when the witness is driving home from Vernal to Roosevelt. Sighting 43 is the first of these in Table 1, and it is a strange one to say the least. It is colorful and bizarre—although of brief duration. I was quite ready to write it off as some sort of pure fantasy, but Tony Zufelt and his wife told a straight story:

It was dark as they drove west along Highway 40 when the surrounding ground started to light up, dim at first and then "as bright as this room." They wondered where the light was coming from, and then they spotted the object about 150 feet above the road. It came around the front of the car and then headed back toward Vernal. Tony stopped the car but couldn't hear any noise. I asked what it looked like:

> Well, to tell you the truth . . . it looked like a boxcar on a train, a train car, only it tapered off too fast, and there was a flame coming out of the rear end of it, but it wasn't in long strips. The first portion of it coming out was in round balls, and they were all colors, and then after the round balls, there were kind of long strips of fire coming out of that, but the darn windows in it were not like they were on a train car. They were more like a house door, just like that and low. Some of them looked like they'd be ten feet long. It had windows all down along it like that, but they didn't have any partitions. Each one looked like one big light, and as they come towards the back, they got smaller. But the front of it looked like it was kind of round like that.

The lights were blue except for the balls of fire out the back, which were all colors. Tony estimated that the object might have been about 100 feet long, but the sighting was very short: a couple of minutes from the time the ground lit up, and then seconds for the object itself.

Sighting 46 includes the only report of a "formation" of objects. This witness was a retired Air Force officer. Sighting 47, involving a landing, looked like a good one, but I didn't have time to investigate either it or Sighting 48, which was a close, daylight sighting that had impressed Junior very strongly.

Junior was away from the Basin during part of the summer of 1967, but apparently no reports were waiting for him when he came home. We draw a blank on that period. Apparently, the UFO occupants, knowing that their cataloger and chronicler was away, arranged for a vacation themselves.

6. Autumn of 1967

The Bow Hunt: Fire on the Hill. Just as we were typing the manuscript for a final time in 1970, I heard of a group of people who had a Uintah Basin UFO sighting on September 1, 1967. These were hunters from the area around Salt Lake City, who knew nothing about the other sightings described here. It seemed worth comparing their story with sightings by Uintah Basin residents. The story matches in close detail. I called Lee Albertson of Kearns, Utah, to interview him; the other witnesses were Barry Bruggeman, DeLoy Densley, and John Savage Jr.

The group was driving on a very muddy road, south of Ouray toward the Book Cliffs (Buck Canyon) about midnight. The sky was exceptionally clear as a storm had just passed. They were going to hunt deer with bows and arrows.

Coming over a small hill, they saw a "fire" hovering above a ridge.

It moved right along with us, and, you know, late at night, I'd been driving, and I thought, what's the matter with me? So I pulled up, and I stopped on top of this hill and watched it, and the son-of-a-gun moved along, stayed on about the same plane, and then it broke the horizon, and there it sat, and gee, we couldn't imagine what it was—and then it hovered there for a minute, and then it went almost straight into the air. It went way up and just continued to go and go and go and just completely disappeared up there. While I was sitting there talking about this—it even makes the old hair stand up on the back of my neck now—the son-of-a-gun came back in another location, and it came right down. You've seen how a big harvest moon is as it comes over the mountain? It was about this size. It kind of sat there like it was watching, you know? And then after a while, let's say a space of maybe thirty seconds, it took off again. . . . The first time it took off just kind of straight out, and it just shrank right up to nothing, quite fast, and the next time it took off, it got right out of there. It was really something—a lot faster.

Lee estimates the distance in the southwest at about a mile; when the object returned, it was in the north-northeast. There was no sound.

Lee then tells about another sighting—ten people in the group this time. It was the same year and the same area, but it was the rifle hunt instead of the bow hunt. "This time when it finally took off, it just kind of hovered out there, and it seemed to be a little bit smaller this time, but when it left, you could see something fall away from it. We reported this at the time. There was a fellow from the Air Force. We didn't know whether to tell anybody, because, you know: 'Ha, ha, what are you, some type of nut?' But we decided to, and he said that there had been other sightings of something similar."

A Burning Haystack Circling the Moon. There were several other interesting sightings during this period, but I found time to talk only to Orvil and Czar Rudy (#52). Originally, when they told their story to Junior a few months after the sighting, they estimated the date as Oct. 5, 1967. Having checked on the position of the moon and discussed the matter with the Rudys, we have corrected the date to Oct. 14, 1967.

Czar Rudy (elderly) and his son (middle-aged) were returning to Roosevelt from Flaming Gorge about 8:00 PM when, in Halfway Hollow, they saw what looked like a burning haystack—although they knew there were no haystacks at that desert location (on the pointed knoll in Fig. 1-10). They stopped to see what it was. "It was flat across the bottom and a half-saucer, and for a minute we thought it was the moon, and then we knew it wasn't. The moon was up above. . . ." The 'haystack' raised up very rapidly and made a half circle around the moon and then was out of sight. "It kind of blinded us, and it traveled at terrific speed." (The moon was full on Oct. 18, 1967, and would have been just east of the zenith on Oct. 14.) "It was large; it was just a glow. It was something like a fire, and yet it was too bright. . . . Take a tumbleweed; did you ever take one of them and throw it on a fire in the evening? You know how they'll just sort of flame, and when the flame dies, there's a glowing." That's a good description!

Dick Hackford's Shifting Gears. This sighting (#53, which took place on October 11, 1967) was another outstanding one in Junior's file. There wasn't time to talk to all of the witnesses, but the more we talked, the longer the list of witnesses seemed to grow. Nearly everyone who was in on the sighting seemed to know of someone else who had also seen the same object that night. Our list of witnesses extended beyond forty by the time I had to leave the Uintah Basin. As indicated in the table (and hexagons in Fig. 1-1), people all over the Basin reported seeing the brilliant reddish-orange object moving from south to north, generally over the Lapoint/White Rocks area. Dick Hackford's wife and three of his children saw the object, parked their car, and watched it for a few moments as it moved toward the mountains. They commented that it was headed right for Dick's truck. As a matter of fact, his brother and his brother's family also saw the object. Mrs. Hackford said other cars were parked along the road with people watching the object. Since we have no reports from that particular location, it is clear that there were many other witnesses besides the forty or so whom we are able to list. October 11, 1967, was an eventful night for UFO watchers in the Uintah Basin.

The object did indeed proceed on toward Dick Hackford, who saw it under spine-chilling circumstances. We have two versions of his story, one carefully written down by Junior Hicks shortly after the time of the sightings; the other taken from my tape, recorded about eight months after the event. It is interesting to compare the two accounts. Here is the report from Junior's file:

> I was driving an old truck up to our camp on the mountain. The truck's battery was dead, and we had to push it to get it started. I hadn't drove the truck very much, and I didn't want to stop it because I would have to walk to camp. I was driving this old truck up the mountain, shifting gears and keeping the truck going, thinking that if it stopped, I'd have to walk to camp.
>
> Suddenly this big ball of light about two hundred yards away started moving toward me. It looked about three yards in diameter, getting bigger, orange in color. My first thought was about what happened to a horse in Colorado. I didn't want to get shot by any ray gun. I was badly frightened and shaken up. The object moved to within thirty to forty feet, lighting up the ground. I was busy trying to keep the truck going. The light began to change color to a fluorescent blue and settled directly over the truck. The area around the truck was as light as day. I could see the leaves of the quaking aspen trees around me. The object stayed just above the truck as I drove up the mountain. I was getting very nervous, hoping it would not stop me. I imagined the truck stopping and me walking to camp with that thing out there waiting for me. I was too busy driving and shifting gears to get any detail of the object. I had both hands on the steering wheel and in low gear when suddenly the gearshift moved from low to compound. When I saw this happen, it somehow assured me that if they would shift my gears for me, they wouldn't hurt me, and I felt a little better. Suddenly some headlights of a car appeared, coming down the mountain ahead of me. It must've scared this thing, cause it suddenly rose up off the truck and left.

When I read the above story in Junior's file, the hair stood up along the back of my neck. I was most anxious to meet Dick Hackford and to hear him tell the story himself. The recorded interview is very close to Junior's report, but there are some interesting points:

> I thought, well, my next bet will be around one of these curves; that will be my destiny. When it came over me, it was right on top of me, and the quaking asps [aspens] just brighted up—and they were lots brighter than the old truck lights. I was giving this old truck the gas,

and I was afraid to shift gears. Now this is something that you might not believe. I never told you [Junior] this, but the truck shifted, and I never touched a gear. Now whether I did or whether I didn't, I don't know, but that truck was in compound, and I had it low gear, see. And I was afraid to shift it to compound, afraid I'd kill my motor, and when I got to the top, that old truck was in compound gear, and I know it was in low gear when I started up there. And this light lit up the quaking asps just as bright as day. . . . But boy, that was something. I still say they're not from this outfit. . . . It was plenty big. A good-sized outfit coming right toward me.

Let's discuss for a moment the interesting little discrepancy in Dick's story. It points out a characteristic of human nature which surely must play an important role in many of the accounts studied by any UFO researcher.

Within a few days after the event had occurred, Dick was so enthusiastic about telling the story to Junior that he added the detail of his watching the gearshift move from low into compound while he had his hands on the wheel. After a few months had passed, however, Dick had apparently come to realize more and more distinctly that he had not actually seen the gearshift move. Rather he "knew" it was in low at the bottom of the mountain, in compound at the top, and that he had not shifted. Even here there is a little doubt. ("Now whether I did or whether I didn't, I don't know . . .")

There certainly are pitfalls and problems in searching the memory for details relating to an account. The passage of time might blur some of these details so that they become less distinct. Here we may be dealing with an opposite phenomenon. With the passage of time and the diminution of immediate enthusiasm, basic honesty begins to prevail over embellishments in a story that were not really known but seemed too good to pass up in the telling.

The concept of the UFO pilot remotely shifting gears for Dick brings up such formidable problems of physics that it becomes much easier to imagine that, in the excitement of the event, Dick did shift the gears himself—but quite unconsciously—so he had no recall of the action whatsoever. (Here, I'm sounding like a debunker with a just-suppose story!)

We spent an hour or two after the above interview talking with the Hackfords about the significance and meaning of UFOs in the Uintah Basin. Several years before, they had been active in the religious group called Jehovah's Witnesses. In the context of that theology (in its 1940s form), they were inclined to think of the UFOs as manifestations of the demons. Everyone seems to have some kind of answer.

We also interviewed David Rasmussen, who with three or four other witnesses, had apparently watched the same object go straight up into the sky with breathtaking speed (like a meteor in reverse) after it had finished frightening poor Dick Hackford.

7. Winter of 1968

Several good sightings occurred during this period, as indicated in the table. Unfortunately, we were unable to find time for any interviews, although the landing described in Sighting 65 was an especially good story.

8. Spring and Summer, 1968

Upon arriving in Roosevelt, I was told that sightings had occurred at the rate of one every week or two for the past year and a half, but there had been no sightings for about a month before my arrival. The last sighting, (#67, of May 21) is an excellent one, however. An English teacher with twenty-two members of her class all watched the large, silver, shining object maneuver, change speed, hover, and drop near the ground.

On Friday morning, June 21, Junior informed me that there had been a good sighting Wednesday night, right over Roosevelt. Some people had seen the brilliant red object hovering over the church for a while. As they drove around trying to get a better look at it, it disappeared. I had made it a point to be outside as much as possible after dark, since that is when most of the sightings had occurred, but, of course, I was nowhere around when this sighting took place.

Then when we were talking to Dick Hackford, his young son came in and told us that he had seen a red, round, glowing UFO on that same Wednesday evening. This time it was up by the slide rock in White Rocks Canyon. He and some friends, driving around in a car, had watched it for perhaps half an hour to forty-five minutes. They had first seen it in the sky, and then it had descended and remained for most of the time over these rocks in an area well known to the boys, and where they knew that there was nothing but rocks. It would change intensity, almost fading out and then becoming brilliant red again. They thought that its diameter might have been about half that of the full moon. In addition to changing intensity, it also changed from a brilliant white to a kind of yellowish-white and then brilliant red.

So that was my luck again. Why wasn't I driving around White Rocks Canyon? Of course, the reason was that there were hundreds of places besides the church in Roosevelt and White Rocks Canyon where I might have been driving around. My only consolation was that Junior, in his then seven years of collecting sightings, had not had a really good one himself. He had seen some lights move in strange and interesting ways—and I would like to see even that much! (By 2009, Junior had had a couple of good sightings to tell about!)

9. Summer of 1968 to Autumn of 1973

When I returned to Roosevelt in April, 1972, I found that Junior had accumulated only about fourteen good sightings during the five intervening years. These are indeed good ones, and they are included in Table 1. Junior found five separate witnesses (mostly his students) for Sighting 70, for example. Three of the sightings had been especially impressive to Junior, and so we made appointments to talk with the witnesses. We were able to talk with at least two witnesses to each of the three sightings. The different accounts gave us an excellent opportunity to compare stories from more than one witness. There was good general agreement, but often details are described differently by the different witnesses, and sometimes an important detail will show up in one account but not in another. All this will fortify the point to be made in Chapter 6 that, while people under the excitement of watching a UFO are good observers, numerous distortions of interpretation and communication (with the interviewer) creep into an account. Unfortunately, space permits only summaries of the actual interviews, but I'll include many direct quotations.

Balloon with Hanging Vacuum Tube. Morlin Buchanan and Richard Faucett were hunting at Pelican Lake on the evening of November 14, 1968 when they saw their marvelous UFO (drawing in Fig. 1-3). We visited Morlin first (Fig. 1-11). He was an industrial arts teacher at West Junior High, where Junior taught.

Morlin remembered:

> We were out hunting geese down by Pelican Lake. It was a kind of enjoyable evening, just about at sundown. Probably the sun had set, but it's difficult to remember for sure. All of a sudden old Richard turned to me and said, "Look at that weather balloon up there, or whatever it is. It's a UFO!" And I said, "No, it's not; that's a plain old balloon down there with a string on it—see the string, how it curves with a little bit of breeze?" It was about time for us to quit hunting geese, so we jumped

Fig. 1-11 (A) *Location of the Buchanan-Faucett sighting.* (B) *Morlin Buchanan (left) and* (C) *Richard Faucett (right). When the object was first spotted from a distance of six to eight miles, it was about even with the horizon. The location photo was taken from the position of the closest approach. The "tube" was hanging so that the bottom was just above the ground in the sagebrush flat at the center and near the top of the picture. (Photos taken in 1972.)*

in the truck, and I looked through the field glasses and said, "It's down there about six blocks; we'll ride on down and grab that string off the ground." So we got in the truck, and we'd drive down the road a couple of miles and stop to look at it through the field glasses. I had these 10-50s, pretty powerful. It kept getting bigger, and that string kept getting bigger around! Pretty soon we'd gone about six or eight miles. I thought we'd just go down there and pick it up, but it got a little big there! Soon we were almost underneath it; not quite underneath, but you looked right up and there it was. The "string" was a great big wind tunnel descending from the UFO down to the earth. Just offhand I'd say it was at least three feet in diameter all the way down to the ground. And it kind of had a breeze that was really blowing it. There was gray matter coming up through this wind tunnel, so I presume it was kind of sucking things up from the ground into the object."

I asked if it was like a tornado spout.

Right! Right! Except it was the same diameter, right from the UFO clear to the ground. By the way, the object up in the sky was very round, sort of like a balloon, but the top of it was glowing—and I mean it looked like the sun was reflecting off the glass—but it couldn't have been, because the sun was down. . . . But anyway, as we jumped in the truck the last time and started off, all of a sudden the light went out and it was gone—just like that! . . . It disappeared. The lights went out, the tunnel was gone, and it just—pshoosh!—away it went.

I pushed the point: "Yes, but 'away it went' is different from disappearing. Were you watching at the time the light went out, or were you driving, and the next time you looked, it was gone?"

"We were driving, and all of a sudden, 'Did you see that?' 'Well, yeah!' I mean it was just gone. That's all there was to it. . . . The lights went out and it was dark all of a sudden. By the time we had traveled about eight miles, stopping to look through field glasses, it was quite dark."

They were close enough to estimate the height with some assurance: "When we got there, we were looking up at a fifty-degree or sixty-degree angle, or more. [It was] in front of the cliffs, the Randlett Ledges." They figured they were within about a block when it disappeared. The light on top was white with maybe a little yellow, not red like light from a setting sun would have been—and it was well after sunset anyway.

Morlin says it was "just a gray column, a white light on top, and a dark object, because it was getting dark," but silver or white when they first saw it. The very round object—not flattened in any way—was at least fifty feet in diameter. When I asked if it could have been some natural phenomenon, like a tornado, Morlin emphatically denied it. "The day had been calm, the sun had been shining, there was a nice evening breeze, a nice fall night." I kept pushing questions along those lines, and I'm glad I did, as this led to some additional information below. The tube had distinct, sharp edges, not fuzzy ones. There was gray matter inside the tube, but Morlin couldn't pin down in his memory why he had the impression that it was swirling.

The interview with Morlin Buchanan illustrates nicely the difficulties of communication. It took a lot of questions to produce a fairly clear picture in my mind of what Morlin had actually seen—and I'm not so sure it is really all that clear now! The interview also illustrates the difficulties of memory. It had been about three and a half years since the sighting, and some of the details presented by Morlin were different from those recorded in Junior's file. For example, the account Junior recorded mentions swirling dust at the base of the cylinder, but Morlin couldn't remember how he got the impression that it was spinning. The drawing in Junior's file also shows the bottom of the spherical object lit up as well as the top, but that was never mentioned by Morlin—or by Richard Faucett. These distortions and forgotten points are what one would expect in a real situation—but maybe not if the account had been carefully memorized as a hoax.

When we interviewed Richard Faucett, the interview began with three other UFO sightings of his before he got to the sighting with Morlin Buchanan.

We called on Richard Faucett, city manager of Roosevelt since 1966. Interestingly enough, he and Morlin had never really discussed their experience since it happened. They had told their stories to many other people, but it never seemed important to discuss their sighting with each other. There are a few interesting little discrepancies. Each one said that the other spotted the object first, for example! But generally speaking, the accounts support each other rather well. Incidentally, Richard Faucett has had a number of UFO sightings, including #48 in Table 1. For some reason we didn't discuss this one with him, although it was a good one.

Except for those little discrepancies, Richard's version of the evening was closely similar to Morlin's version, so I won't repeat those similar details, but there were some interesting new points:

> When we got about halfway to it, these two—I'm not sure if it was two or just one kind of oblong light—came out of it and shined down. It kinda spooked us. We stopped the truck and looked at it through our binoculars, and we could see that the thing hanging below it looked like it was oh, possibly four inches in diameter. And the darn thing was spinning—looked like it was turning, you know, rotating—but yet whatever it was with the light on it there just held real still.
>
> Then, when we got up about to where the old Young place was, it was about a quarter of a mile from where this thing was hovering.

I guess they must have gotten scared—whatever it was—because this light went out all of a sudden, and there was just kind of a flash, and it disappeared, and we never saw it again. But this thing that was underneath it—when we got up there close—was big. It was huge—looked like it was probably three or four feet in diameter, and it went clear to the ground. Finally the darn thing sucked right up inside of it, and it just flashed and disappeared. . . . I turned my spotlight on and looked all around in the sky, but we couldn't see it.

Richard emphasized that "it looked like the bottom of a tornado coming out of it, but instead of being funnel-shaped it was even all the way to the ground. When it went in, it was really fast! As I remember it—yes, the whole tube coming from the vehicle was turning. But the light was just as stationary in the sky as anything you've ever seen. I don't think it was over a quarter of a mile high; in fact, it looked like just a couple hundred yards up to where it was." As to the tube, "At first it appeared blurry, and even as close as we got, it still looked blurry, like it was really spinning. You couldn't see through it, but it looked kind of gray and blurry."

Richard agreed with Morlin that the spherical object was high in the sky when they were close: "Maybe sixty degrees or seventy degrees even, from where we were at . . . . We went down the next day—I don't remember if it was me alone or if I had somebody with me—we went down and looked around on the ground to see if we could find any disturbed earth or anything. We couldn't find anything."

The details of Faucett's sighting are interesting. Again a strong impression of movement of the tube hanging from the object is mentioned, but again the witness isn't exactly sure of how he got this impression. The estimates of distance are also significant. In the accounts, they vary from two hundred to nine hundred yards (unless the object moved between the two estimates, which isn't clear in the interviews). Distance is always difficult to estimate, but in this case, if we really wanted to know how close they got, we could probably find out, because they had a strong impression of where the tube was touching the ground (probably obtained from their seeing swirling dust as reported at first but then apparently forgotten).

I got the feeling that I was pushing Morlin Buchanan to the point where he was uncomfortable and kind of gave up trying to answer my questions. But I'm glad that I did push him a bit! Some time after the first edition of this book had been published, I read an article about dust devils in the desert.[2] There were photos, and the string of dust going up was indeed about the same diameter all the way up! By the time I read the article, I had forgotten many of the details of the interview, and I began to have grave doubts about the Buchanan/Faucett sighting. Maybe it was just a dust devil, and I hadn't been suspicious enough! Reading the entire interview, however, I clearly already suspected that it might have been a miniature tornado (forgetting that there were such things as "dust devils"), and I pushed pretty hard to check that out.

This sighting is an excellent example of how ambiguous a sighting can be. My first inclination is to play the role of a debunker. The "just-suppose" story would be that the witnesses simply saw a dust devil, common in desert regions. If ever there was a case that, on the surface, sounds like a natural phenomenon misinterpreted, this is it. The "string" below the "weather balloon" sounds exactly like a dust devil. Dust devils can be inches to several yards in diameter, but a typical diameter is three to four feet. They can be just a few yards to over a thousand yards high, typically with a curve like a string in a light breeze. They can be seen from as far as ten miles away. They spin just like Richard Faucett described, and the edges can be quite fuzzy—although they can also appear to be surprisingly sharp. There is almost always a cloud of dust surrounding the bottom. They can last from seconds to twenty minutes or half an hour. When they collapse, it is sudden! It's as if they just disappear.

There are some serious problems with the dust-devil hypothesis for the Buchanan/Faucett sighting, however. Perhaps the most serious problem is the time of day—something the witnesses cannot be mistaken about! Dust devils occur in summer, under clear skies, in early afternoon when the ground is heated by the sun—and probably not on an evening and as late as November 14, when it is likely to be quite cool. (Tornados, which apparently were in our minds during the interviews, form as part of large storm systems.) I cannot find any mention of a dust devil beginning just after sunset and lasting until it was quite dark. The second serious problem is the "weather balloon," the object at the top of the "string." The witnesses both report seeing such an object clearly, at least before it got dark. None of the photos of dust devils that I've seen have anything at the top; that is, there is never even a cloud (as with a tornado). Indeed, usually the dust becomes thinner near the top until there is just blue sky. A third problem concerns the light that "flashed" and then went out. Dust devils do generate electro-magnetic charges, but I find no mention of lightning from a dust devil.

Now it's time for a different kind of just-suppose story: Just suppose that a genuine, Uintah Basin-type UFO hovered over the desert near Randlett, beaming energy down to heat the earth until a dust devil formed! That's a good probable explanation—except, perhaps, for the energy beam and the UFO with such capability! Are there really such things?

Faucett Family Sightings. Richard Faucett's other sightings are far less spectacular. The first one was seen by his wife from her father's porch. It was a fairly large, amber-red object high in the sky. It disappeared and then reappeared closer to the ground.

The second sighting was at Halfway Hollow. It was a bright light in the west, but Richard remembers it as being about "the size of a three-quarter moon when we first saw it, then as it disappeared, it got smaller and smaller until, as I remember, it finally went behind the mountain." In his file for this sighting, Junior lists the date as August 24, 1967. Venus was dimming and close to the horizon at that time. Since it was in the proper position, it must be considered as a possible explanation for that sighting. Apparent size can be deceiving (see Mable's story in Chapter 6).

The third one was another light in the sky, but at one point it sent out a beam of spliced light. Was this one of the strange beams that Junior recorded, or was it a spotlight striking layers of clouds?

The Distant Red Giant with Swirling Dust. The vision described in this account is one of the most colorful that I have encountered in UFO lore. The episode was in my mind for days after hearing about it, and it was especially vivid when Junior and I drove out to the area in his Jeep. Leland Mecham (Fig. 1-12) lives five miles west of Roosevelt. He and his son Jody were riding after dark on September 5, 1970, when they had their sighting.

Leland: [We] looked up west and saw this big red glow with a big dome-shaped light over the top of it to the ground. It was behind Carl Richin's house—which is at least a mile away—and I would say it was a half mile [past] his house. It looked about ten times bigger than his house. Down at the bottom of this glow there were long streamers of red coming out the bottom, like sun rays—that's what it reminded me of, but they were red. And where they were hitting the ground, the dust or smoke or something was boiling, just flying like that. You could see it roll way up in the air and then come back down; it would never go clear up to the object, but it was rolling way up and coming back. We watched for probably three or four minutes, and finally we decided ([since] there was a car coming) we better stop somebody, to

Fig. 1-12 (A) *Approximate position of the Mecham-Hullinger sighting, photographed after driving close to where the object might have been (opposite page, top);* (B) *view from where the object was first seen (arrow) by* (C) *Jody and Leland Mecham (1972).*

get somebody else to see it. So we stopped them, and they said yeah, they'd just seen a flash of it. So we took off for home.

When we got down there by the neighbors, we went behind some big cottonwoods and were blocked from view of it. When we came out, the red object was completely gone. Where it went, I don't know. But the light—the dome light—was still there, and this, whatever it was flying in the air, was still a-boiling up, flying, and going up and settling. And it did that for quite a while. We came clear over here and through the gate and over to the house, and this light just gradually kept shrinking and coming down like this, just shrinking to the ground. When we got up here, I got Norma [Leland's wife]; she came out the back door, and the glow was still there, but you couldn't see this, whatever it was—it wouldn't come up high enough to see it above the hill. It's really kind of hard to explain without seeing it. I don't know; it was really something. Jody, I think it kind of scared him."

Jody: "Yeah, it was kind of spooky."

Leland: "The ridge north of Carl Richin's would be at least two miles, and we could see the cedars [junipers] on that ridge just like it was daylight. It is sand dunes kind of spotted with cedars, and you could see the individual trees just as good that night as you could in the daytime. . . . Just the red object itself was at least ten times bigger than Richin's house, and he's got a big house. It was on the other side of his house. The rays that came out of it were just as bright red as the object itself—they were just brilliant red. The rays weren't coming straight down but out about like this—like the sun was shining down through a hole in the clouds. . . . It looked to me like whatever it was coming out of the bottom of it was a thrust, letting it down or putting it in the air. It reminded me of smoke at first, but if it was smoke it would have kept going.

Whatever this was, it only came up about halfway to the object, and then it would go back to the ground. It looked like a big cloud, only it was boiling. I figured from the height of that ridge, this side of it, probably the object itself must have been four hundred or five hundred feet in the air. The dirt or dust or whatever it was flying went up in the air half that distance. . . . This dome light over the object just kept going toward the ground, getting dimmer and dimmer and smaller until it was completely gone after maybe half an hour. Everything just indicated that it set down like that, and if it had gone in the air, I don't know why this light wouldn't have gone with it. It looked like something hot that was cooling off."

Jody said the object reminded him of the moon, and Leland agreed that it was like the moon but more oblong and a little larger than the moon appears. Leland and Jody didn't see the object leave, but they were behind the trees and couldn't see it for a short time.

A month later, Leland and Junior drove in a Jeep to where the object appeared to have been, but they couldn't find anything. In the interview, Leland tells about someone from Texas who came into the saddle shop where Leland worked. The stranger had a tale about an object he had seen that had a "thrust out of the bottom of it" that dug its way into the ground. The object went into the hole and disappeared!

Like so many other Uintah Basin witnesses, Leland goes on to tell

Fig. 1-13 *Dee Hullinger (1972).*

about other sightings. His brother and his wife were present for one of these rather good sightings—which I won't bother to recount here. On another occasion, with others present, Leland saw an object, flashing brightly and then dimly, that appeared to be sitting on some power lines at a distance away.

"But when it went across the field, it sounded just like when you get one of these little toy tops going like heck and they hum, just a 'hmmmmm'—a steady whir sound. It didn't sound like a motor." I asked how these sightings impressed Leland compared to the big one. He answered, "Actually, these little lights you see moving in the sky, at the time you think there's really something to it, but after it's over for a while, probably somebody could talk you out of really believing. It might have been anything. But after we saw that big one up here, why, they couldn't talk me out of that one!"

The dazzling big object with the red rays, boiling "dust," and a "dome" of white light must have really been something to see! I would have liked to have seen the one sitting on the power lines, a feature common to other sightings around the world, especially in New Hampshire in 1965 (Fuller, 1966a), which then came humming across the nearby field. But it pales to relative insignificance compared to the big red one.

In the interview, Leland said that he stopped a car coming along the road, but that was an example of faulty memory. Actually he tried to stop Dee Hullinger and his wife, but they thought he was just giving a friendly wave and went on. After they saw the UFO, they turned around and drove back to where Lee was coming out from behind the trees. Even that bit wasn't clear in our interviews with Dee Hullinger (Fig. 1-13), but Junior returned to get the details straight after I began to worry about the discrepancy in the two accounts. Dee generally confirms Leland's story without, however, confirming some of the most spectacular points. Dee did not have a strong impression of red color, possibly because the redness had become less intense by the time he noticed it. Nevertheless, the "dome" of light remained to the end, according to Leland; yet Dee did not describe this the same way Leland had—again possibly because it was less noticeable when he saw it. Dee speaks of a "glow" instead of a dome. He also failed to see the rays and the boiling "dust," but he confirms that it was "as big as a full Moon." This was apparently due to position and possibly due to time—which in Dee's case was relatively short. When Dee saw the object, it appeared to be right on the horizon, and he couldn't see anything below it. Actually, Leland and Jody were a few feet higher than Dee, for they were on horseback. Dee does clearly confirm the glow that remained after the object left, and he adds one most significant detail: The object certainly didn't bury itself in the sand; it spun on its axis and then shot up into the sky with a high velocity—probably while Leland and Jody were behind the trees. Dee's father-in-law also saw the glow, which gradually faded away. "It was really something to see!"

Typically, Dee had another sighting to tell us about, this one just two weeks before our interview. Junior and I were looking the area over at that time, but as usual we missed the sighting.

Combining the accounts of Leland and Dee, we were able to determine the location of the large red object a little more accurately, the area shown in Figure 1-12 A.

Chased Home by a Big, Flashing Convex Plane. The third sighting that impressed Junior occurred at Christmastime, 1970. The main witness was David Martin, but his parents saw the object as it was leaving. We first got the story from David's mother, Ruth Martin, and then I talked with David on the phone. He lives in Salt Lake City and was visiting his parents when he had his sighting. It is interesting to compare the stories as told by Ruth and by David. They are alike in virtually every detail. This may be because Ruth is telling the story as David had told it to her (except for the few moments when she saw the object herself). She obviously has a good memory. It may be significant to note here that while a person can remember a story almost exactly, his interpretations and the things that he happened to notice may alter his account in several often important ways from that of another independent witness, who noticed other things and interpreted them differently.

Here's Ruth Martin's story:

He had been stargazing for years in hopes he'd see something special, and he had been out parked with a friend, talking, when they saw this light going back and forth between two peaks [Squaw Peak by U Hill—east of Roosevelt]. They had been up to Hilltop, and when they came back, they just sat for a while and watched this light. He had borrowed our truck, and his friend said good-bye and got in his car and left. Well, David decided that he would just sit and watch the light for a while and see what would happen.

When he got his cigarette lit, he looked up, and here it was coming toward him from the east. He decided that maybe he'd better go! So he turned the truck around and started home on a cross road, which was a real rutty, bumpy road. He barely got started down the road, when he looked back, and there was this light, right above him, to the side of him. He said it was around two hundred to three hundred feet up. You know how you can't get traction on a bumpy road—and he got real excited and oh, my word! He decided that he would just try to ignore it—but there this light was, following him, staying about the same distance above the ground.

When he got onto the road going home—we live on the road that runs north and south—he decided that he would turn south and go to some friends that lived closer. This light just followed him right around! So he decided that he better back down and then go on north, towards home, and this light followed him right around north! When he got to the driveway, this light just turned right in with him! And he came banging on the doors—we usually keep our front screen locked—and he yelled, 'Mother! Daddy! Get up and see what followed me home!' Of course we didn't know what in the dickens—it was about one o'clock in the morning.

Anyway, he ran in the back door, and I never knew anybody to get that door open as fast as he did. He grabbed us—we were at the bedroom window, looking out to see what was out there that followed him home—and he said: 'See that up there; it's up there!' Then we ran quickly to the front door and opened the screen, and we saw this diffuse white light, just drifting lazily back to where it started from. He was real shook up about it, and the next morning he could hardly wait to call Junior and tell him about it.

I called David Martin, introduced myself, and told him of my interest in UFOs and my connection with Junior Hicks. His story is very close to his mother's version. Here is part of his interview:

I kept looking over my shoulder as I was coming across the road, and it kept getting bigger and bigger and closer and closer. I tried to turn left to go over to Dale Galley's place, which was the closest between my Dad's and where I was, and it turned with me to the left. I jammed on the brakes and slipped the wheel and turned right, and it made a right turn, and made an arc out in the field across the road. I scrambled up the street there in the dark, turned into my Dad's place, honking and flashing lights, hoping that someone would be up to see it. I stopped the truck, shut it off, and looked up. It was up in the field about three hundred feet above the ground—and it was at about a forty or forty-five degree angle from where I was. I rushed in the house and got the folks up—Mom was the first one out—and I looked out the window just before she did come out and it was still hovering. When she came out, I rushed her over to the window, and all we could see was this one little white light which appeared to be on top of the unit. Before, it was triangular in shape and had a big reddish-colored light on one side and a green light on the other side. I thought it was an airplane, but there was no sound at all. The white light—the dull white light—came from on top. It was no light like I'd ever seen before. It was really different—like looking at a diamond without the light shining through to give the fire effect. We sat and watched it go east, straight east, until it went out of sight.

David described the UFO's shape as planar convex. He says it was four or five times as large as the full Moon but much smaller when he first saw it—maybe a tenth the size of the Moon.

Then came the usual second story. Driving near Fruitland where Red Creek Draw is, David's lights kept going on and off. He pulled off to the side of the road, and when another car came by, he followed—which apparently stopped the lights from going on and off! This is just about the only account in the Uintah Basin of the so-called electromagnetic effects so often mentioned in UFO literature. David says he saw a light that could have been a UFO, but that part of the story is not so clear.

10. Junior's Early 1994 Report.
Late in 1973, I called Junior Hicks to check on recent events. He had a few more sightings in his file and agreed to tape some interviews for me. I received a cassette in February 1974. Like so many other Basin stories, these are unique in some ways and thus quite interesting.

The first of these sightings took place in October of 1972. The witness was a Native American, Frank Myore, who lives at Randlett, Utah. The sighting took place about fifty to seventy-five miles south of Ouray. Junior heard about it from Myore's son who was in Junior's science class. The boy told Junior that they had seen the UFO during the deer hunt and that it came so close that his father had shot at it. They had heard the ricochet from the UFO, after which it rapidly took off. Another Native American boy, Lynn Sandios, also told of a UFO sighting during deer hunting, and his father had also shot at the UFO with a rifle. It also left rapidly but came back and followed them all the way home from Hillcreek, a distance of about seventy miles.

The interview with Frank Myore was disappointing. He never confirmed that he had taken a shot at the UFO, although Junior brought this up. He did talk about the object appearing as a disc, coming close, taking off rapidly, and so on. The whole party had jumped out of the car and watched the object for a while. "The kids said: 'Mars people! Mars people coming! Let's get out of here!' "

Junior comments on the tape before the interview that it is very difficult to get detailed information from the Native Americans. The children are much more ready to talk than the adults, but by the same token, they may be less reliable. We should be grateful for anything we learn from these people. We have many reasons to believe that they have had numerous sightings, the vast majority of which have never been reported. We'll encounter this conclusion later in this book (see Chapter 8).

Rearview Lights. Jessie Pickup, the wife of LaRu Pickup, also lives at Randlett. She had a rather interesting encounter with a UFO on November 1, 1972. The locale was close to where Joe Ann Harris had her sighting: a little south of Fort Duchesne.

> I was just getting ready to go around this hill, and the lights were so bright in my rearview mirror that it attracted my attention to what might be behind me. It was slate color and I'd say the two lights were each about twenty-four inches in diameter with a bright red light and maybe a four-inch halo around each one of them. There were two lights, quite a bit like the headlights of a car only much lighter and much brighter . . . they lit up the inside of the car; that's why I saw it . . . . It was sort of like a puppet on a string, just bouncing around, sort of moving up and down as it came down the road like a pogo stick.

She watched the strange lights in her rearview mirror for a few seconds, and then when she "looked in the mirror it had completely disintegrated." She thought the slate-gray object might have been about twenty-five feet in diameter. Jessie Pickup said she was "kind of numb, if you know what I mean. It kind of puts you in a spell." The brilliance of the lights and their interesting motion make the case interesting.

Dave Hunt's Morphing UFO. Dave Hunt had been teaching mathematics at Union High School for about ten years. Driving south toward Roosevelt on his way to work at about 8:00 AM on March 16, 1973, he "saw a large object floating in the sky approximately three miles down south." It was somewhat elongated horizontally and moving toward the west. He thought it might be a weather balloon but could see no package hanging below. Some trees obstructed his view, but as he broke over a hill, he looked up in the same direction and saw it again, only much higher:

> I observed a triangular-shaped object, kind of dark gray in appearance . . . I drove about two and a half miles or more while I watched this object. It was out to the southwest at about a thirty to forty degree angle in the sky. It was shaped very much like a kite, only instead of having the elongated part on the bottom, it was about a perfect diamond, and it was rotating on a vertical axis. As it rotated around, it changed shapes from a diamond and then to a kind of cigar-shaped thing, and then right while I was watching, it rotated right back to the exact same diamond shape again . . . Either it moved into a distant cloud cover or the clouds moved in front of it; the shape could be seen as it was going into the clouds. It was a very well-formed object with a definite edge. Judging by trees that appeared to be in front of it, it must have been very large—perhaps 60 to 100 feet.

David Hunt, with his analytical background in mathematics, has done a lot of wondering about what he actually saw. When he arrived at school that morning, he called Junior, and the two of them went down to the shop. They made a model with a piece of wood that was kind of elongated and oval-shaped, with some sides flattened with the sander. "We could look at that model, rotate it at the various angles, and all the shapes in silhouette would fit very well . . . . It seemed rather puzzling at first that I saw a definite oval-shaped object and then a diamond, but in experimenting with models, we did come up with a type of model that would have given those views."

The Burdicks' Upside-Down Moon. On March 23, 1973, Max Burdick, his wife, Fern, and Elva Gardner, his sister-in-law, were returning to Roosevelt from Vernal where they had been attending a square dance. It was about midnight, and no other cars had been seen for quite some time:

> We came around a turn in the road; the road was straight then

for perhaps three hundred or four hundred yards; and up about two hundred yards in front of us there was a bright orange object that was sitting off to the left of the road. It was shaped like the moon upside down with a circle on the bottom. It was between us and a hill behind it, because I could see the skyline of the hill on the opposite side of it. [We were near] Halfway Hollow. It moved across the road in front of us, and I drove as fast as I could to try to catch up with it. It kind of hesitated over the road a second, and then it went to the right and on out parallel to the road. Then it moved away instantly. It just disappeared. It didn't go out, it just moved away so fast that it pin-pointed out. When it was over the highway, it covered the whole right-away, maybe two hundred feet. It was kind of an orange, a light orange, like fire—not as bright as the sun but still brighter than the moon. It wasn't so bright you couldn't look at it.

Although the time of the sighting was very brief, this is a fairly impressive story because there were three witnesses, the object was brighter than anything that might be expected in the area at that time of night, it was large, and it moved much faster than a speeding automobile.

11. Years 1974 to 2009

By the time I contacted Junior in 2009, his files of good sightings had grown to about 400. He generalized that most of the sightings he had investigated since 1974 were similar to ones that I have presented above, but he agreed to check his files and his memory and make some suggestions about other interviews. This he did, and I arranged to visit the Uintah Basin again from September 7 to 11, 2009. I had given a talk at the annual MUFON Symposium in Denver, Colorado, on August 9, 2009, and I had had lunch with James Carrion, then the director of MUFON, headquartered in Fort Collins, Colorado. (Incidently, this was the first UFO meeting I had attended in about thirty years.) James was interested in visiting the Basin himself—mostly because he was quite familiar with *The Hunt for the Skinwalker* (Kelleher and Knapp, 2005), which concerns the goings on at a ranch in the Basin, as we'll see in Chapter 8. He arranged to go with me and Junior Hicks as we interviewed witnesses.

I bought a fancy new digital recorder, and the three of us were able to interview eight sets of witnesses in the relatively short time period available to us. There were others that Junior hoped we could visit, but we were unable to arrange times with them. A few of the interviews concerned truly spectacular sightings, but rather than including them in this chapter,

I have incorporated them into chapters where they illustrate the points under discussion. However, here is a brief preview of those cases as well as a summary of cases that I otherwise won't present in this volume:

Marjorie Beal and her daughter Rebecca were coming home from an honors dinner way back in the spring of 1966. Their sighting was truly spectacular as I'll show you in Chapter 6. I'm saving it for that chapter because that is where I talk about the Betty and Barney Hill case in which there was a loss of time. Marjorie and Rebecca clearly had a loss of time, although they have no idea of what happened during the period. About a month after our interview with Marjorie, my wife, Mary, and I visited Rebecca Crandall and heard her version of the event, as you'll see.

Junior had received a letter from Russ Perry in Vernal about an experience he had with Alicia, his date for the high school Sweetheart Ball back in 1968. One aspect of this experience was so unusual that I have decided to present his account in Chapter 7 as an illustration of just how some of these events—and the accounts of them—can test your sanity!

We interviewed a man who had been a deputy sheriff and a tribal policeman. He didn't want us to use his name. He not only had sightings (similar to others in the Basin) to relate to us, but he had personally investigated about a dozen cattle mutilations from the early 1970s to 2000. (I won't further discuss his stories.)

John Garcia owns the ranch adjoining the skinwalker ranch to the east. He also had several stories to tell, but I'll present only one of these (in Chapter 8) because it took place about 1990—before the *Skinwalker* events.

Charles Winn, who owns the ranch west and north of the skinwalker ranch, had a frightening experience in the summer of 1997. I'll present that interview in Chapter 8.

We interviewed Craig and Dee Ann Mitchell and their daughter, Mindy Mitchell, who described a number of sightings over a period of several years. Mindy told Junior that she had had a time-loss experience, but that was not clear from the interview. She had a series of sightings and experiences from about 1995 to 1999, but I've decided not to include them. The objects seen by the parents are similar to other sightings in the Basin, but Craig told us about a night sighting near Las Vegas where an object seemed to fly right into a mountain!

Another witness did not want us to use his name. His sighting was probably in June 2006. An object approached with tremendous speed from a great distance, dived toward the earth, and landed about 200 yards away, stayed for only a few seconds, and then took off again at high speed. The witness told of a kind of reverse crop circle that appeared a few weeks later when the grass where the object had landed grew three or four times as tall as the surrounding grass; there was also a smaller circle of the very short grass inside the large circle of tall grass. This strange growth persisted for a couple of years but is no longer visible. Junior observed the phenomenon on several occasions.

The most recent sighting among our interviews took place in July 2009. Nellie Barney and her husband, along with several of their children and grandchildren, live on a ranch north of Pelican Lake. At a family get-together on a Sunday, they saw a huge pink object (hundreds of yards in diameter) a couple of miles away, hovering over high-tension power lines. The entire family watched the object until it disappeared after a short time. As was typical, Nelly also told us about several other sightings going back to 1966.

Now it's time in Chapter 2 to stand back and examine this large body of data.

Notes

1. "Uintah" is sometimes spelled "Uinta." Kelleher and Knapp (2005) use Uinta for the Basin, but half the Basin is located in Uintah County, and the Native American Reservation in the area is called the Uintah and Ouray Reservation. Kelleher and Knapp note that the "h" might be dropped for physical features such as the Uinta Mountains, which makes sense, but I've always spelled it Uintah Basin, and that's what seems common in our newspapers and such.

2. I've long since lost the article, but Wikipedia has a good discussion (see http://en.wikipedia.org/wiki/Dust_devil). That article leads to some wonderful pictures at another website, and it is clear that the dust devil itself often closely matches the "string" described by Buchanan and Faucett. See also http://www.inflowimages.com/ChaseReports/DustDevils/dustdevils.asp.

2

Some Thoughts on the
Uintah Basin Sightings

So what are we to do with these stories you have just finished reading? They must have literary—or psychological—value as accounts of human experience, regardless of what they mean. But do they have any scientific value? Surely they might have had more scientific value if it had been possible to check conditions during the sightings, to verify the presence of other witnesses, or to see if all the alternative explanations had been rendered impossible. Regardless, the sightings obviously raise many more questions than they answer—but then, most scientific progress is based upon discovering good questions. Certainly, answers are not likely to appear until suitable questions can be formulated.

The purpose of this chapter, then, is to extract scientific information from these reports by evaluating the witnesses and their stories, looking for patterns in their reports, watching for isolated but perhaps significant events, to see if any conclusions might be justified, and even brainstorming a little. Please note that this evaluation must be limited almost completely to the sightings listed in Table 1. We will consider some sightings that occurred after 1974 in later chapters, but my records are not complete enough to look at the more recent sightings as a whole (nor do I have the time to go through Junior's massive collection!). Furthermore, Junior tells me that the post-1974 sightings would follow patterns similar to those of Table 1.

So before proceeding in Part 2 with a consideration of the UFO phenomenon as a whole, let's pull these Table-1 sightings together a bit so they will provide a better frame of reference.

The Uintah Basin Residents as Witnesses

How do the Uintah Basin residents stack up as witnesses? Basically, they are good witnesses, probably as good as one could hope to find by taking a sample of a population at large.

The Mormons are considerably more sophisticated and better educated than their rural environment might lead one to suspect. Of course not all Basin witnesses were/are Mormons, but the influence of the Church has been, and still is, considerable. The Church has long emphasized education and culture, and many of the people in the Uintah Basin may have a working knowledge of drama, for example, or they may speak some foreign language fluently, having spent a couple of years as a missionary in some foreign land. Utah State University has been conducting classes in the area, and these are well attended. Yet at the same time, these witnesses tend to be a bit naive about some things. They keep abreast of scientific developments by watching TV, but few have any scientific training, Junior Hicks being a notable exception. But the farmers and deer hunters in the area are certainly well trained at estimating distances and sizes. They know the size of a forty-acre field, and they are good at estimating yardages because they must set the sights on their rifles accordingly.

Why so many recorded sightings? Obviously Junior Hicks' numerous contacts provide one of the best answers. Furthermore, many people of the Uintah Basin are outdoor people. They do their farm chores every morning and every evening, and many sightings have occurred in conjunction with these chores. They also drive long distances through open, treeless country. Nevertheless, the percentages are quite fantastic. The good sightings in Table 1 represent 6–8 percent of the people in Junior's part of the Basin. Furthermore, in virtually every interview, the witness told of other people with similar stories. We were surprised that there were so few repeats in Junior's file, but in the course of our interviews we found that many, if not most, people had had more than a single sighting. They simply didn't bother to report more than one—and their reports went to Junior Hicks, not to any official authorities. In the 35 years since the first edition of this book was published, the number of sightings may have dropped a bit, but the percentage of people who are acquainted directly or indirectly with UFO sightings has probably gone up. One reason might be the popularity of *Hunt for the Skinwalker* (Kelleher and Knapp, 2005), which reports UFO and other phenomena on a ranch in the heart of the Basin (Chapter 8).

The "Noise"

One problem in science is to separate the "signal" from the "noise": the meaningful information from random and distorted material (see Chapter 3). As noted, the following sections are based on Table 1. To extend the generalizations to 2009 would require a careful analysis of Junior's files for that time interval. The scientists at the National Institute for Discovery Science (NIDS), which I will discuss in Chapter 8, did compare Junior's extensive files with their own data on the skinwalker ranch. Junior has copies of the results, and in general they show a similarity over much of the applicable time interval.

How much noise is there compared to the signal in the sightings of Table 1, especially those that we have presented in detail? No doubt, noise is included. We can't help but be a little suspicious, for example, about Sighting 32. Changing direction is not typical of a satellite, but then it would be easy to mistake such details if careful reference points were not established. Sightings 27 and 55 could have been reflections. Yet most of the sightings just don't seem to be misinterpretations of natural phenomena, as I'll discuss further in Chapter 3.

Could we explain the sightings as psychological phenomena? Hardly— unless we are badly mistaken in the limitations that we presently place upon psychological experiences. Nevertheless, the importance of psychology in the many sightings should be amply clear after reading the interviews. For example, people's memories of a given event may differ in detail. Accordingly, I'll discuss the role of psychology in Chapter 6.

What about hoax? It is virtually inconceivable that so many people, many of them church and community leaders, none of them seeking outside publicity, could be conspiring to tell lies. The variety of the sightings also speaks against this. It is equally fantastic that anyone could have devised contraptions capable of fooling that many people so many times. The objects described in the interviews clearly are not polyethylene bags supporting burning candles!

What about the secret weapon or government development idea? Although several witnesses consider this possibility and tend to accept it, I must reject it for the simple reasons discussed in Chapter 5.

So the likelihood of a clear and present signal, rather than a lot of random noise, seems high.

Patterns

1. Shapes as a Function of Time

Interestingly enough, two specific kinds of UFOs, the convex planar and the double convex, seem to have disappeared almost entirely for a year and a half, beginning with the January 15, 1967 sightings. Two other sightings did occur during that period (#44, #56), but the vast majority of sightings after that time were of round or perhaps oval-shaped objects, glowing evenly all over and with no sign of windows or other specific markings. Kent Denver's second account (pp. 35–36) might lead us to believe that the orange ball is really the double convex object but completely illuminated and seen perhaps from the "top" or "bottom." Nevertheless, the essential lack of accounts describing a double convex or convex planar object from January, 1967, to October, 1968, is a striking observation.

This pattern is all the more interesting when we realize that Junior Hicks, deeply impressed by the stories he had heard, built his models of these two most common shapes and began to exhibit them around the Basin at about that time. From the psychological standpoint, we might expect more witnesses to be generated by this. Yet such was not the case. It was as if the UFO squadrons stationed in the Uintah Basin had received their orders from headquarters (xeroxed in nine copies, no doubt) to transfer out the assigned spacecraft and to replace them with others of different designs!

When I returned in April 1972, I learned that the orders had been changed again. Nine of the thirteen cases that had accumulated since the summer of 1968 involved either convex-planar or double-convex UFOs.

2. Speed, Pulsating Lights, Color, and Lack of Sound

Four features of the Uintah Basin sightings are typical of other sightings reported from all over the world. First are the maneuvers in general, but especially the speed of the takeoff. This instant departure is a most common feature of the Uintah Basin UFOs. It is nearly as common for UFOs in general. The pulsating lights are a second strikingly common feature of sightings in the Uintah Basin, as well as of other sightings all over the world. The reddish-orange color provides the third common feature. Sometimes the lights are described as being a deep red color, but the yellow or amber red—which witnesses had difficulty describing— is more common. The general lack of sound, except in very close encounters, provides the fourth common feature.

3. Locations

Junior has plotted the location of the sightings on a map, as shown in Figure 1-1 (p. 22). Quite clearly, they are clustered over the Native American communities of Lapoint, White Rocks, Fort Duchesne, and Randlett. Junior was impressed with this distribution before he actually plotted the sightings on a map. He had begun to think that the stretch of country from the desert south of Randlett to the mountains north of White Rocks constituted a sort of UFO alley, through which the objects were often seen to move. Did they have a base out in the remotest part of the desert and another high in the Uinta Mountains? Or was the distribution of sightings more closely related to Junior's circle of acquaintances in the Uintah Basin? It is from this area that most of his students are drawn. Furthermore, there are many other sightings that fall outside this area. My luck at running down sightings in Duchesne, for example, indicated that a thorough search might well change the apparent distribution on the map. Thus Junior and I feel at the moment that any such UFO alley is probably an artificial phenomenon and not something that needs explaining in terms of the motives of UFO pilots.

4. Car-Following

There are almost enough sightings (#21-B, #30, #41-F, #42, #44, #48, and #78) to constitute a sort of pattern of car-following. This is not an unknown phenomenon in the rest of the world, but the percentage here seems to be rather high. We are then faced with the question of why UFOs should want to follow cars. Car-following is certainly impressive to a witness. This seems to be a clearly discernible pattern, and it plays an important role in my thinking that the UFOs wanted to be observed; that is, that they were putting on a display.

5. Landings

As a percentage, the number of landings, or at least near landings, is also exceptionally high. The following sightings constitute examples, and those that are underlined seem to be especially good examples: #6, 8(?), #10, #13, #15, #16(?), #19, #21, #22, #23(?), #37, #39, #42, #47, #48, #54, #61, #65, #66, #67, #69, #71(?), #73, and #75(?). These constitute about 25–30 percent of the sightings.

6. Reaction to the Witness

Many witnesses reported the feeling that the UFOs seemed to react to their actions or even to their thoughts. This was mentioned, for example, in the interviews with Verl Haslem and Estel Manwaring. The witness turns his lights on or off, shouts loudly, or perhaps merely says something to his companion in the automobile, and suddenly the object blinks out its light or leaves in great haste. Reaction to thoughts would be difficult to prove, and until better evidence comes along, we will suspect that this is a sort of coincidental event, which is given more significance than it merits. Nevertheless, there are many cases in which some action taken by the observer (e.g., coming around the bend, flipping headlights, and so on) resulted in rapid departure of the UFO.

7. Some "Expected" Patterns that are Absent

A few features of other sightings around the world fail to show up in the data. Except for one recent sighting, which Junior couldn't run down, and Sighting 2, which occurred three years before the current wave of Uintah Basin sightings, no UFO occupants are mentioned. Since many of the sightings included windows or transparent domes, and since in a few cases these were even observed for long intervals of time, and with binoculars, this lack of comment on occupants could be significant.

Although the number of sightings that involved binoculars was unusually high (#13, #19, #29, #40, #45-B, #46, #49, #58, #63, #70-A, #71—about 15 percent of all of the reported sightings), it is interesting that no physical evidence, such as photographs, burned grass, or holes in the ground, were reported in the Table 1 sightings. The lack of markings on the ground is particularly striking in view of the number of landings and reports from other parts of the world.

And why were there no photographs? Being deer hunters, people in the Uintah Basin carried binoculars, but few, if any, carried cameras in the 1960s, though this is no longer true, thanks to camera cell phones. After all, they were out in that beautiful country every day, so why should they be taking pictures of it? Cameras were used to take pictures of relatives at family reunions but not to carry around in automobiles as any dude tourist might.

Hundreds of sightings around the world have involved stopped cars and other so-called electromagnetic effects (static on the radio, dimming or flashing house lights, and so forth). These don't show up in the Uintah Basin, except for David Martin's flashing car lights, and no UFO was clearly involved in this incident. (Our eight recent interviews uncovered one and perhaps more possible effects on automobiles.)

It is interesting that there are no physical traces such as "landing-gear" holes in the ground in Junior's early files. The "reverse crop circle" mentioned near the end of Chapter 1 is an interesting possible example of a physical effect.

So the signals coming through the noise seemed to include specific shapes that changed markedly in January of 1967, interesting maneuvers, rapid takeoffs, pulsating lights, orange-red color, lack of sound, a cluster of sightings in UFO alley (probably due to sampling error), following of cars, landings or near landings, reaction to the observer, lack of occupants in spite of windows and transparent domes, and near lack of electromagnetic effects or physical evidence, including photographs.

The NIDS Study

As we'll see in Chapter 8, there is a ranch in the heart of the Uintah Basin where a family experienced a considerable number of UFO sightings and other strange events. These events took place during the second half of the 1990s, beginning in the late spring of 1994 when "the witness" (as I call him in Chapter 8) and his family bought the ranch. By August of 1996, the family members were so distraught by their experiences that they put the ranch up for sale. The National Institute for Discovery Science (NIDS), financed by Robert Bigelow and located in Las Vegas, Nevada, purchased the ranch and moved in to carry out a study of the phenomena. They worked with Junior Hicks (and the first edition of this book) to learn about the history of UFOs in the Uintah Basin. In 1998, Junior gave 106 of his original, handwritten files to NIDS for analysis. The plan was to continue the analysis of the remainder of Junior's approximately 400 cases, but the project was apparently terminated with the 106 files. (Junior feels, however, that the results are typical of the rest of the cases.) The cases studied were essentially all those included in Table 1, plus some more closely related cases. Junior gave me a copy of the report, a series of graphs. NIDS also studied some cases they had themselves assembled, but that part of the analysis is considered confidential and won't be considered here. Speaking of patterns, the NIDS study illuminates a few. Here are some interesting numbers (but remember that these numbers and other patterns are based on witness memories and interpretations):

1. Only about 36 percent of Junior's cases involved just one witness; the rest of the cases included two or more witnesses.

2. Two thirds of Junior's cases occurred between 6:00 PM and midnight.

3. Some 35 percent of Junior's cases involved silver or metallic objects; 20 percent were orange-red; and 26 percent had pulsating lights. As you've seen from the cases described in Chapter 1, there were also other colors, such as colors changing from red to green and back.

4. About 22 percent of the UFOs sighted were disks (saucers), 18 percent were domed, and 42 percent were round or egg shaped.

5. The weather was clear in 85 percent of Junior's cases. (Chapter 8 notes that many of the ranch events were under cloudy or stormy skies.)

6. There is a wide variety of durations of sightings: 15 percent lasted less than a minute; 48 percent, a few minutes (usually less than 10 minutes); 22 percent, between 11 and 30 minutes; and 15 percent longer than half an hour.

7. There is also a wide variety of movements, from hovering or moving slowly, to the very rapid departures that we saw in Chapter 1 ("like a meteor in reverse").

8. Some 10 percent of the objects were estimated to be within 100 feet of the witness; 19 percent were less than 500 feet from the witness; and the rest were observed at varying distances from over 500 feet to 2 miles or more.

9. The vast majority of the objects were silent, with a very few producing various sounds.

10. About two fifths of the objects were thought to be from 10 to 100 feet in diameter; and most of the rest were said to be very large—"as big as a house" or sometimes much larger than that.

Isolated Events

There are some other features of the sightings that may well be nothing more than noise but that are a bit difficult to forget. Kent Denver's "rocket" (#6), for example, is not matched by any other sighting known to me, but his story is a straightforward one, and we can't help but wonder if a ship assigned to duty somewhere else happened to be visiting in the Uintah Basin that evening. This also comes to mind with the "train windows" (#43) sighting, as well as the "formation" (#46), a feature often mentioned in

1947 and for a few years thereafter, but seldom recently. The "busy signal" sound of sighting #33 is unusual but well documented, and not without precedent, as is the green color in the bedroom (#39). Color changes are not uncommon but especially interesting in a few sightings, such as #61. The orange "tail" (#28) is interesting. I was also quite impressed with the maneuvers around the moon described in Sighting 52, clearly an evidence of the display. To make an apparent circle around the moon, the UFO drivers would have to be well aware of the witnesses' exact position on the ground.

Most of these things, while not typical of the sightings in the Uintah Basin, are not atypical of sightings in general. On the other hand, we have a few features here that are really strange. What about Tony Zufelt's "train windows" in Halfway Hollow (#43)? And while we are wondering, let's wonder about the ouija board question (#41) or the "red beam" (e.g., #10) whose builders don't seem to know that once a beam of light starts on its way, it has to keep going until it hits something. The trouble is, there are no good hypotheses for such things.

The sightings of Morlin Buchanan and Richard Faucett, Leland and Jody Mecham, and Dee Hullinger were unusual and seem to me to be without precedent. "Airships" with hanging ropes (often with anchors on the end!), cables, or tubes were reported in 1897, but I know of nothing comparable to the spinning "wind tunnel." The rays of light with billowing "dust" described by Leland and Jody are also unique, as far as I know. (However, I strongly suspect that similar things have been observed but simply haven't come to my attention.) The variety of sightings around the world is truly fantastic, yet virtually any sighting anywhere has its counterpart somewhere else. (Among our eight recent interviews, two had powerful elements of strangeness: one related in Chapter 7 and the other in Chapter 8.)

Conclusions

What can we say about all of this? Are there conclusions to be drawn? We might argue that a researcher's obligations have been met after the facts have been presented. But a creative scientist must go on to interpret, or he is really not doing much more than is expected of the instruments. Yet how can one interpret what has been described above?

I must admit that the objectivity that has protected me from ridicule by my fellow scientists is, in the face of overwhelming data and the necessity for honesty, beginning to dissolve. Say, for example, a scientist tests a hypothesis, one that may seem unreasonable but that cannot be disproved. How long can the person continue to remain open-minded about it as evidence piles up in its favor? How long were scientists two centuries ago justified in ignoring the accumulating evidence in favor of the oxidation process, only to cling to their archaic and subsequently disproved theories of phlogiston? Certainly for a while, but how long? As for the problem at hand, how long can I (or you) resist the idea that some real objects have maneuvered in our skies in ways completely beyond the ability of any physical objects with which we are presently familiar? The data have now piled up. I must accept the stories of the Uintah Basin witnesses as actual events or call them liars. I cannot call them liars. I cannot reject these stories simply because I cannot understand them.

My first conclusion is then, and I believe I have been forced into it by the data at hand, that the people of the Uintah Basin have indeed seen real objects that I cannot explain in terms of any human constructions or natural events known to science. Could they be explained by a talented debunker? Obviously, if I thought they could, I would have explanations myself.

What are these objects? The possibility remains that they consist of some natural phenomenon that science does not yet comprehend. Is there perhaps a fantastic combination of physical forces and material that will in some manner, some day, be understood and described in textbooks, to account for the experiences of Joe Ann Harris, Dean Powell, Thyrena Daniels, or Dick Hackford? Maybe so. We must realize, however, that these experiences are completely beyond our modern science, and that the chances that we will discover physical explanations seem extremely slim. On the other hand, the chances that intelligence exists on other planets in the universe—or in some unseen-by-us extra dimension or parallel universe—are extremely high. We know that intelligence exists in the universe because we are it! We cannot understand how "they" could manage to visit us, nor why they would want to visit us without formal contact. But our lack of understanding does not eliminate the possibility that this very thing has occurred.

For these reasons, my imagination is now severely limited by this possibility. In 1974, I could not think of any reasonable explanation to account for the objects sighted in the Uintah Basin, except for extraterrestrial machines; that is, machines not produced by any human society.

Some of my thoughts now complicate this idea, as I'll explain in the Epilogue, but in a sense I'm stuck with the notion. And I'm not alone. Most ufologists will admit that they can't see any completely satisfying explanation for UFOs. But then in the history of science, the inability to see a true explanation is not at all rare. Once a reasonable explanation is at hand, it becomes extremely difficult to think of any other. Perhaps, then, there is some other explanation for the objects in the Uintah Basin. At the moment, however, the extraterrestrial-machine hypothesis, with its dimensional complications as I'll explain, seems the most reasonable one to account for the sightings.

But why the Uintah Basin? Here science leaves us, and we can only make the purest of conjectures with no assurance whatsoever of their validity. Have they been making a survey? Leah Haslem thought that extraterrestrial beings coming to earth to live might put quite a strain on an earth already facing famine because of a population explosion. Would they, she suggested, have technical means available to tame and make productive the desert regions in the Uintah Basin? This is an interesting idea.

As noted already, I, and some of the witnesses as well, couldn't help but be impressed with the idea that the UFOs wanted to be seen. Otherwise, why should they dive on Joe Ann Harris, follow Thyrena Daniels' and many other cars, dance around in full view of dozens of witnesses for fairly long intervals of time, and so forth? Why indeed should they execute these intricate and involved maneuvers? Why do their lights flash or change color? It is as though they have been putting on a display. Often they seemed to stay around only until they could have been quite certain that they had been observed (e.g., Dean Powell's sighting and many others). On a few occasions, they even stayed around long after they had obviously been observed (e.g., with Thyrena Daniels, Dick Hackford, and Garth Batty). But why? Could it be that they do intend to eventually make formal contact with mankind, and that they want to prepare the way psychologically beforehand? Many UFO writers have discussed the tremendous cultural strain placed upon a lesser society as a result of visitation by a more advanced one. One need only observe the Native Americans in the Uintah Basin to be aware of this possibility. Yet obvious changes have occurred among this population since the reservations were partially opened to settlement.

Could the same thing happen, but on a more dramatic scale, even to our sophisticated society? Perhaps not so readily if the process were an extremely gradual one, occurring over an extended interval of time. Many of the witnesses in the Uintah Basin were clearly frightened by their experiences, yet as they tell them over and over to each other, and as more and more of them partake of these experiences without any harm, the subject becomes more widely accepted and more commonplace. It is becoming legend or folklore. People in the Uintah Basin may be backward in some scientific respects, but they are probably about as sophisticated in regard to UFOs as any group of people on earth. One could hardly imagine a better place than the Uintah Basin for the extraterrestrials to study the effects upon mankind of a carefully controlled UFO display. A national highway crosses the Basin, but otherwise, it remains relatively isolated. Desert is to the south and high mountains to the north. The people are intelligent and cultured, probably as much as any people in a comparably isolated situation, yet they are indeed isolated. Are the UFOs attempting to bring about positive changes? How about negative changes?

While the lack of harm to the witnesses is a general observation in the sightings recounted in Chapter 1, animals have not escaped such harm (e.g., cattle mutilations and other reports from the skinwalker ranch). Vallée (2008 b.) reports many incidences of harm to humans in northern Brazil.

Brainstorming with the Uintah Basin Sightings

Let's consider some final points that aren't exactly conclusions. The sightings have two kinds of value. First, they contribute to an evaluation of the phenomenon's reality. The overwhelming impression of story after story, each told by some ordinary and apparently credible person, is that the UFOs surely must exist as real objects—or at least real visions perceived by the witness (more about this possibility later). Yet I don't feel fully confident in using the sightings as strong primary evidence for the existence of the UFOs as physical objects. To do so, one would need to make a much more thorough investigation. Whenever a second witness was indicated, he should have been sought out. Neighbors might have been interviewed as character references for important witnesses. Weather and astronomical conditions and other circumstances surrounding each event should have been intensively studied, with a careful view to possible alternative explanations. I couldn't bring myself to do all this. My time was limited, and I was not willing to make the sacrifices required to obtain more time (such as quitting my job or giving up my other interests). Besides, the people told such straight stories and seemed so personally convinced that I simply could not strongly doubt the substance of their stories. I also wanted to obtain all the stories I could find to round out "the big picture."

Which brings me to the second value of the accounts. Say we quit worrying (for a while, at least) about the reality of the objects, and even assume that they are extraterrestrial or dimensional visitors. What can we learn about them from the reports? In recently reading over the accounts with this in mind, I felt that there must be a veritable wealth of material in these interviews. We have learned quite a bit by studying the accounts without worrying about their reality. Yes, it might turn out that the garnered information is not true—probably some of it is not true in any case—but if it does turn out to be true, it would be of the highest significance. That is the challenge to science.

I hope you will take this approach to the interviews as you study them yourself. It is a lot of fun! The idea is to have a brainstorming session in which any idea is considered, regardless of how absurd it might seem. Just be careful not to really believe your speculations! I'll illustrate by going over the accounts myself and listing some examples of what I mean:

UFOs clearly have some strange propulsion system or systems, since they are normally perfectly silent (Dean Powell) or only make a little humming (Priscilla Sireech) or buzzing (Leland Mecham) sound when the witness is very close. They may move in a most singular manner, either with a sort of start-stop motion with lights or flames on when stationary and off when moving (Kent Denver and Joe Ann Harris), or with tremendous velocity from a standstill (many Uintah Basin witnesses). Often they leave so rapidly that they seem to vanish. Or do they really vanish? UFOs come in all shapes and sizes, although the size is usually large in the Uintah Basin. There was Dean Powell's strange shiny craft, Kent Denver's "bowling pin," the flat-on-the-bottom-with-a-dome-on-top object seen by many witnesses, the double-convex (sometimes with windows) shape also seen by many, the red ball of fire that was perhaps the most common UFO, the train-windows-with-balls-of-multicolored-fire of Tony Zufelt, the balloon-with-a-string (or wind tunnel) of Morlin Buchanan and Richard Faucett. Or the fantastic apparition of Leland and Jody Mecham: the red ball with rays of red light, boiling "dust," and a dome of white above.

Could they be some kind of light images? This would readily account for the bizarre and "impossible" movements, the fantastic sizes and shapes, and the sudden disappearances. Using lasers and principles of interference, three-dimensional photographic holographs can now be made. The product is a projected light image that doesn't require a screen and appears differently when viewed from different vantage points (as Princess Leia's image in Star Wars). Say an advanced extraterrestrial technology wanted to impress us with fantastic visions. With perfected, multi-colored holographs, they could produce the shows seen in the Basin by a sort of trick photography. In this case the witnesses would be totally convinced they were seeing real objects, although they were really seeing only an other-worldly super-movie, projected into the sky rather than on a screen. This way the "objects" could appear to do things that we think of as completely impossible! (This idea was suggested to me by Dr. J. Allen Hynek in an informal conversation and later in the *Playboy* panel.)

There is a problem with this brainstorming idea, however. Junior says that he had a recent case where the witness saw the object while deer hunting, and that he shot it with his rifle—hearing the bullet ricochet off the metallic surface! So our visitors must ride around in real vehicles sometimes. Or else when they project holographic images, they are prepared for the eventuality of being shot at, and hence they provide recorded sound effects to fool the hunter into thinking he really hit something! (But remember that we were unable to get a good interview on this case anyway.) Outside of the Uintah Basin, there have been many cases in which impressions are left in the ground where a UFO landed (e.g., in Socorro, New Mexico).

What about the beam that stops in midair or even appears "spliced," as though it were in segments? I've wondered again if we could duplicate that with superimposed and carefully tuned lasers, set for slightly different wave-lengths or frequencies. Two tones with slightly different frequencies will produce a beat, alternately reinforcing and cancelling each other. With the coherent beams of a laser, this might be done with light, which can be considered to be a wave phenomenon similar to sound. The beats would be the segments in the beam. The effect might also be produced by holographic technology as discussed above, or perhaps a plasma effect.

What about Dick Hackford's gear shifting? Of course, it might have been only a faulty memory. But say it wasn't. In addition to the obvious possibility that the visitors have some super technology that will direct "magnetic" beams into Dick's old truck, moving his gears around (a truly fantastic idea), there is the possibility that it did indeed happen only in Dick's mind, but that it was put there by the visitors in the craft above Dick's truck. Maybe their super abilities are in the field of mind control—which would be another way to account for all the spectacular sightings. Maybe they project the images seen by the witnesses not into the sky but directly into the witnesses' minds! This would explain cases where some witnesses see an object but other people not far away do not (e.g., the Pascagoula case mentioned in Chapter 6).

See what I mean by brainstorming? Try it.

PART 2

What's It
All About?

3

Natural or Conventional Phenomena Misinterpreted

What Is the UFO Evidence?

The Uintah Basin reports provide an excellent cross section of the raw material for UFO study. In many ways they are highly typical of sightings that have been experienced (although seldom reported) by millions of people living today. Few are reported to anyone "in authority"—and as a matter of fact, the vast majority are not even reported to local authorities like Junior Hicks. The UFO witnesses include a cross section of the population, from common laborers to airline pilots and scientists. J. Allen Hynek, a longtime special consultant for the Air Force's Project Blue Book study, had good reports of UFO activity from a number of his astronomer friends, and I have picked up a few from some of my colleagues, both in biology and in other fields. It is perfectly apparent that the reports are not restricted to crackpots, psychotics, or other abnormal individuals. And the witnesses in the Uintah Basin are a good cross section of the people there, although the area is too rural to be typical of the United States as a whole.

The Uintah Basin sightings are also typical when they are atypical. As we noted in Chapter 2, certain aspects of the Uintah Basin sightings don't have their counterparts in the sightings recorded in the rest of the world, and some of the things reported in the rest of the world do not show up in the Uintah Basin accounts. But then, that is typical. For example, South American sightings sometimes involved hairy bipeds that are peculiar to

South America, and the 1965 sightings around Exeter, New Hampshire, seemed to be concentrated around power lines (Fuller, 1966a). So the UFO phenomenon is a widespread occurrence, exhibiting many common features everywhere, but typically a few features are unique to a given locality.

So what's it all about? Why have these UFOs been flitting around in our skies? What do they mean to us? What are the implications for science, technology, philosophy, sociology, religion—or your sanity? Should we be afraid of them? Should we ignore them?

As a scientist, I would very much like to know how they fit into the scientific picture of the universe that has developed during the past few centuries. I would like to know whether they are real objects and whether they can really accomplish the maneuvers so often described by witnesses. Do the witnesses really see all they claim to? Or does the mind of the observer create many of the details? In short, I am filled with scientific curiosity about the phenomenon—and I must say I'm also intrigued by some aspects of the problem that may not be exactly scientific in the usual sense. (But then any attempt to understand anything about the universe can be considered scientific if it is carried out in the right way—can't it?)

Science

Let's examine how science works. There are complications, but in an ideal application of the scientific method, obtaining truly objective data is a necessity. This means that the data (observations) must be available to anyone who is willing to apply the same efforts that were required to get the data in the first place. Maybe that will only require direct observations with the human senses. Other times human senses are aided by microscopes, telescopes, pH meters, lasers, sensitive microphones, rock hammers, voltage meters, artificial satellites, or a huge myriad of other instruments that have been developed since science really got going. Although many of these instruments are extremely complex, it is still possible for anyone willing to make the effort to understand how they work—even if that effort requires several years of graduate education. (I have only the most rudimentary notion of how my computer works, but somebody—or some group of somebodies— must understand such things well enough to build them.) The key word in the definition of objective data is *repeatability*. In principle at least, it must be possible for anyone to obtain the same data that the first observer reported.

Yes, there are many complications. The procedures to obtain the data may be so complex that experimental error always enters in. Statistics are used to study the variability in experimental data, and you may justifiably be skeptical of conclusions supported by statistics. Be that as it may, the goal is always to obtain repeatable, objective data.

Yet there are certain situations in which it is impossible to repeat an observation. For example, an astronomer may happen to observe a celestial phenomenon that lasts only a brief time. There is no way to repeat it for others to see, so we are dependent on the astronomer's witness account. And for the most part, such accounts are accepted without question. Obviously, the reported observation might have all the shortcomings of any witness accounts: The astronomer might have been drunk or hallucinating—or he might have lied to enhance his reputation. The same could be true when a witness reports a UFO sighting—although the astronomer has presumably been trained in the observation of astronomical phenomena, whereas a UFO witness probably has no training in UFO watching. But it boils down to a matter of how others subjectively judge the witness. This leaves a big escape hole for the UFO debunker.

Next come the attempts to interpret or understand what the data mean. Sometimes the data fall into a pattern that makes sense. In 1869 the Russian chemist Dmitri Mendeleev saw that the elements known in his time fell into a pattern that became the periodic table. The beauty of his "empirical generalization" was that there were blanks in the table, and Mendeleev could predict that those blanks would fill as new elements were discovered and studied. This proved to be the case, strongly confirming the principles of the table. By now the periodic table has been refined and extended in ways that would certainly have pleased Mendeleev—and that nicely illustrate how the scientific method continues to build upon earlier results.

Step by step, all the sciences usually follow such a pathway: Data are accumulated, and hypotheses (or theories, if you will) are formulated to understand the data. A good hypothesis will predict something (like Mendeleev's missing elements). Then the hypotheses are tested by going after more observations.

What happens when this process doesn't quite work? What happens when no one can think of a way to truly test the hypotheses? I call such untestable—but not totally unreasonable—hypotheses just-suppose stories (or what-if tales). They are generated especially when only witness accounts are available (i.e., there is no or only questionable physical evidence) and when the would-be interpreter (UFO debunker) has a mind-set either for or against a given interpretation. The UFO debunker will make up just-suppose stories (hypotheses) to debunk a UFO account, and a UFO believer will do the same to support the account.

The point of the "just-suppose" or "what-if" story—terms that I'll use frequently in this book—is that there is no absolutely compelling evidence that one or another interpretation of a phenomenon is correct. Objective, repeatable data are lacking. So the debunker says (or implies), for example, remembering a couple of cases from the Prologue: Just suppose Father Gill thought he saw humanoids on top of the New Guinea object because he wasn't wearing his glasses. (Ah, but he says he was, we note.) What if his memory is faulty? Or what if the witness misinterpreted a lighthouse beyond the Rendlesham Forest? Or just suppose that the whole show was staged. On the other hand, the UFO investigator might say: Just suppose the witness really saw what he described, albeit with a few minor distortions caused by imperfect memory. (That's the sort of thing I find myself saying—and will often say in this book.) For both the debunkers or the believers, the tendency is to express their guesses—their just-suppose stories—and then consider the case closed.

So what is scientific proof in the UFO field? If a UFO sighting cannot be repeated at the will of the investigator—and it surely cannot—then what is to be done? As should be clear, things often boil down to one's personal evaluation of witnesses, even one's gut feeling. Much of this book is a discussion of how to interpret witness accounts. I'll do the best that I can to evaluate objectively.

The few scientists who have been interested in the problem of UFOs have independently and almost invariably come up with about the same approach. One formulates broad hypotheses designed to explain the phenomenon and then one tests the hypotheses insofar as possible. Usually we talk about five hypotheses. They clearly overlap, and it isn't difficult to combine some of them or to subdivide them to come up with some number other than five. The fifth one would be especially easy to break into two or more other hypotheses. In my own thinking I get along pretty well with these five basic ideas. Let's introduce them by stating them as questions:

1. Are the UFOs natural or man-made objects or phenomena that are misinterpreted by the witnesses?

2. Are the UFOs lies or deliberate hoaxes concocted by the witnesses, or perhaps by someone who wants to fool the witnesses?

3. Are the UFOs the result of a secret government project? If so or if not, what does the government know about them that it is not telling us?

4. Are the UFOs only in the mind of the beholder—psychological phenomena such as hallucinations or vivid dreams? What role does psychology play?

5. Are the UFOs the products of extraterrestrial intelligences (from a distant planet or even from some kind of parallel universe), vehicles whose occupants are keeping our planet under surveillance—or even holographic images meant to influence our thoughts?

Positive Identification

Is it possible for someone to see one of these things without knowing what it is, and to become convinced that it is a spaceship from some other solar system? Are the UFOs really only the planet Venus or some other bright planet or star? Are they meteors, weather balloons, reflections of light from airplanes, artificial satellites, sundogs, mirages (e.g., car lights refracted at night by a warm layer of air), flocks of birds, ball lightning (Klass, 1968), lens-shaped clouds, reflections on windows, or a host of other natural phenomena or man-made objects that are misinterpreted by the witness? After all, seeing an extraterrestrial machine is not exactly an everyday occurrence, and it ought to awaken decidedly uncommon emotions of awe and wonder in the observer—overlapping with the psychological phenomena discussed in Chapter 6. Is it possible for someone to have such a feeling when a witness is only observing the planet Venus or a weather balloon but thinks he is watching a spaceship?

We can provide an unqualified "yes, in a great many cases" to answer these questions. I said that a sighting usually cannot be repeated. But sometimes it can, making identification possible. Consider the following interview as recorded on December 6, 1970 (the name has been changed—almost the only name in this book changed or withheld, except for some in Table 1):

> **Mable:** As I came out of the door and looked to the east; there was something just as big as that, and I thought, "Well, that doesn't belong

there." And it made me feel kind of funny, and I looked across the mountains—I have a bad habit of looking up when I come out at five-thirty in the morning on my way to work in the [university] cafeteria. It was, well, it was so bright, I can't tell you what would describe it. The intensity of it was just magnificent. It was just about that far above Mt. Logan, and it looked so close that it looked like it could just set down.

Frank B. Salisbury (FBS): Did it have a shape, a depth, or was it a point of light?

Mable: I picked up my girlfriend that was going to go to work, and I said, "I'm going back home to get my field glasses. I don't know if I'll see any more with them, but I'm going to get them anyway." I said, "That's something that someone's sending or something from some-where else." So I came home and got the field glasses, and when we got to the cafeteria, we were in the east dining room, and it was dark in there and you could get a better view. It looked just like one of these big fish that you see in an aquarium. They're about this wide, and they have a big tail and fin that comes like this and one like this. It was just about that shape, and then there was the mechanical part here, whatever it was. And it looked like it had just a little streamer out of the side. And it looked for a while like on the lefthand side, right in the middle, was a little streak of red, and the intensity of that was just great. I'll tell you, it just made you feel kind of weird.

FBS: It was above Mount Logan. Did it change its position?

Mable: No, it didn't seem to. It was so brilliant, it's just a shame that someone didn't get a telescope so you could bring that right up to see. I took the glasses out just before we went out for breakfast about five after nine, and at that time it was higher up here in the heavens, and it was still quite bright, but it was about the size of a pinhead. Of course, the sun was up then. It was daylight, real bright. But it was something fantastic. As a matter of fact, it made you feel just kind of insignificant. I wasn't alone. There were all the people eating breakfast, and some of the others that came on duty went out and looked at it. But it was huge. It didn't travel too fast. It looked like it was going in the same pattern that these jets fly. If it was daylight and those jets were going over, I imagine they'd get a pretty good look at it. The black background maybe made it look bigger when it was dark, but it looked like it was going in the same path as those jets that come from the east and go right over Mt. Logan.

FBS: Well, I hate to have to tell you what I think it is, but it sure sounds like the planet Venus. You'll know tomorrow if it's in almost exactly the same place and looks almost exactly the same way.

Mable: [After a disappointed pause.] If it is, I'll call you. Maybe it'll be out.

FBS: Venus is the morning star, you know. It was the evening star until about two months ago, and it's the brightest object in the heavens next to the sun and the moon—most spectacular if you haven't ever happened to notice. Why, it's very breathtaking.

Mable: In the summertime, you'll notice this evening star out in the daylight.

FBS: That was last summer. Venus was a beautiful evening star, and now it's moved around and is coming up ahead of the sun, so you can see it in the morning instead of in the evening after the sunset. It's been cloudy for the past few weeks, so this morning was your first chance to see it as a morning star.

I had the illusion once, very strongly, so I know exactly what you mean. You saw a shape in the binoculars, and it could have been because they weren't focused properly. What you should do is focus on the top of Mt. Logan and on the background stars that you know are points. If you really have it focused, then Venus ought to be pretty much a point of light—unless you had a telescope. The main thing to watch for is that it's in about the same place tomorrow morning and that it appears to move the same speed as the sun—all due to the Earth turning. The other test would be that it ought to appear farther above the mountain from here than it does when you get up there closer to the mountain. When you get close enough, it ought to go below the mountain.

I had heard that Venus was visible in the daytime, but I had never seen it. I watched it carefully off and on the next morning, before and during sunrise, so that I could determine its apparent distance from the sun. Then at about ten o'clock a few of us from the office went out into the parking lot, and sure enough, we were able to find Venus in the clear blue sky with sunlight blazing around us. I have now seen it on several other occasions in the daytime. It does have to be near its maximum brightness, however, and the real trick is knowing where to look.

My view of Venus as a UFO came early one morning in the autumn of 1962 in Germany, where I was on sabbatical. It was an interesting experience. My three boys (then ages six, eight, and nine) had heard me discussing UFOs, and so they were properly conditioned. After watching some time, they ran in and woke me, telling me there was a UFO maneuvering out there, over Österberg in Tübingen. I grabbed my binoculars on my way into their room. They said they had seen it flying around, and especially that it appeared to be flying rapidly toward us and then, after a few moments, away from us. I saw both of these illusions clearly. The apparent lateral motions, as I have since learned, were probably an example of autokinesis. If one sits in a dark room and can see only one small point of light, it will appear to move around after a few moments. If reference points are illuminated, the first point then holds still. Apparently the boys and I concentrated so intently upon Venus that we became unaware of the surrounding stars or lights in the town below (we lived on a hill). When I calmed down after my one and only really convincing UFO sighting, I stepped back in the room and lined Venus up with a window frame, after which it remained properly stationary. As the sun came up, we could see that there were thin, rapidly moving clouds in the sky. When one of these moved in front of Venus, it appeared to dim and retreat—advancing again at high velocity when the cloud moved away.

These stories could be multiplied indefinitely. Donald Menzel and Lyle Boyd (1963) have done a thorough job of explaining numerous sightings in terms of natural phenomena, as did the Condon Committee (1969) and the Air Force's Project Blue Book. Of course, these groups often got carried away and "explained" sightings when such explanations were not warranted, but in general, their writings make sobering reading when one is over-impressed with witness reports. In any case, sightings often have astronomical explanations.

Here is one more story. The explanation was not readily apparent but required a little lucky knowledge. It is also a good story because it illustrates again the psychological mood of UFO watchers—even when the witnesses aren't watching a spaceship but think they are.

Two families southwest of Fort Collins, Colorado, observed a "flying saucer" that hovered about four miles away above the north end of Horsetooth Reservoir for several hours during the day. Its distance could not be disputed, since it was seen in front of the foothills behind the reservoir. It had a brilliant, silvery, metallic appearance and seemed at first to have the shape of two saucers placed together face to face. Careful observation through binoculars finally revealed that it was not circular in shape but square and exhibited a fluttering motion similar to a falling leaf. The witnesses (two mothers and several children) became quite excited. They were tense, their voices uneven, and they commented upon their "unearthly" feeling.

When they called me, I was unable to see the object from my home, so

I drove over to where the two families were watching. After some moments of observation through binoculars, I remembered that the Atmospheric Science Department at Colorado State University had recently purchased a large (fifty feet across), square, polyethylene-coated-with-aluminum, inflatable weather kite. To confirm this diagnosis, we drove to where we could clearly see the kite and the cable holding it in place.

Probable Identification

So there are many cases in which a UFO can be positively identified. It might be that if an investigation could be made soon enough after every single UFO sighting, the number of UFOs that would turn into IFOs (Identified Flying Objects) could exceed ninety percent. The Air Force Project Blue Book usually claimed percentages this high, although many of their identifications were only probable and certainly far from convincing—but then many sightings of the planet Venus and the like were probably not reported to the Air Force.

An example of a probable identification is the Mantell case, well-known to earlier UFO buffs. At about 3:30 PM, on January 7, 1948, Captain Thomas Mantell was flying a plane in an area over Kentucky where a large, shiny UFO had been sighted near the towns of Maysville, Owenboro, and Irvington. Mantell kept climbing toward the object in his plane, although he had no oxygen. He radioed that he was getting close, but was going to 15,000 feet. Less than an hour later, Mantell's body was found in the wreckage of his plane. Of course, numerous rumors circulated to the effect that he had been zapped by a Martian. Several years later, when Project Skyhook was declassified, it was revealed that huge, silvery balloons had been released in that area from time to time. Unfortunately, no record was available indicating that a Skyhook balloon was in the vicinity on the day in question. It is reasonable, however, that such a balloon was floating rapidly in the jetstream at perhaps 60,000 feet, and that Mantell climbed high enough to black out from lack of oxygen. The details have been published in several books (e.g., see Menzel and Boyd, 1963), so there's no point in going into them here. The fact is, we have a probable identification of an important UFO, but at this late date it is apparently impossible to be certain. This is typical of many cases.

In their interviews, Thyrena Daniels and Dick Hackford mentioned Snippy the horse, whose body was found near Alamosa, Colorado, in 1967.

All the flesh and hide were missing from Snippy's head and neck, and a line of demarcation at the collar bone was so well defined that it appeared to have been made with a razor or scalpel. One pathologist who examined the carcass concluded that its condition could be accounted for by wild animals and decay. Others were totally convinced that the carcass could not be explained in this way. No UFO was ever seen with Snippy, so the connection with UFOs was strictly an assumed one. After reviewing the details I felt at one point that it was indeed an explained case—but after further study I was not so sure because several details were not easily accounted for. Here was another of many cases in which the evidence is suggestive of a scientific explanation but is far from conclusive.

Poor Snippy's mutilation was a forerunner for thousands of cases that were reported throughout the ranching part of North America during the 1970s and that still continue at a somewhat slower rate up to the present (see Chapter 8). Typically, these were dead cattle that had been mutilated by removal of teats, rectal areas, sex organs, lips, and tongues. Typically there was no blood and no tracks made by the mutilators, and the mutilations appeared to be performed with surgical precision. The economic losses to ranchers were sometimes considerable. As you can imagine, this situation has sparked considerable controversy that has continued for decades. To begin with, it is rare that the mutilations have any relationship with UFOs, although in a few cases UFOs were reported from the general area and general time of the mutilations. Still, many UFO buffs wonder if visiting aliens were responsible. Or is there some kind of Satanic cult that has perfected the mutilation techniques to obtain organs for use in secret rites? Or is it all a secret government project? Or is it simply a matter of attacks by predators or scavengers, as many skeptics have suggested? The topic is far too large for us to consider in any detail here, but it illustrates another case of unsolved mysteries that just might have an explanation in natural phenomena (i.e., predators) or in UFOs. (Wikipedia has a long article on cattle mutilations, noting that some reports go back to the late 19th Century.)

Recently (November 2009), I had the opportunity to discuss cattle mutilations, particularly in the Uintah Basin, with Dr. Daniel S. Dennis, a retired veterinarian who practiced for many decades out of Roosevelt. This was a somewhat sobering interview because Dr. Dan could remember only two cases, out of dozens, of his investigations of dead cattle that just might have been mutilations in the sense that they are discussed by investigators of the paranormal. He is by no means a UFO debunker. In Chapter 6 we'll present a most impressive 1966 UFO sighting, including a prolonged, very close encounter with a loss of time. The participants were a mother and her daughter, and the mother, Marjorie Beal, is Dr. Dan's sister. He is as impressed with the encounter as I am, so he is convinced of the reality of the UFOs, whatever they are.

He thinks, however, that the cattle mutilations often have quite natural explanations. Why are there seldom signs of attack by a predator? Because the typical cause of death is a cattle disease caused by clostridium bacteria, he says. This disease is always fatal once the animal contracts it, and ranchers must vaccinate their animals twice a year—a task that is often forgotten or postponed indefinitely. Why is it that certain areas on the cow appear to have been mutilated? Because the skin covering those areas is only about a fifth as thick as the hide on the back of the animal. Furthermore, it is typically some time before the dead animal is found, and by then these soft areas are protruding because of the gasses of decay produced inside, providing the target areas for scavengers (especially coyotes) who find the dead animals before the rancher does. Why are there no signs of blood on the ground? Because the blood coagulates inside the animal very soon after death. Why is the upper eye (as the animal lays on its side) the apparent target of mutilation? Because it is easy for magpies to get at. Dan says he has witnessed the birds pecking away at the eyes of dead animals, often searching for the soft tissue there. How about the surgical precision of the mutilations? In Dan's opinion, that precision can well be in the eye of the beholder. He remembers one case where he was accompanied by another veterinarian who was a "believer" in the paranormal explanation for cattle mutilations. He says the man kept pointing out the areas that supposedly showed the laserlike surgery, but Dr. Dan just could not see it that way. And he can't help but wonder why the UFO occupants, or even the satanic cult members, would need to collect so many of those special samples. But we don't need to wonder very long about why hungry coyotes might be attracted to dead cattle!

Most of my reading about cattle mutilations has been in the UFO literature. When skeptical veterinarians are mentioned, they are presented as being a trifle stupid to miss the clear signs of paranormal mutilation. Dr. Daniel Dennis is by no means stupid. But he readily admits that there might well be cases of mutilation that can't be explained—except for two possible cases, however, he just hasn't seen any.[1] And he has seen many dead cattle. The important thing is to keep an open mind.

Back to The Signal and the Noise

The really interesting cases are the ones that seem to defy explanation in terms of natural phenomena. These are the ones that keep UFO researchers interested. If all UFOs could be identified as the planet Venus or ball lightning, it would still constitute an interesting phenomenon for psychologists to study—but it would not hold much interest for many of the rest of us. When one hears a report of a flashing object "as big as the church at Randlett" diving down to within fifty feet of the car, then one can usually assume this report is not a misinterpretation of the planet Venus.

What about the Uintah Basin sightings? How many can be explained as natural or man-made phenomena misinterpreted by the witness? A few of them probably can. I have suggested that two UFOs—Douglas Horrocks and Richard Faucett's sightings—were most probably the planet Venus. But most of the sightings reported in Chapter 1 cannot be explained this easily. Often they describe large nearby objects behaving in most unusual ways ("Close Encounters of the First Kind," Hynek, 1972). Of course, the fact that the witness claims to see an object with some form is not itself convincing, as we saw earlier from the weather kite and from Mable's story. She saw a fish-shaped spaceship by looking through the binoculars at Venus. That is readily explainable, however, and anyone can more or less duplicate the phenomenon by looking at a star with binoculars and adjusting them so that they are out of focus. In any case, while many Uintah Basin sightings were probably misinterpretations of natural phenomena, these are for the most part the nocturnal lights and other apparitions that Junior Hicks didn't bother to investigate. With the few exceptions included in Chapter 1 as examples, the sightings in the Uintah Basin do not fit well in this first category.

When we are considering the question of natural phenomena misinterpreted, we need to think in terms of the signal versus the noise, as mentioned in Chapter 2. In information theory it is often necessary to separate a meaningful signal from the random noise. A good example is the bar-code checker in the grocery store. The red laser beam is constantly producing many random reflections from its environment (the noise) picked up by the detector, but the computer behind it is programmed to constantly respond only to a pattern that is recognized as a bar code (the valid signal). Then the bar code is translated into numbers that are further translated into the price and description of the item. (I'm amazed at the technology!) In the case of UFOs, we might think of the noise as the misinterpreted sightings of natural and man-made phenomena. Hence, the question: Is there some kind of genuine UFO that comes from an other-worldly place—or perhaps has some totally unexpected origin? If so, in this analogy, such a phenomenon would constitute the signal.

The important thing to realize is that the presence of noise does not negate the existence of a signal. If spaceships are visiting us from the Zeta Reticuli star system and being witnessed by inhabitants of Earth, we might, based upon our present knowledge of psychology, expect the accounts of the witnesses to generate additional reports that involved only misinterpreted natural phenomena. This would be noise obscuring a signal. As a matter of fact, our current interest in the space program and our long-standing interest in science fiction might also be expected to generate such "noise" sightings. And of course, there *could* be noise without a signal.

Any way we look at it then, we should not be surprised to discover that numerous UFO sightings have perfectly reasonable, natural explanations. The assignment of the UFO researcher is to determine if there is a signal amidst the vast quantities of apparent noise and what that signal might be.

UFO Evidence: The Ideal Witness

Let us, then, consider an ideal UFO witness. He is not so subject to panic that his powers of observation and memory are impaired; rather, the excitement increases his observational abilities and his tendency to remember what he has observed. He looks for details and tries to think of ways to remember them. Ideally, he even makes sketches and jots down notes during the sighting itself or immediately thereafter. (This has occurred in only a few instances.) He tries to identify colors by comparing them with other colors in his field of vision (perhaps street lights or neon lights), or if no other colors are visible, he tries to mentally make such comparisons. He is extremely careful in his observations of size and distance. He realizes that, in the absence of reference points, distance observations are only valid when the object is extremely close—close enough to allow his stereoscopic depth perception and other depth clues to be valid. In other cases, he hopes to see the object behind or in front of some other object (trees, mountain peaks, or even the horizon, as in a few Uintah Basin cases). If he can observe such a situation, then he can place maximum and/or minimum distances on the object. If the object is simply in a cloud-free sky, then he must realize that there is no way whatsoever that he can know the distance. Yet he will be tempted to guess. When I saw Venus over Oesterberg for those few seconds, I was certain that it was only a mile away. Of course, it was several million miles distant, and it could have been many light years (e.g., if it had been a supernova).

If our witness is positive of the distance, he can then make reasonable estimates as to size. If he is not positive of the distance, he should only record the apparent size—the angular dispersion. This is difficult for most observers to do, as is clear from the Uintah Basin interviews. They insist on saying that the object is the size of a basketball or a football, for example. The only valid thing to do when the distance of the object is not known is to compare its apparent size with the apparent size of some object that is either constant or that can be reproduced exactly later. The diameter of the full moon varies only slightly from thirty-one minutes of arc, or about half a degree of angular dispersion. (Because of an optical illusion, it appears larger when it is near the horizon. See Rock and Kaufman, 1962.) If a TV antenna is silhouetted against the object, then it is usually possible to return to the point of observation and measure the angular dispersion by measuring the portion of the TV antenna that covered the object. Thyrena Daniels estimated the size of her UFO by comparing it to the width of the highway and the distance between the fence lines. A perfectly simple procedure would be to hold one's hand at arm's length and measure the size of the object compared to the size of the thumb, finger, or fist. The size could even be marked on the thumbnail with a handy ballpoint pen. I know of one case where the witness measured the size of the object with a ruler held at arm's length. This would be an excellent procedure if a ruler were available.

The best possible solution for size and distance estimation is to triangulate; that is, to make observations from two points, preferably widely separated. The object must have been located where the two or more lines of sight (from the observation points to the object) cross, giving an accurate measure of its position and hence its distance from any observation point (as in Dick Hackford's UFO with its many witnesses). Once distance is known, actual size can readily be calculated (estimated) from apparent size. If our ideal witness is lucky enough to have a camera at hand so that he can photograph the object, he will do so from two or more locations, including as many foreground and surrounding objects as possible, and trying to have as much distance as possible between the different points of observation. If the object was holding still, this would later allow accurate triangulation (but few really good UFOs hold still!).

The duration of the sighting is important. A familiar object can be identified in a hundredth of a second, as shown by speed reading and aircraft identification experiments. It would certainly take longer, however, to fix in one's mind the size, shape, color, velocity, and so forth, of an unfamiliar object. Nevertheless, much can be observed in five or ten seconds, and a thirty-second sighting can produce a lot of mental information (as with Tony Zufelt's "train windows" in Halfway Hollow). Of course, I am always impressed when a witness is able to watch the object for half an hour or longer (e.g., Thyrena Daniels), especially if he has the presence of mind to take notes.

The ideal witness might carry not only a camera but also some other UFO observing equipment. Binoculars are especially handy, and many Uintah Basin hunters were able to use them in watching their UFOs. In one California case, Polaroid glasses showed haloes of light around a UFO that were not visible without the glasses (Harder, 1968). These haloes could indicate an extremely powerful magnetic field. An observer who has been in the near vicinity of a UFO should have any gold objects on his person tested for radioactivity (e.g., gold teeth, watch, or rings). The nucleus of a gold atom is large and readily captures high-energy radiation, itself becoming radioactive. Residual radioactivity in such a gold object could indicate certain kinds of radiation from a UFO. Furthermore, it is now possible by thermoluminescence measurements to tell whether many materials have been previously irradiated with high-energy photons or particles. It may also be possible by this method to tell whether a given substance has been previously heated to a high temperature. Nearly anyone might have gold, binoculars, or at the very least, a thumb. A really dedicated UFO watcher would also carry a pocket spectroscope or a wedge interference filter, either one of which would allow a more accurate analysis of color than would otherwise be possible. With these available, it would even be possible to look for distinct spectral lines.

UFO Evidence: Physical Traces

In a few cases, such as with cattle mutilations, we have the tangible remains of a possible UFO visit but no human witnesses. The vast majority of cases are exactly the opposite: We have the story without the physical evidence. Still, even in cases involving tangible evidence, the account of the witness remains paramount. Tangible evidence could almost always be fraudulent—in a philosophical sense, perhaps it always could. Thus it is really no better than the story of the witness—which, of course, could almost always also be fraudulent. Almost or just always? You tell me.

Dozens of UFO photographs have been taken. How valuable are they as evidence? Virtually any photograph could be faked—even before the days of Photoshop! Indeed, I have never seen a UFO photo that could not have been faked. If there were one, we would not be speculating about the existence of UFOs. Still, good photos combined with good witness accounts become especially impressive. For example, consider a photo taken in 1958 from the deck of a Brazilian ship off the coast of Trindade, an island east of Brazil. (Fig. 3-1 is the best of six photos that were taken.) The photographer was Almira Barauna, and his story was backed by several sailors who said that they were watching the object before and while Barauna photographed it. The sailors report that they called the object

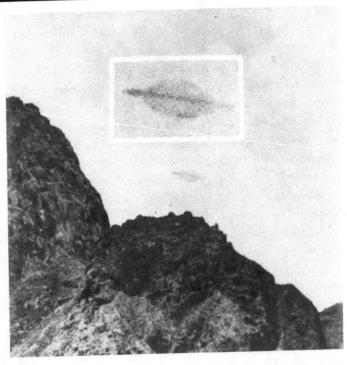

Fig. 3-1 *The third, and best, photograph (of six) taken by Almira Barauna from the deck of the Almirante Saldanha, as the object hovered over the island of Trindade, a Brazilian possession off the coast of Brazil. The photograph itself has been enlarged, and the inset shows the object enlarged to the point of obvious grain in the negative.*

to Barauna's attention. The film was developed in the ship's darkroom almost immediately, and on the negatives, Baruana and the sailors were able to make out the tiny object in the sky. (There was no printing paper, so prints were made later.) Because of the witnesses, I find the photo quite impressive. Of course the photos could have been faked—I once managed to fake one like it myself, even in the presence of a witness (Fig. 3-2). Did the photos and the witnesses prove the existence of the UFO? No, because the sailors could have been part of a conspiracy—or have been taken in by a conspiracy (see Chapter 6). There are just-suppose stories that suggest that they *were* part of a conspiracy, noting that Barauna had the skill to fake the photos and had even written an article about such tricks! Others present evidence that the basic story is correct and that the object really was seen. I tend to side with those who accept the account, but I surely cannot prove it to be true.

Fig. 3-2 *A fraudulent UFO photograph that I created. Insert is an extreme enlargement of the photograph. Note in this and in the Barauna photo that a simple double exposure must always produce an object that is lighter than its background—in these cases, the sky. Faking a photo with an object darker than the background is a bit more involved than a double exposure.*

Still, if a story itself is credible, a photograph can be valuable because it might provide detail at a level of accuracy that could not be supplied by the witness. But most UFO researchers have had to conclude, after years of study, that photographs by themselves are seldom, if ever, convincing evidence. This is simply because a capable photographer can do just about anything with his equipment to produce fraudulent UFO pictures. Some rather impressive UFO pictures, claimed for years to be genuine, were finally admitted to be frauds. Anyone who watches science fiction movies or television programs is aware of how convincing fraudulent UFO photos can be. Probably the best UFO photos I've seen were in the movie *Close Encounters of the Third Kind*. Photographs simply cannot be accepted as absolutely convincing primary evidence—especially in the days of Photoshop! And many photos of "UFOs" not seen by the picture taker prove to be lens flares.

In a sense, radar is in the same category as photography, although fraudulent radar returns are unlikely. More likely are radar returns that are not generated by real objects in the sky (as they appear), but that are radar mirages due to the beams being defracted by layers of warm air (as is a visual mirage), or "radar angels" due to defects in the equipment itself. This evidence could be summarized at great length (and has been—see, for example, Condon, 1969; Hall, 1964; and Menzel and Boyd, 1963). Nevertheless, to put it briefly: Numerous radar returns have been observed of objects traveling in the manner typical of UFOs (extremely high speeds, sharp turns, and so on); some of these could have been false returns due to mirages or defects in the set, but some of them might just as well have been returns from genuine UFOs (whatever they are).

There have been a number of excellent radar cases where the UFO was visually observed, as well as being picked up on radar, and in a few cases photographs were also taken. In some of the best radar cases, observations were made on several radar sets, located both on the ground and in the air, with observations extended over fairly long intervals of time (up to hours). My neighbor, Raymond Alvey, worked as an air-traffic controller for many years. He has one good story of a UFO that was seen on radar and by a plane that was scrambled to go after it.

In many cases throughout the world, so-called electromagnetic effects have been observed. Most typically, a car engine stops in the presence of a UFO (see interviews with Larry Sorenson, pp. 171–72, and Marjorie Beal, pp. 166–71) and then starts up again when the UFO leaves. Since no abnormalities can be detected in the car after such an experience, this detail is in the same category as any other detail reported by a witness—we are completely dependent upon the veracity of a report. Numerous other effects have also been observed, such as static on a radio, a spinning compass needle, dimming car or house lights (house lights even changed color in one instance), and the failure of power systems. Again, these effects have been discussed at great length in the available UFO literature. Often they have a powerful emotional impact upon the witness, and they provide fascinating details for a story. Seldom, however, can they be studied in any concrete way by the UFO investigator who comes upon the scene after the event.

Physiological effects of UFOs on witnesses sometimes provide a better opportunity for subsequent study. Several witnesses, for example, have exhibited a severe "sunburn" after witnessing a UFO at close range. This typically persists for several days, and in a few cases it has been studied by medically trained personnel who were interested in UFOs. Various forms of nausea and other sicknesses have also occurred in UFO witnesses, following close encounters. Sometimes these have exhibited the characteristics of radiation sickness, but usually the symptoms are unfamiliar to medical personnel. Again, these effects have been widely documented in the UFO literature. These examples are impressive because, while they might conceivably be fraudulent, it seems unlikely that a witness would subject himself to such misery just to perpetrate a hoax. Of course, they could also be coincidental with a cause other than the UFO sighting. In some of the best cases, the witness was even quite reluctant to tell the story; some friend or relative brought the witness's physical condition, as well as the UFO story, to the attention of the investigator. Of course, symptoms caused by some natural phenomenon might be unfamiliar to some medical examiners—but why would the victim decide to tell a false UFO tale in such a case? (In later chapters, we'll encounter two cases of physical effects on a witness: Villas Boas in Chapter 6 and Dr. X in Chapter 7.)

There are hundreds of cases where a witness has reported that a UFO landed, and traces were subsequently apparent on the ground (Phillips, 2009 and Sharon Peterson's story in Chapter 1). Sometimes these were deep impressions in the soil, purportedly made by the UFO landing gear, as in several cases discussed in the Prologue. Occasionally, holes of a most intriguing sort have been observed. In one case the soil was removed from the hole, leaving the roots of plants at the edge of the hole connected across it (Michel, 1958). It is difficult to imagine how this could be done—unless the UFO beamed the ground with some kind of anti-gravity beam so that soil particles flew out one by one, whereas the attached roots could not. In a few cases, the soil appears to have been markedly changed where the UFO has purportedly landed. (In Chapter 4, we'll discuss the famous Delphos, Kansas, case, which included a ring of soil that proved to have special properties. The residents of the farm claimed that a UFO had hovered over the spot.)

There were early cases in which it was reported that grass or other vegetation had been crushed to the ground in a circular pattern (Rutkowski, 2008). For example, in 1966 in Tully, Queensland, Australia, a witness claimed that he saw a saucer-shaped object rise from a swamp and, upon investigation, he found grass crushed in circular patterns—later called "saucer nests"—where the saucer had been. In 1975, circles of crushed crops began to appear in England. By now, these crops include wheat, barley, rye, corn, linseed, soy, and rapeseed (canola). These patterns in fields were simple to begin with but became increasingly complex. Many of these "crop circles" now have highly complex, geometric designs, and they have been found all over the world—but especially in Great Britain and the United States. According to Wikipedia (which has a long article with many references and a few photographs), by 2009 approximately 12,000 crop circles had been reported and usually photographed from the air. In 1991, Doug Bower and Dave Chorley from Southampton, England, claimed that they had been making the circles by using only a plank and a rope. Although they could not have made all 12,000 circles, it is easy to imagine that others were inspired by their actions and took up the challenge to make increasingly complex patterns (often at a significant cost to the farmer whose harvest is thus reduced). A few others have admitted to their hoaxes. But investigations have turned up characteristics of the plants in some crop circles that are difficult to account for if they were made by human hoaxers. For example, the nodes of the grasses seem to have been heated to the point where steam forms, causing the nodes essentially to explode. This can be duplicated with microwave energy, but could an everyday hoaxer take a microwave generator into the field? Furthermore, there are very few instances where hoaxers have been caught in the act.

Of course, it has been suggested that the circles not produced by hoaxers were formed by our UFO visitors, and some ufologists are convinced of this. But, as with the cattle mutilations, we must note that UFOs are seldom seen in relation to the circles—with the saucer nests in Australia being one exception. Obviously, with all the swirling controversy, crop circles cannot be cited as convincing evidence for the existence of extraterrestrial visitors.

Another interesting observation is that some admitted hoaxers who claim to have made some of those highly intricate crop circles are unable to tell how they did it. Does this mean that the hoax was a hoax? Or is it an example of a UFO projecting the pattern and method into the minds of the hoaxers without them being fully aware of what was going on? Always questions with no answers! (This observation is based on personal communication from Ted Bonnitt.)

In Chapter 1, I mentioned that one witness (anonymous) observed a UFO landing and then a kind of reverse crop circle where grass grew taller in the doughnut-shaped circle, an effect that lasted for a couple of years. The circle was witnessed by Junior Hicks. Again, it could be fraudulent: fertilizer spread by a hoaxer.

Radioactivity is not common in UFO sightings, although it has occasionally been reported. One witness seemed to suffer extreme symptoms of ionizing irradiation. Samples of gold have seldom been checked for radioactivity, although Geiger counters have often been used to check the site of a purported UFO landing (as in the Massey-Batty sighting—#13). Since radioactivity is always part of our science-fiction dreaming nowadays, it is perhaps remarkable that so few examples of radioactive UFO traces have been reported.

There are a few tangible objects alleged to have come from UFOs. Particles of magnesium obtained in South America, along with a story of a UFO crash, were analyzed carefully in several laboratories. Some of the analyses seemed to show magnesium at a level of purity not yet obtainable by our earthly technology. Other samples, however, had the usual impurities (Lorenzen, 1962 and 1966). Even a pancake was once analyzed by the Air Force! The witness said that he obtained it from the occupants of a UFO that landed near his home. Although it contained the usual ingredients of earthly pancakes, this proves nothing, since UFO occupants could conceivably make pancakes in the same manner as ordinary earthlings (Vallée, 1969, 2008 a., b., c.; we'll return briefly to this story in Chapter 4).

The point of the whole matter is that it is extremely difficult even to imagine a completely irrefutable kind of UFO evidence. Nearly anything might be produced fraudulently by someone who wanted to perpetrate a UFO hoax. Indeed, you might imagine that such a hoaxer would want to provide something to go along with his story. Even if a UFO witness comes up with an intricate piece of machinery made of alloys totally unknown to our technology, someone could always say that the witness or some acquaintances had personally created the alloys and then decided to use them in a UFO hoax.

What kind of tangible evidence would be absolute proof? What about some intricate object removed from the brain of a person who claimed that it was placed there by an extraterrestrial visitor? That has not happened, but it would certainly be impressive if it did. Still, if someone were intent enough on carrying out a hoax, almost anything could be done. Given any single case, the debunker has the advantage. All the skeptic has to do to cast doubt on such an event, at least in the minds of other skeptics, is to imagine a just-suppose story that is not totally implausible—and skeptics are very good at producing those what-if tales. Other skeptics are credulous enough to accept their plausibility. On the other hand, the debunker is at a disadvantage because the skeptic faces thousands of well-documented cases that have no obvious explanation. Imagine all the just-suppose stories that would have to be devised to cover such a large field. Who has the time to do it?

I would personally be impressed by a perfect cure for cancer obtained from a UFO occupant. Certainly there must also be propulsion systems (if the UFOs are tangible machines) that are completely beyond anything of which we are capable. If a UFO witness could produce one of these, I might well be impressed. But basically, it is most difficult to think of any absolutely convincing UFO evidence, produced by one or a few witnesses, and intended to convince the rest of us. A scientific UFO investigator can only deal with probabilities. How reasonable is the story? How difficult would it be to concoct the evidence? Are there patterns that can be discerned in the sightings that would be difficult to account for on the basis of fraudulent reports or natural phenomena misinterpreted?

A televised demonstration by the extra-terrestrials themselves might be convincing. That would be a bit difficult to fake, but it could be done. I would want really credible witnesses present during the demonstration—maybe presidents, kings, or the Pope! The fact that there never has been such a demonstration certainly suggests that our visitors must like the current status of things; it seems that they must be happy to display themselves to us, but with our not being able to prove that they exist.

Mind-set: Conspiracy Theories & the Difficulties of Objectivity

Rereading the *Playboy* panel transcript (discussed in the Prologue) recently brought home to me again how difficult it is to be truly objective about UFOs. Most of us studying the field have an attitude of strongly set minds. Nothing could have convinced Klass or Taves that UFOs were anything but misinterpretations or hallucinations. They had answers (just-suppose stories) for all the facts and reports the rest of us brought up. We had our own mind-set: Klass and Taves were blind to the facts, and UFOs were in some way real—although we were objective enough to admit that we didn't know how it could be.

One consequence of set minds is the formation of conspiracy theories.[2] Some may turn out to be true, but for years I shied away from them. Is the government really in possession of all the answers? I spent over thirty years in contact with NASA personnel, including serving on three or four NASA advisory panels, and I also had close contact with those studying Mars at NASA Ames. I could never see evidence of conspiracy. At one point, I asked if NASA might fund a UFO project if I could submit a good proposal. They said they might, but I never prepared such a proposal. Hynek worked with Blue Book but concluded that the participants were basically just stupid—and that they never really investigated the good cases.

Still, my respect has increased for those who think the government knows. Junior Hicks has become a believer, and I have great respect for him. Most of the UFO community is totally convinced that the governments of many countries have quantities of UFO information that they will not divulge. The evidence held in secret leaves no doubt about the reality of the UFOs, they say. We'll return to this topic in Chapter 5; the evidence presented there is quite convincing.

One Consequence of Mind-set: Debunk

The skeptical, positivist, secular mind-set (as seen in the journal *Skeptical Enquirer*) wants to debunk everything that cannot be proven scientifically: superstition, astrology, spiritualism, religion, belief in God, creationism (now intelligent design), psychic phenomena, fortune telling of any kind, pseudoscience of any kind, and not least of all UFOs. Actually, it is pretty easy to agree with the skeptics on most of those items. I can get pretty worked up about astrology—it just ain't so!

The skeptics claim they are defending reason above all. Well-educated, reasonable persons (all of us, of course!) go along with much of this, but some of us think the skeptics throw out one or more babies with the bath water. For example, I do not believe reason has proved atheism or evolution only by the natural selection of random mutations (my other hobby), nor has it proved the non-existence of UFOs.

Perhaps the first weapon of the debunker is to claim that people who believe the things listed above are simply ignorant of natural science—they are not educated. If we look at the debunked items, we have to agree in some cases and disagree in others. To an extent, it depends on our mind-set, but it is valid to be reasonably skeptical of the skeptic. Actually, various polls show that the percentage of UFO "believers" is greatest among educated people (see Friedman, 2008).

Because we are discussing evidence that UFOs are just natural or conventional phenomena misinterpreted, let's return to that favorite weapon of the debunker: the just-suppose or what-if story. Here are two examples, one is Menzel's and Taves's debunking of a "legend" and the other is Philip Klass's debunking a UFO story—there are, of course, many such examples.

Walking on Water. The basic data pertaining to a given case are not always agreed upon by all the believers, let alone the explainers. There is often room for argument about what really happened because different witnesses bring up different and sometimes conflicting points. However, I found a nice example in a book by two debunkers, Harvard astronomer Donald H. Menzel and psychoanalyst Ernest H. Taves (1977, pp. 20–21). They not only explained the UFOs; they took on some of the miracles of the Bible as well. One was the "legend" (their term) of Jesus walking on the water. They devote a page and one photograph to the phenomenon of the inferior mirage, in which a person standing on a spit of land at some distance from the observer is both magnified in apparent size and seems to be standing on the water. The conclusion: The "legend" originated as an inferior mirage.

Well, that's nice, but it has little relevance to the only data available: the accounts in Matthew (14:24–31); Mark (6:44–51); and John (6:16–21). There can be no argument about the basic data because we all have access to the same information. Whether the event actually occurred as described is irrelevant to this example; the point is, there can be no disagreement about the story itself. This story says that Jesus approached the boat in the middle of the night when winds were high. As he approached the boat, Peter asked if he, Peter, could also walk on the water. Jesus said yes, but Peter soon sank and had to be rescued. (Read the verses if you are interested.)

To "explain" this "legend" as an inferior mirage, Menzel and Taves had to multiply the "just supposes." Inferior mirages occur under a warm sun and involve objects far enough away so that the atmosphere can have its lensing effect. They don't occur at night and they certainly don't involve someone appearing to walk on the water right up to the boat. Hence, Menzel and Taves by suggesting the mirage implicitly said: *Just suppose that it was really day and not night, that there wasn't a storm, that Jesus was a few hundred meters away, and that Peter's experience was added as the legend grew. See, the legend is explained!* This is a typical what-if-it-happened-thus? story, just like the ones applied by skeptics (and believers, for that matter) to UFO accounts.

Captain Coyne and his Helicopter Crew. Here is a good UFO example of the just-suppose approach. The following has been taken from the first edition of this book (Salisbury, 1974):

> The case involved Captain Lawrence Coyne, an Army helicopter pilot, who was cruising at 2,500 feet altitude with three other crewmen at 11:10 PM on the night of October 18 [1973] near Mansfield, Ohio. The crew chief spotted a distant red light off to the right on the eastern horizon. The light appeared to be moving directly toward the helicopter on a collision course at high speed. Captain Coyne put the copter into a shallow power dive, trying to evade the oncoming red light. "But it was traveling in excess of six hundred miles per hour," he said, "and it came from the horizon to our aircraft in about ten seconds." Coyne held the chopper in the dive down through 2,000 feet. "At 1,700 feet, I braced myself for the impact with the other craft. It was coming from our right side. I was scared. There had been so little time to respond. The thing was terrifically fast."
>
> There was no impact, and the men looked up and saw it stopped above their helicopter. They said it had a big, gray, metallic-looking hull about sixty feet long and was shaped like an airfoil or a streamlined fat cigar. There was a red light on the front of it, the leading edge glowed red, there was a center dome, and a green light at the rear swivelled like a spotlight, completely flooding out the red instrument lights in the helicopter. There were no windows or other markings on the object itself.

The radio in the helicopter suddenly went completely dead. After hovering over the helicopter for a few seconds, the object sped off into the north.

With the danger of a collision over, Coyne turned his attention to his controls in order to pull the helicopter out of the dive. The crew then discovered that the altimeter indicated an altitude of 3,800 feet. Apparently, the helicopter, set for a dive, had been raised by the object over 2,000 feet in a few seconds—an accomplishment that would have torn the helicopter apart unless the air surrounding the vehicle moved along with it. This is not the only case in which a vehicle seems to have been levitated by a UFO—in one experience, an automobile was lifted off the road and dropped in a field on the other side of a fence—but it is surely one of the best cases on record. All four crew members told exactly the same story, and they were in touch with the Mansfield Air Force Base except for the few moments while the radio was dead. An impressive report, indeed!

Philip J. Klass (1974) took on this story. He actually spent many months running down interviews with Coyne and his crew, talking to radar and radio operators, and checking with airports and people on the ground. His was a model of what a UFO investigation should be. It is also a model of what one must do to maintain one's mind-set; great skill is required to find plausible(?) just-suppose stories that will support the foregone conclusion that there is no such craft as the Coyne crew described.

Here's *my* fictional story: Just suppose that Philip Klass's train of thought over those several months went something like this (based on Chapter 29 in his book):

Hmmm . . . They said it was a bright light in the dark sky coming at them very fast. Spectacular meteors—fireballs—do that. Just suppose they were really seeing a fireball. Let's check the calendar for meteor showers. Wow! The Orionids (rocks left from Halley's comet) can be seen from about October 2 to November 7, peaking about October 21. The Coyne crew saw their UFO on October 18, which fits nicely. Let's suppose they saw an Orionid fire ball.

But wait a minute. The way they described their experience doesn't really match a fireball. But just suppose that they were misinterpreting what they saw. Maybe their minds were playing tricks on them. Let's look into it.

The crew thought the "craft" was very close, within 500 feet. But there was another flight crew that misjudged the distance to a fireball in broad daylight by 125 miles. So just suppose Coyne's crew was also way off in their distance estimate. Coyne's crew thought the cigar-shaped object was about 50 feet long, but if they didn't know how far away it was (and we've established that because another flight crew made a mistake!), then they couldn't know how large it was. They thought it had a gray metallic structure, but suppose that their minds played a trick on them. What if the tail of the fireball gave the impression of a craft, and it produced the green light in the cockpit, while the red light was only on the front of the fireball, caused by the heat of friction with the atmosphere? And suppose that the excitement of the encounter caused the crew to temporarily lose their sense of direction so that they thought the UFO had turned to go north after approaching them from the east—something meteors do not do.

The "levitation" is a bit harder to explain, but what if the pilot's instincts took over while he was preoccupied with the UFO so that he really set the controls to climb instead of to dive? Subconsciously controlled actions can be very powerful. There could be various reasons that the helicopter was unable to gain radio contact during the event. What if the Mansfield tower operator was simply preoccupied with another aircraft?

In short, this case can be "explained" by postulating a number of supposes and what-ifs. And that seems to be the situation with almost any UFO case. The events can't be repeated, and human memories and interpretations are far from perfect. So we are left with our own assessments of the probabilities that a just-suppose explanation comes close to the truth or does not. Klass's mind-set allowed no unexplainable UFOs. My mind-set finds it difficult to think that the helicopter crew could be as wrong in their memories and interpretations as Klass's story requires.

The interesting thing is that Klass's scenario could be true—but there is no way for us to be sure that it is or that it isn't. Such are the problems that we face when we try to understand UFOs.

As a last resort, a debunker can always suggest that the UFO account is a hoax: a lie or trick played by someone who, for example, sends up a balloon with a flare attached. We'll take a look at the Travis Walton case in Chapter 6. In that case there were many details that didn't fit any just-suppose stories that Klass could conjure up, so he called the whole thing a hoax. Was it? It is never easy to be sure one way or the other.

The Believer Mind-set: Defend!

In my opinion, UFOs are a truly important phenomenon of our time—and earlier times for that matter. So how can we keep intelligent minds interested enough to perhaps one day find a solution? One way to turn off good minds is to insist on debunking every case, regardless of what it takes to do so, as we've been seeing. Another way is to believe and defend with so much zeal that reasonable people again are turned off. I had a recent encounter with a case in which a good and intelligent man had become such a total believer that he was willing to go way beyond reason into pseudoscience. The case itself was fascinating, but this man went far beyond the evidence to postulate energy rays and beams that could analyze and interpret the chemistry of a leaf.

Another defense is to claim that the debunkers just don't really understand the evidence. And that is often the case—most scientists who reject all UFOs out of hand have not gone beyond rumors and news accounts—and the statements of the debunkers. But I couldn't accuse Philip Klass of not digging into the facts. It's just that even if the debunker does have all the evidence, if at all possible, he will eliminate all the unexplained details with just-suppose stories, as in the examples above. And there is always the hoax to fall back on. It's a matter of mind-set.

Carl Sagan (much as he bugged me) was right when he said that extraordinary claims require extraordinary proof. I don't see the extraordinary proof that UFOs and all they imply are bunk. In any case, we must be most careful not to jump to far-out conclusions. Although it is extremely difficult, we must maintain an objective mind-set. When we don't, we lose credibility.

Notes

1. In Chapter 8, we'll talk about the role of cattle mutilations in relation to the skinwalker ranch. Some of those cases were very impressive because there was less than half an hour from the time the animal was seen alive until it was found mutilated. Dr. Daniel Dennis was not called in on those cases because he had retired well before they occurred. Nor does he recall being called to examine dead cattle on the ranch before the *Skinwalker* events were claimed to occur.

2. An example of a possible conspiracy theory concerns the possibility of life on Mars; that is, highly advanced or even intelligent life. Do those working with the thousands of close-up photos of Mars have proof of developed life forms that for some reason they refuse to share with the world? Elaine Douglass called my attention to www.marsanomaly.com whose webmaster, Joseph P. Skipper, has no doubt that the Mars photos he has looked at represent higher life forms—that's his mind-set.

   The idea of mind-set works in either direction. There are certainly good reasons to doubt that there is any life, other than perhaps microbial life, on Mars: extreme low temperatures, scarcity of water, very low atmospheric pressure, only CO_2 with a few traces of other gases—O_2, methane, and so forth.

Hence, mainstream science is conditioned to believe that higher life on Mars is impossible—and this seems to be confirmed by all the close photos that mainstream science sees. The mind-set is simply against higher life forms on Mars. (Contrary to the days of Lowell and his canals.)

What about the things on Skipper's website? Some of them are indeed impressive enough to convince him that science is censoring the truth. It's all a conspiracy to keep us from knowing! As a mostly mainstream scientist, however, I tend to share the no-higher-life mind-set. But I surely don't know. I shy away from a conspiracy theory in this case for two reasons: First, that Martian environment is a huge problem. Second, it seems that if the photo analysts knew there were higher life forms (e.g., plants) on Mars, they would be extremely eager to tell us. Think of how their grant funding would skyrocket! It is difficult for me to think of a plausible explanation of why they would not want us to know—this idea might not apply to UFOs; maybe the public would panic or something—but I doubt even that. It would surely unite us!

What about some of the photos (available to anyone willing to go to the trouble to get them) that show amazing things that look like advanced life forms on Mars? Well, with our mind-set, the photo analysts and I make up just-suppose stories in an attempt to explain those photos in some way other than advanced life on Mars. That's also what happens (I think) with what many in the government know about UFOs.

4
Lies or Hoaxes

There are basically two ways that a UFO sighting can be fraudulent: The witness may be lying or the sighting itself might be fraudulently arranged to deceive a witness. There are a few known examples of the second situation. Students at Caltech in Pasadena, California, were apparently the first to hit upon the idea of suspending a candle beneath a plastic dry cleaner's bag to produce a lighted balloon. These were released over Pasadena in about 1966, generating a number of UFO reports. I also heard that certain teenagers in Vernal, Utah, prepared a big plywood disc with railroad fusees and rolled it down a slope during the height of the UFO wave in the Uintah Basin. Predictably, this generated a few local stories. Such tricks have been repeated many times. Perpetrators in New Jersey used railroad fusees and balloons to produce a "formation" of brilliant red UFOs. It is interesting that nearly all the New Jersey witnesses recognized the nature of the flares and did not think they were watching UFOs (see Randle, 2009, pp. 129–34).

It is difficult to imagine how many UFO sightings could fit in this category. If objects were built that fooled Dean Powell, Joe Ann Harris, Thyrena Daniels, or Leland Mecham, just to name a few examples, they would have to have been nearly as spectacular as the proverbial spaceship from Zeta Reticuli! But I'm not about to say what can and what cannot be done along these lines. I watched a stage performance of The Great Blackstone in which he passed a spinning bandsaw blade through the neck of a lovely young lady who had been placed in a proper trance. A piece of hardwood flooring below the young lady's neck was cut in two, amidst much flying sawdust—but of course the lady was unhurt. Blackstone would readily admit that this was an illusion, yet from the audience I was convinced (well, nearly!) that I was watching the blade itself actually pass through the subject's neck. So when a really ingenious person wants to perpetrate a hoax, it is not always easy for others to see how it is done. I doubt that scientists are the best-trained individuals to investigate UFO sightings. Magicians are probably better at providing explanations, and perhaps trial lawyers should handle the interviewing of witnesses.

A fictional story presented as a valid UFO sighting is a much more likely form of hoax. It is not difficult to imagine that many individuals might get some kind of mental reward from fooling the public with such a story. Certainly it has been tried many times, and certainly it has succeeded in some cases. It is probably the most difficult thing for a gullible scientist like me to disprove. Often, the best that an investigator can do is to state the possibility that the UFO might really be a fabricated story. Of course, the witness is always aware that the story might not be believed.

In regard to the Uintah Basin stories, I can only say that I don't think they are lies. I have no idea how I could really prove that they are not. I only know that lies seem extremely unlikely because of the large number of witnesses involved—most of them unknown to each other and none of them in a position to gain anything from their reports. Furthermore, their stories are similar in many ways to stories told by other witnesses all over the world, and, as a rule, most Uintah Basin witnesses were quite unaware of these other stories. In many cases these people were outstanding citizens of the community and leaders in their congregations. To me, they just don't sound like liars.[1] But how can I prove that they are not liars? I suppose that I cannot prove it. You will have to decide for yourself—or, if you are really going to be scientific about the matter, don't decide: keep an open mind.

The Carlos Allende Hoax

Still, as we've indicated, there must be numerous cases in UFO lore where the witnesses told deliberate falsehoods. I'm not referring, of course, to the distortion of truth that may enter into any UFO report. Memories are not perfect, and observations are often colored by conscious or subconscious interpretation, as we saw with Mable (Chapter 3). But in this case, I'm talking about conscious and deliberate lies.

A classical case is that of the so-called Carlos Allende letters. Here's the story: The Office of Naval Research received a copy of a UFO book written by Morris K. Jessup (1955), an astronomer. This had been annotated by comments in the margins, written in three colors of ink and apparently written by three different annotators. The comments described two subcultures of space people and implied that the annotators belonged to one of them—although there were also implications that they were gypsies. The "people" moved in various vehicles from space to cities below the sea. Numerous strange things unexplained by conventional science were "explained," such as unusual objects falling from the sky, strange marks, and footprints. Before the book was received by the Office of Naval Research, Jessup had received two letters, one signed Carlos Allende and the other signed Carl Allen, but both in the same style. It was apparent upon comparison that at least one of the annotators must be Allende/Allen. The letters told of top secret experiments in teleportation of a ship with its crew from one harbor to another.

The whole thing was most cleverly done. The Navy had the book copied on mimeograph stencils and prepared so that several people could study it. I had one of these copies for quite some time. Apparently it was carefully studied at the Office of Naval Research. At least three authors of UFO books (Sanderson, 1967; Steiger and Whritenour, 1968) commented upon it in a favorable way, accepting it on a tentative basis.

In the fall of 1969, Carl Allen, alias Carlos Allende, walked into the office of the Aerial Phenomena Research Organization in Tucson and admitted his hoax (The APRO Bulletin, July–August, 1969). In discussions with him it became quite apparent that he was indeed the author of the annotations and the letters, and that all was fictitious. He took seriously the teleportation experiment, which he had heard about in a brief newspaper article. He wanted to "scare the hell out of Jessup," because he was afraid Jessup's research into unified field theory was dangerous. When Steiger and Whritenour published a sensationalized account, Allen tried to stop publication and then admitted his hoax.

Incidently, Morris Jessup committed suicide, and UFO buffs have developed conspiracy theories, of course. Vallée (2008 c., pp. 180–89) relates a long correspondence with Allen/Allende. Vallée even includes a photo of Allende taken by one of Vallée's associates.

So hoaxes can certainly play a role in the UFO phenomenon. But to have set out to prove Allende's story a hoax would have taken much more time and money than is available to most UFO researchers. And besides, his tale sounded too fantastic to be taken seriously, anyway.

The Contactees

As a matter of fact, hoaxes could play a large role in another aspect of the UFO phenomenon: the contactees. These are individuals who claim to have been contacted by flying saucers and their occupants. Usually they tell stories of trips in the saucers. The "space brothers" they meet are nearly always perfect specimens of mankind, although they sometimes differ in physical detail from the human prototype (e.g., narrow eyes, round face). In most stories I have encountered told by male contactees, at least one of the extraterrestrials is an indescribably beautiful woman—again often with some special feature such as blood red hair or translucent skin. Beautiful music is also common in the accounts. Most typically, the contactee is informed that he was chosen to present some special message to the inhabitants of Earth—and usually the message is to love one's neighbor and destroy all atomic weapons! Unfortunately, the messages vary tremendously in detail beyond this rather obvious admonition (Rutkowski, 2008; Vallée, 2008 c.).

By now there are thousands of contactees. Several years ago I had a list that approached one hundred, and they seemed to be multiplying at an exponential rate. They are scattered all over the world. Although their heyday might have been the time while I was writing the first edition of this book, they continue to appear—although it now seems to be much more common to hear about abductees who are taken against their will, as we'll see in Chapter 6.

What do we make of the contactees? On the surface, the problem seems to be an easy one to deal with. Nearly always the contactees report on a "science" received from the extraterrestrials that makes our science obsolete. The trouble is, their "science" includes "facts" about the universe and how it operates that are simply not true—and that differ greatly from contactee to contactee. Nevertheless, the contactee is often able to gather a following, a cult of believers.

Practically any contactee could be taken as an example, but the George Adamski story is a great illustration of a point I want to make—although by now his three books, which circulated widely during the 1950s and '60s, have pretty much dropped out of sight. Adamski was the first contactee to reach prominence. In addition to UFO photos (which, it turned out, looked like a chicken incubator hung from a string), he had stories to prove his contacts. Consider an example from one of his books (Adamski, 1967, pp. 118–21, 169): George was taken on a trip to the moon (not to mention Venus and other distant places!). This was in the early 1950s, well before our lunar explorations. One UFO in which he was riding went around to the back side of the moon, the side that is never visible from the earth. Adamski reported that this was quite unlike the side that we see. In addition to snow-capped peaks, there were rolling hills covered with lush forests. There were rivers and lakes and small towns nestled in the valleys. Happy people could be seen walking along the roads and pathways. The atmosphere on the moon, Adamski tells us, was indeed thinner than it is on earth, but one could learn to breathe it with a little practice.

We all know that the moon didn't turn out to be this way. The back side has even more impact craters than the side we see, and of course in the absence of an atmosphere it is just as lifeless. Even after genuine photos of the moon's far side were published, some Adamski followers continued to believe in him by saying that the moon people camouflaged their side so that it looked to our astronauts just like our side! That would take some doing.

It is quite apparent that Adamski was not telling the truth about the moon. But was he lying in a conscious sense? Just suppose that the UFO drivers wanted to remain anonymous for as long as possible. Probably they would realize that scientists and engineers might be the ones most likely to detect them and destroy their anonymity. How could they keep scientists and engineers from doing this? They would achieve their goal if they could keep scientists and engineers from even being interested in them, regardless of numerous reports from ordinary people (including a few scientists and engineers). How to go about it?

One way to convince scientists and other educated people that UFOs don't really exist might be to make many contacts with people on Earth, but to choose people (assuming they had knowledge and ability to choose) who have no eminence in human society and who have little or no scientific or engineering training. Always their egos could be built up by telling them that they were the chosen ones, and that in spite of persecution and ridicule, they were to carry the message of loving one's neighbor and destroying the Bomb. But different contactees could be told different things about how the universe functioned—clearly, they do all have different stories.

Some might even be taken for rides in UFOs. Adamski, for example, might have been taken for a spin in the scout ship up to the mother ship, as he claimed. But instead of going to the moon, his hosts conceivably could have shown him northern New Hampshire or somewhere on Earth that looked like how he described the lunar landscape. I suppose Adamski would have believed whatever his hosts told him, but if there were any doubt, they could easily have resorted to hypnotism, special drugs, or another method, to convince him beyond any question that he was seeing the far side of the moon. I suppose hypnotism could be used even without the UFO trip. When he and his fellow contactees told their stories, it would be immediately apparent to most of us that the stories didn't make sense, and that they were full of out-and-out untruths. The sincerity of the contactees might be highly impressive, but even in 1955 when Adamski's book was first published no one could have convinced me that the other side of the moon had rolling hills, lush forests, lakes, small towns, and so on. For numerous reasons, this was contrary to so many scientific facts that it had to be impossible, even then. What scientist or engineer is going to take a contactee seriously when he tells such stories? (Vallée, 2008 c., makes this point with many other contactee examples.)

Now, let's get one thing straight. I am not suggesting that Adamski and his ilk had genuine contacts as they claimed. I am not even suggesting that Adamski was sincere. The most logical explanation is that Adamski and all the other contactees made up their stories just as Carl Allen, alias Carlos Allende, made up his. Adamski's book certainly reads like fiction.

The world is full of people with psychological and mental problems. It would not be at all surprising if a certain portion of these told contactee stories. Certainly the contactee nearly always exhibits symptoms of paranoia. What I am trying to do is to illustrate the difficulty of really coming to grips with the UFO enigma. Probably the contactees are the best example of lies in the UFO business, but I can't prove this because there is the alternative explanation that extraterrestrial beings use the contactees to mislead the scientific and engineering communities. Even when you have something as blatantly phoney as lakes and forests on the far side of the moon, you still can't come to a positive and final conclusion about the storyteller.

The Raëlian Movement

As far as I know, Adamski's cult has faded away, but similar cults are going strong and even make the daily news now and then. One is the Raëlian movement. In May 2003, the movement claimed 60,000 members who adhere to the doctrines of "Raël," the former Claude Vorilhon, a French journalist and race-car enthusiast. Raël claims to have been twice contacted by an alien in a flying saucer who revealed to him the true story of the creation of life on Earth. Raël's accounts of these visitations were published in 1974 (with an updated version in 1986). The Raëlians were recently in the news for their claim to have cloned a human infant.[2]

According to Raël, eons ago on a distant planet, these aliens—the Elohim (Hebrew plural for God)—advanced in their science until they could create primitive cells in the laboratory. They were afraid of contaminating their own planet with these cells, however, so they found another suitable planet, our Earth, of course. As their science advanced (presumably while countless generations came and went), they were able to create all kinds of plants and animals, and with the help of their artists, some of these were spectacular indeed. There was not only a great variety of flowers, but some birds were so adorned with colorful feathers that they could not fly. Their greatest challenge was to create beings after their own images, but there were some failed attempts along the way (the fossil pre-humans). They ended with what we recognize as the races of humans, but all were in the fundamental image of their creators.

The Raëlians consider evolution to be a myth. The increasingly complex fossils in the geological column are the evidences of how the Elohim scientists improved in their special creations. Raël relates all of this to the Biblical account of the Creation as you have already guessed. Raëlians hold that the Bible contains a partial but somewhat corrupted version of the true story of the Creation. Although the Biblical authors had been told the story of their creation, they were too primitive to understand it correctly. This is a story by a special, "scientific" brand of UFO contactee creationists who reject both the more traditional religious accounts of the Creation and the theories of modern evolutionists!

Another current contactee cult is built around "Billy" Eduard Albert Meier, a farmer in Switzerland. Meier says that he was in contact with extraterrestrials, called Plejaren (from the constellation we know as the Pleiades). Meier's contact began when he was five years old and continued with an eleven-year break, which ended in 1975. After 1975 the Plejaren again made contact and continued with messages about world peace and such, differing of course in detail from the messages given to other contactees. Meier offers over a thousand very clear photos of the UFOs that visit him, most being taken in the late 1970s and set at his farm in the Swiss Alps (see his website www.steelmarkonline.com). Their beauty certainly makes Adamski's photos look like those produced by a total amateur. It is interesting that none of his neighbors see the space ships in spite of their numerous visits—although there are other witnesses to some of the phenomena that Meier reports; for example, an extremely loud sound that was recorded and that bothered Swiss residents a few kilometers away. Meier has also traveled the world, and lost one of his arms in a bus accident in Turkey. His supporters note that a one-armed man could never fake such beautiful photos—although with two arms and proper control of depth of field, it is not difficult to fake such beautiful, daylight photographs with a well-made model on a thread. Meier has strong supporters and also detractors, such as James Randi and Jacques Vallée. (See Wikipedia and many websites; also Vallée, 2008 c., who visited Meier in Switzerland.) There are plenty of other modern contactees as well as the ones mentioned here.

One thing is absolutely certain. Regardless of the educational level of the contactee, his sincerity is almost always as overwhelming as that which I encountered in the Uintah Basin. While I was still in Colorado several years ago, I received a number of letters from a young lad who had a contact story to tell. The story could either be a fantasy or a semi-accurate report of the extraterrestrials' overwhelming impact on one pathetic witness—who would never be believed. His first letter is attached as an endnote to this chapter to illustrate what I am talking about when it comes to sincerity and lack of education.[3]

Captain Franch

There is an interesting story that has entered into the classical UFO literature (e.g., Rutkowski, 2008; pp. 47–49; Vallée, 2008 a., pp. 49–51) and that leads to the story that I want to tell in this section. Joe Simonton is a sort of contactee although he didn't have messages to save the world; instead, he had pancakes! They were given to him by occupants of a UFO that hovered close to the ground near his home in Wisconsin just before lunch on April 18, 1961. A hatch opened in the egg-shaped object, and three "men" who "looked like Italians" motioned that they wanted Simonton to fill their pitcher with water, which he did. Perhaps as a reward before leaving, the UFO occupants gave Joe three "pancakes." One of the pancakes, which Joe said tasted like cardboard, was eventually analyzed by the Air Force and declared to consist of substances just like those found in our own pancakes. All this was so strange that it got quite a bit of publicity at the time.

Let's return to the *National Enquirer* panel described in the Prologue. One of the letters from UFO witnesses (during our first meeting) led to an interesting experience for me: Captain Guido Franch promised to take us to Mars in the Space Ship Neptune, owned by the Black Eagles and responsible for many UFO stories! The ship was kept in a secret hanger in the Andes. The letter included photos of a couple of sexy young ladies from Mars. One was a Martian brain surgeon! When we on the panel read his letter, we had a good laugh. But to be truly objective, I had to admit that if he took me to Mars, I would vote to give him the reward! In his letter, Captain Franch told about how he and his fellow Black Eagles (who might well have looked like Italians) visited a farmer in Wisconsin in the space ship Neptune. Since they were eating breakfast, they gave the farmer three of their pancakes! J. Allen Hynek and I played along with Guido for awhile, and then I continued my contacts with him for quite some time after Hynek decided he had better things to do.

Hynek and I visited Guido Franch's home and his "secretary" in Chicago. I was traveling a lot, and Guido would arrange to meet me at the O'Hare Airport. On one of those visits, I went with him and two of his "secretaries" to first buy a bottle of distilled water from a drugstore and then to rent a lawnmower. We went to a park where I "watched" him turn

Fig. 4-1 *Captain Franch and the lawnmower, which ran on gasoline made from water (he claimed!). (Date unknown; mid 1970s.)*

Fig. 4-2 *Captain Franch's lady from Mars visiting at O'Hare International Airport.*

---

some of the distilled water into gasoline with a little black powder, a nice trick the Black Eagles had taught him. We ran the lawnmower with the gasoline (Fig. 4-1; previous page). (During the time I was in Maryland at the Atomic Energy Commission and the first edition of this book was being published, I was actually contacted by a group who wanted me to evaluate the gasoline-from-water process! Apparently, there were serious people who took Captain Franch seriously. I declined the invitation.)

Although it would be nice if we could get our gasoline from water, Captain Franch probably cheated. When it came time to add the black powder to the water kept in his trunk in the back of the car, he said I had to stand back a hundred feet because it might explode! So much for the demonstration, but I acted convinced anyway. Unfortunately, he never gave me a sample of the black gasoline-powder as he kept promising to do, although he did give me a small bottle of the "freshly created" gasoline. On other occasions, I met sexy ladies from Mars whom he brought to O'Hare (Fig. 4-2).

He kept promising the trip to Mars, and he was so cool in his approach that I finally had to realize that *I* was cancelling the Martian visit, so I decided to push him to the limit. I would go along with anything that he suggested. He was so slick that I began to wonder if I should write a will and buy lots of film to use on Mars! His secretary had always wanted to see Mars and was planning to go on this trip. The scam went on right to the day he was supposed to pick me up in the Neptune. At the last minute, the trip fell through—he actually backed out—the Black Eagles had expelled him as their publicity man! On the phone, the secretary sounded truly devastated. She really wanted to go!

Years later at O'Hare, I met with two business men who appeared to be convinced of Franch's stories. Franch also made one more pitch to me, which was like a Nigerian scam. There was gold buried by the Black Eagles in an abandoned Illinois coal mine, and if I would help him retrieve it, I would get a share, and an equal share could go to my church! I finally told him that I had been leading him along the whole time, which ended the adventure.

I'm a bit embarrassed to tell this story, but I had to lay over at O'Hare anyway! I think the story illustrates the complexities of human minds. Why would Guido Franch want to carry on such a charade? He never asked me for money (but he apparently wanted to use what reputation I had, judging by the people who called me). Why would I let it go on so long? I don't know.

Delphos, Kansas

I'm also a bit embarrassed to tell you the next story. As noted in the Prologue, I spent five years on the *National Enquirer* Blue Ribbon Panel to evaluate UFO reports. In early 1972, the *Enquirer*, a weekly with its head-quarters in Lantana, Florida, decided to offer a $50,000 reward "to the first person who could prove that an unidentified flying object came from outer space and was not a natural phenomenon." When it became clear that proof was going to be very difficult to come by, we felt that a number of good cases were not being submitted because the witnesses realized that they did not quite constitute proof. So we suggested that the Enquirer establish a second prize of $5,000 for the case with the most scientific value. In March, 1973, after several meetings and much deliberation, we awarded the $5,000 prize to the Durel Johnson Family of Delphos, Kansas. My reason for embarrassment in telling the story is that I voted with most of the panel in favor of the Delphos case (Bob Creegan abstained) although I was not intimately familiar with the details—and by now some doubts have crept into my mind! Here's the story:

On November 2, 1971, at about seven in the evening, sixteen-year-old Ronald Johnson and his pet dog were tending his flock of sheep at the Johnson Farm near Delphos, Kansas. As he approached the back side of the barn, he heard a rumble and proceeded toward the sound. He was startled to see a brilliant, mushroom-shaped object on or near the ground, illuminated by multicolored lights over its entire surface. Although he was stunned and somewhat blinded by the apparition, he watched for perhaps five minutes. The object brightened on the bottom, ascended over a low shed, and headed south. Ronald called his parents who both saw a bright object in the southern sky. By then, however, it was far enough away so that it might have been an airplane, satellite, or something similar. During the sighting, Ronald reported, the animals were upset.

Upon returning to the area where the object was sighted, the Johnsons found a glowing, ring-shaped area on the ground (actually more of a horseshoe, open on one end). They also noted that portions of a tree, dead sticks, rocks, and so forth, in the adjacent area were glowing too. Photographs were taken that night with a Polaroid camera, and these clearly showed the glowing ring as well as the other glowing materials. Mrs. Johnson touched the soil (which was not warm), and her fingers became numb. This numbness persisted for about a week. Ronald suffered eye irritation and difficulty sleeping for a couple of weeks. (James Harder, who visited nine months after the original sighting, said that his finger also felt numb after touching the ring material—but many others handled the material without reporting such a response.)

The story was given to the papers, and many people viewed the glowing ring. It was thirty-two days later, however, before Ted Phillips of APRO arrived on the scene to take samples and further investigate the case. The ring soil proved to be impossible to wet. It was a lighter brown color, almost white, than the surrounding soil. Phillips found that the whiteness extended some fourteen inches below the surface. There was also whiteness on nearby trees. Numerous analyses were made of the soil material by many laboratories (supported by the *National Enquirer* and others). The ring soil contained fairly high concentrations of salt, and the samples we investigated also included numerous "fungal" hyphae (Nocardia, actually, a bacterium that forms hyphae; common in soils). Some extracts with organic solvents seemed to indicate the presence of fatty (lipid) materials, which could account for the inability to wet the soil particles. Thermal luminescence tests indicated that the soil had never been irradiated with high levels of ionizing radiation nor raised to a high temperature. Nor was the soil radioactive. No satisfactory explanation for the soil condition has been found, although numerous theories have been considered. The ring luminescence was never accounted for, although bioluminescent fungi were suggested. In view of these and several other facts (which are reported in detail elsewhere), our panel felt that this sighting had much scientific value for UFO investigation.

Enter Philip Klass, the dedicated, almost fanatic, UFO debunker. He first heard about the case some months after the event, but he visited the Johnson farm and interviewed the family as well as others involved in the case such as Sheriff Ralph Enlow, who visited and photographed the site the day after the alleged event, and Mrs. Lester (Thaddia) Smith, a reporter for the local paper, who had also visited the farm on that day (Klass, 1974, pp. 312–32). Klass notes that the most thorough investigation was made by Ted Phillips, and Klass obtained much information from Phillips.

The sighting seemed impressive for two reasons: the accounts of the witnesses and the horseshoe ring of white material on the Johnson farm. Klass questioned the witness stories and recounted several discrepancies, most of which could be accounted for as distorted memories and the like. But a few problems seemed serious to Klass (and now to me). For example, the ring was surrounded on three sides by trees so the UFO would have had to come from only one direction. A dead tree was laying on the open side, and the Johnsons claimed that the UFO must have knocked it down—but it was positioned at a right angle to the direction that the UFO would have followed to enter the area. The photo taken by Mrs. Johnson shows the ring, but a stick in the foreground is the brightest object in the picture, and the ring darkens with distance from the camera—as if a flash had been used to take the photograph, in which case the white material would look like it was glowing brightest closest to the camera. Mrs. Smith saw the glow when she visited in the evening, but there was a nearly full moon, which would have made the white material stand out against the darker soil. And of course, some kind of bioluminescence could have accounted for the glow if it were real. On trees that were far from the ring, Klass also found white material like that on the nearby trees.

Klass recounts several other discrepancies, but one key point should have kept us on the panel much more alert to the possibilities of a hoax: There was a strong motive to perpetrate a hoax; namely, a prize of $50,000 when the Johnsons first submitted the story, and later a still substantial prize of $5,000 (which they did collect). Klass found that the Johnsons also had financial problems: The farm was about to be sold out from under them, although they thought they had an option to buy. So Klass's implied conclusion: Just suppose the Johnsons perpetrated a hoax (a lie) to obtain the reward money! With hindsight, I must suppose that this explanation just might be true![4]

But what about the white ring? Klass supposes that it might have been there long before the alleged UFO sighting. To find out, he obtained aerial photographs of the area taken in 1965 and 1971, but leaves on the trees obscured the area so he could not come to any conclusion. So he came up with a rather compelling just-suppose story: Suppose there had been a round watering tank for sheep or other animals located inside the white ring, with the water supply on one side accounting for the horseshoe shape. Suppose the animals frequently urinated while standing around the galvanized tub (i.e., coated with zinc to prevent rust). One analysis showed zinc to be 100 times more concentrated in the ring than in the soil outside the ring. Urine could account for the high salt, and organic material in the urine could account for the growth of the special bacteria. The high lipid content of the soil would make it very difficult to wet. Could the lipids be from the urine or perhaps a product of the bacteria? Obviously, it would have been a good idea to check with former owners if possible to see if a watering tank had ever been at that location, and Klass most likely would have done so if it were possible. Certainly, he followed the guidelines for a careful ufologist, investigating carefully. But in his final chapter, he makes clear his overwhelming conviction that if UFOs were real, they must be from some other solar system, and that is not possible because of the impossibilities of traveling across space with technologies that he knew or could even imagine. His conclusion was final before he began his excellent investigation.

I couldn't buy Klass's just-suppose story about the Coyne helicopter case (Chapter 3). But I must admit that his what-if story about the Delphos case makes a lot of sense—which doesn't mean that I accept it as a final explanation. Klass himself did not claim it to be the final answer. Actually, Ronald Johnson might well be alive somewhere. His confirmation of a hoax could settle our minds. His denial would be a repeat of the original story and still possibly a fabrication. Who knows? I don't, but the role of hoax in ufology is something to worry about.

With hindsight, I must admit that it is easier to imagine a flock of sheep producing the characteristics of the soil in the ring than it is that a UFO produced those characteristics. But again we encounter difficulties in deciphering events in the past. What if the ring had been there for many years, caused by a watering trough as Klass suggests, but Ronald saw a real UFO that night—although the UFO had nothing to do with the ring! It's that old correlation versus cause-and-effect problem!

Pseudoscience and the UFO

Speaking of false stories, anyone who is interested in the UFO story must be prepared to meet pseudoscience, not only in the contactee tales, but frequently in other places as well. Some of the most "respected" writers in the UFO field fill their writings with a pseudoscience that descends to the level of Adamski's productions. For years I had heard of Brinsley Le Poer Trench. He had apparently contributed several things to ufology. Finally, on my second visit to the Uintah Basin, I saw one of his books as a paperback and purchased a copy. I managed to read it, but it was most disturbing. Not only were several facts distorted regarding specific UFO cases that were familiar to me, but the pseudoscience was there in copious amounts and presented with much arrogance. If the contactees drive away the serious scientific investigator, imagine a scientist's reaction upon reading the following:

> And then, what about man himself? What kind of current is he generating? So far, we know all life forms (including planets and suns) generate electromagnetic energy, and that every time man's electrical output has been measured, the amounts registered at about 1/10 of a volt, Direct Current. My, what an insignificant amount! But wait. There's always a compensatory law, and this one says: The lower the voltage, the higher the amperage. Now what do you say? Exactly! With a voltage so low, his amperage must have potential to stagger the imagination.
>
> Now, shall we stop a moment to recall our definitions? Amperage and voltage are merely terms of measurement. The amount of current in use is measured as so many amperes, or "amps," while the voltage is a measurement term designating how much pressure is being applied to the current to make it move. There, it naturally follows that man must be moving a fantastically high current under the minute pressure of 1/10 volt, Direct Current! (Trench, 1966, p. 87)

Apparently Mr. Trench had somewhere heard of Ohm's Law and gained the impression that voltage and current are inversely proportional to some kind of universal constant. But the work done by an electric current is measured in watts, and watts are the product of the volts times the amps. A very low voltage and a very low amperage (as in the human body) simply produce a very low wattage. Brinsley's statement is worse than the worst of Adamski. It lectures with arrogance, presenting as fact something that the most elementary science book clarifies as foolishness.

In any case, the world is full of self-made scientists, people who never really liked science, perhaps, but who later learned all about it anyway by reading a few books. It isn't difficult to learn the terminology of science and even a few principles. Anybody can pick these up with a minimum of effort. Unfortunately, however, there is no real road to a scientific education except by the expenditure of a great deal of effort. After one has worked through the mathematics, physics, chemistry, and biology courses, then one begins to see the whole picture at least as well as it can be seen at a given point in historical time. Without expending this effort and spending these years of study and evaluation, it just can't be done—which is not to say that it is impossible for a person to learn science on one's own; only that systematic study and years of effort are required. One may get the impression of an overall picture from a few books, but invariably they constitute only a small part made up of specialized terms and a few principles. In a haphazard approach, one not only hasn't put the puzzle together correctly; one is missing many significant pieces.

I believe this is an important problem in our modern world and especially in the field of ufology. It divides rather sharply the scientist from the non-scientist. This doesn't upset the scientist much because he is acutely aware that the non-scientist is just as "smart" as the scientist is, knowing a great many things that the scientist doesn't know about business, art, politics, history, music, and so on. One can appreciate a lack of knowledge in those fields, perhaps, because of the rudiments of knowledge about non-scientific matters that one does have. Yet the non-scientist often does not understand the position of the scientist, feeling that the scientist must be something very special indeed rather than just another human being who has paid the price of years of intensive study.

Sometimes the non-scientist reacts against all of this, and this seems to be the situation with contactees and pseudoscientists like Le Poer Trench. Indeed, the contactee cults constitute a protest group. They rebel at the apparent sacred position of the scientist but attempt to assume a comparable position themselves. They believe that they can achieve this by learning certain words and a few ideas. Interestingly enough, they will often do this in all fields of science. But the scientist knows better. Having devoted the time and the effort, it is possible to speak intelligently with other scientists in fields related to one's own—or in a field that might be a very serious hobby. In other fields a scientist is a layman, and that is that.

So watch out for pseudoscience in the UFO business. And try to distinguish between pseudoscience and good, honest scientific mistakes. The differences are not easy to describe. Science has made immense strides in understanding the universe in which we live, but that understanding admittedly still has a long way to go. It is full of error and untested theory, and much of that will show up in any of its writings, particularly when these are examined many decades from now. The pseudoscientist, on the other hand, is something else. His mistakes are not the mistakes of an incomplete search for knowledge; a pseudoscientist's mistakes are the mistakes of someone who would assume an appearance without the substance.

Notes

1. Incidently, Patricia Hagius, who transcribed my tapes, became a solid believer in the sincerity and veracity of the witnesses. So did my fifteen-year-old son, Clark, who went with me on my second visit to the Basin in 1968. Listening to the witnesses tell their stories "made me [Clark] a believer that these folks had seen what they said they did," he recently told me.

2. *Raël* (1986) is an official account of the movement. There are many details on the Raëlian website: http://www.rael.org/english/pages/home.html. A website designed to counter the Raëlian movement is: http://skepdic.com/raelian.html. This website says, among other things, that "Raël's success seems to derive from providing a structured environment for decadent behavior: He offers a no-guilt playground for hedonism and sexual experimentation." My brief summary here is modified from Salisbury (2006, pp. 197–98), which is from a longer account found in Pennock (1999, pp. 233–40).

3. Here is the letter from a young contactee. The letter doesn't put the young man in a very good light, so I have not given his name. Incidently, it was a real challenge to type his version:

[Postmark, 12 February 1965]

Dear Dr. Salisbury.

I am writing you about the article which apeare'd in the sept pageant. Concerning life on mar's, there is something I'd like to tell you about first, about my self.

I am 22 years old and have always believe'd what I've seen for myself not just rumour's. I work for _____ _____ in downtown Denver as a shiping clerk. And have been on my own since 16 and i believe you might not be afraid to listen.

I don't expect you to believe it, if not that's that, the F. B. i. suggeste'd i forget it and acted like i hit a nerve. But the people involve'd want me to do this.

I hope I've been fairly clear so far this hard in any speech. I can show you some thing's that might ring a bell for you.

Your be'life of life on mars is true, let me start at the beginning.

The time June 62, Estes park Colo, i was just about to go to bed.

The house had a balcay on the red room i starte'd to go in, a blue white flash made me stop dead. I turned and saw a blue globe come to rest on a mountain top about 1/4 mile away.

I was pretty nervous by this time and could int move a muscle, It move'd against all laws of motion i ever saw, it came left to right, right to left, up and down like a bubble.

You think thats to much, now it stoped not a ft. in front of me, a music'le voice kind of man, women, said, Do not be afraid Enter the shell, it is attune'd to your vibrational field.

Now i stood in the thing, just an empty blue, glassy Bubble no more, it move'd out and up and i felt that my body belonge'd to some one else.

Then how much later i can't say it entere'd a giant black object. It opene'd a bar like a hand rail snaped down so i could cross a gap.

Looking down there were other level's, and above me too.

If you think I've blown my cork hear this. upon gaining the other side a lift with two petel's on it was there, the one i steped on had a mark like this,

I hope your still reading.

I went up to the top it stopped, here a blank wall suddenly a door like a cambra's eye was ther'e, i went in.

The door was gone a very beautiful girl was there, Blond hair blue eyes, about 5.4. She was colour of copper.

She only smile'd and pointed to a large room, with 3 men all in black uniforms i think. The room was filled with odd music it came from every where, I felt very good as they meant me.

The first man answere'd a question before i even aske'd it. He said i am 7. ft 4. in. by your standards, these are my Brothers of far galaxies.

They are Saurians who are anxious to converse with you. Their clothes were black with silver disk's on the shoulder's.

As with the first man whom they calle'd the master. Oh, on the left hand shirt pocket was this

anyway i can't write it all down here they put picture's in my mind they didint speak by mouth.

Near the last i saw an airforce jet which was apparently comeing up, the master said we could go into space, but there was no time, and they would help me remember, when i meant some one who would believe me.

And they would give me ways of contact, and help me write a language for proof.

I hope it helps you, I've also learned other startling things one they called Electrophys, cametory

If you can belive any of this i can meet you here, next Wedsday, or the Saturday of next week. You would not be disapointe'd.

I hope you can read this i never could get the hand of it as they say.

I mostly would like to talk to you about the new satillite they plan to launch. I can pretty well say it will be destroye'd.

Before 13 hrs, of its life, about every major city being observe'd and about the great pyramid you might like to see an ancient map i have.

If you do wish to see my address is _____ _____ _____ _____ my name _____ _____

One condition i have you may tell one person and when you come here if someone ask's, you're my mother's friend, and you belong to the same writer's club.

I have to be careful, I've been threatene'd and laughe'd at. No more.

Thank you very much

_____ _____

[Two pages of strange language omitted here.]

PATHOS SARONDOS
This is not copye'd from any book.
I can write it all day in front of you.

4. While I wrote this second edition, the media reported on a family that built a helium balloon and "accidentally" let it escape, telling the media that their six-year-old son might be inside. Helicopters followed the saucer-shaped balloon for sixty miles across the Colorado plains. The boy was found at home, hiding in a box in the garage attic. The family is now facing felony charges for perpetrating a hoax. Apparently, they wanted to catch the public's attention so they could get on reality TV shows. They had a motive for their hoax, it seems. The Delphos, Kansas, case is similar in many ways, including the motive (money!) and the possibility that the sixteen-year-old was coached to tell a story. As far as I know, no one checked on his eye and sleep problems—nor the mother's numb fingers. (James Harder's numbness adds an interesting psychological dimension!)

5

Secret Government

Projects and Cover-ups

You'll recall that several of the Uintah Basin witnesses suggested that what they had seen might be some kind of secret government vehicle or weapon. Dean Powell was quite convinced of this, and even Joe Ann Harris considered the possibility. Thyrena Daniels thought this was the answer to her sighting until Junior Hicks talked her out of it. For a long while, many people liked this secret-project explanation. Except for a few with a pseudoscience or contactee mentality, most Americans had a great deal of faith in the technology of their scientists, especially when they were working in secret, as on the Manhattan Project that produced the atomic bomb.

In the first edition of this book, I wrote: "Interestingly enough, after our recent failures in world markets and world battlefields, this explanation is less likely to be suggested." And that should be true today, but there are still many people who hold to this idea—except that it is now common to suggest that the government developers are receiving guidance from the extraterrestrials who visit us in their UFOs! Some conspiracy theorists tell us that extraterrestrials are working side by side with government technicians, as we'll see below. Of course in America, that usually means United States technicians, but what about the Russians or maybe the Germans?

A large portion of the UFO community is convinced that the government is guarding secrets from the rest of us: secret weapons maybe, but especially secret knowledge about the UFO phenomenon. I have long avoided getting too deep into these ideas because they can be highly distracting to research of interesting UFO cases, but the case for the cover-up is becoming overwhelming. That topic moves us a bit far from my goal in this book, which is to show you the evidence that some kind of real UFO phenomena have long been active in the Uintah Basin. But we'll take at least a brief look at the cover-up evidence.

Problems of Keeping Science
and Technology Secret

There is one good reason why secret weapons are not a likely explanation. If we'd really had those super machines stashed away somewhere at least since 1946, why would we have taken such a propaganda beating in relation to Vietnam or even Korea, let alone the Middle East and other trouble spots? The UFO machines were developing very well in 1947, according to the best witnesses. They didn't seem to need much more development. Why would we have kept them under wraps all this time?

The same argument applies equally well to the Russians (who were taking the propaganda beating twenty years ago and who publicly stated their desires for world domination), or to any other power: the British, whose empire has been shrinking and who have been beset with other problems; the French, who want to be number one in science and technology; or even some relatively small and obscure nation such as Cuba, who would prefer not to be so relatively small and obscure. It is even difficult to see how Canada, having captured the secrets developed by Nazi Germany during World War II (Jungk, 1958), could manage to keep their UFOs concealed in laboratories under the Canadian Rockies (Vesco, 1969). It just doesn't make sense that the UFOs are some secret development of any nation on Earth.

It has been suggested that they might be a development of some secret society (Steiger and Whritenour, 1968)—perhaps even one like Captain Franch's Black Eagles! This idea is a little more difficult to refute on the above grounds, although it also seems extremely unlikely in terms of how science and technology work. To produce any major scientific or engineering achievement on the magnitude of the UFO in this day and age requires a tremendous expenditure of capital and manpower. It doesn't seem likely that this could be done by any private organization—although this cannot be rigorously denied. Furthermore, engineering progresses by building one technique or item of knowledge upon another. These are shared worldwide. Even in 1974, the rocket programs in the United States and the

Soviet Union were not as independent as one might have imagined—and of course today other countries such as China and France are in the space and rocket business. In addition to the transferal of information through espionage, data relating just to the performance of one country's rocket is bound to provide technological clues to other countries. Ideas must build upon each other in the global community of scientists and engineers—even if the countries to which they belong are at war with each other. This was true of the development of the atomic bomb in the United States and its near development in Nazi Germany. The essential basic research was done in various countries and was well known to us and to them. (I remember, as a teenager in the early 1940s, reading in *Newsweek* magazine about the possibility of nuclear fission.) The point of all this is that it is extremely difficult to carry out really sophisticated engineering in secret with the likely limited resources of a private and secret group.

The UFO in History

All of these arguments may be compelling, but none is really conclusive. The following argument does, however, seem quite conclusive to me: the UFO phenomenon didn't really begin in 1947. That was simply when the news media of the world began to discuss UFOs extensively. Actually, they have been around almost since the dawn of recorded history. Because this has been amply documented by several other authors, only a few high points will be reviewed here (see especially Vallée, 2008 a., as well as his earlier books).

To begin with, it has been suggested several times (e.g., Downing, 1968) that the Bible includes a number of UFO accounts. Quite a yarn can be spun about the parting of the Red Sea, which allowed the crossing of the Israelites (Exodus 14:13–31). The story goes that there was a UFO involved (the pillar of cloud by day and the pillar of fire by night), and it must have had some kind of gravity beam that forced apart the waters of the Red Sea. The mud on the bottom of that swampy area was so compressed that the Israelites said they crossed on dry land. When the Egyptians followed them, they were apparently forced to the ground—at least the wheels broke off of their chariots, as if the gravity beam that was focused on the sides of the channel, holding back the waters, was suddenly focused on the Egyptians themselves. Then it was switched off and the waters rushed in to cover the Egyptians! This is pretty wild, but it makes such good science fiction I can't resist presenting it.

Ezekiel's UFO sighting (Ezekiel 1 & 2) is somewhat more clear cut. Here a definite machine is reported ("a wheel in a wheel") although the description is so obscure that a clear mental picture does not seem possible. There are also many interesting sidelights, such as beings accompanying the mighty machine, who were covered by domes of glass. "And the likeness of the firmament [the big, blue dome that we now call the sky] upon the heads of the living creature was as the color of the terrible crystal, stretched forth over their heads above" (Ezekiel 1:22). There was much fire, wind, and speaking with the voice of thunder. The object was encompassed about by "eyes" (lights?). Ezekiel obviously didn't have much technology to use as a precedent for describing his sighting; we might have done a bit better based upon our ideas of jet airplanes, rockets, and science fiction devices of all kinds (Blumrich, 1974).

The Romans often reported flying shields, sometimes with flames spitting out from the sides (Wittman, 1968)—like Thyrena Daniels's traveling companion on the way to Roosevelt. In 1561 and 1566 the inhabitants of Basel and Nuremberg reported all kinds of objects flitting around in their skies: discs and long tubes (Vallée, 1965, 2008 a.). These were witnessed at least by hundreds and perhaps by thousands of individuals. Several similar instances have come to light in recent years.

Numerous UFOs were sighted during the 1800s. Jacques Vallée (1965, 1969, 2008 a.) has documented many of these sightings. Particularly interesting are the "airship" sightings of 1896 and 1897. A large airship was reported at nearly two hundred sites in the United States. Approximately sixteen of these sightings involved landings, and in several of these cases the witnesses conversed with the occupants of the vehicles. Although there was much typical UFO behavior (rapid departures, powerful beams of light sweeping the countryside, and so forth), the fascinating thing is that the airships had the characteristics of science fiction devices common to that time—although it is now quite apparent that such devices (built by us, at least) could never perform the maneuvers ascribed to them! That is, the wings, motors, and other parts would not be capable of producing flight at the velocities and maneuverability reported by the witnesses.

Hundreds and probably thousands of other cases could be mentioned. The point should be quite clear: It hardly seems likely that Ezekiel's wheels, the Roman shields, the Nuremberg discs and tubes, or the 1897 airships were really secret developments of the United States Air Force—or of the

Soviet Union. If they are developments of some secret society, it is indeed an ancient one (a possibility that cannot be rigorously excluded but that seems extremely unlikely—although it has been defended by some writers). Actually, if we approach the history of ufology with a completely open mind, we encounter disturbing instances that seem to be part of UFO lore but that bear little relation to technology. Jacques Vallée in his *Passport to Magonia* (1969) considered folklore, especially the fairy faith, in this light. He does so again in *Dimensions: A Casebook of Alien Contact* (Vallée, 1988/2008 a.). Again, there are numerous parallels to the modern UFO enigma. Suffice it to conclude that the secret-government-project idea cannot readily be accepted as the explanation for the UFO phenomenon—even though an occasional government project (e.g., weather balloons, rocket shields, or high-altitude atomic bomb testing) might have given rise to a few UFO reports.

Area 51

Perhaps today's most widely known conspiracy theory about secret projects—and this one strongly implicates UFOs—is the U.S. Air Force base in Nevada known as "Area 51." The base is part of the vast Nevada Test and Training Range. It is situated by Groom Lake, a dry lake bed about 85 miles west of Las Vegas. The U.S. government barely admits that it exists, although there are satellite photos that show the base, mostly long runways, hangars, and assorted buildings—nothing of obvious interest to ufologists. It is heavily guarded, and it has been (and is?) a base for the development of new military aircraft such as the U-2 and the Blackbird spy planes. It is surrounded by a carefully monitored no-fly zone and signs that not only say "No Trespassing" but also specify that this will be enforced by "deadly force," if necessary. It is probably the most heavily guarded air base in the United States and possibly in the world.[1] When UFO buffs became aware of the base and tried to get views from distant hill tops, the perimeters of its boundaries were extended. Clearly, it provides an ideal situation for conspiracy theories.

And such theories abound! It is said that the hangars at Groom Lake or at another facility called Papoose Lake, some six miles to the south contain the remains of flying saucers that have crashed, including material supposedly recovered at Roswell, New Mexico (as discussed in the Prologue). If not in the hangars themselves, these remains might be in underground laboratories, connected perhaps by an underground transcontinental rail system! Our engineers are said to be reverse-engineering these alien spacecraft so that we can learn the propulsion systems of the UFOs. There are alien bodies being studied as well, and, for that matter, alive-and-well aliens, who are working with the engineers and scientists in Area 51. Exotic weapons are being developed as are means to control the weather. Even time travel and teleportation technology is being studied. Part of the secrecy is to cover the existence of the Majestic 12 organization (see below).

Actually, veterans of experimental projects such as OXCART and NERVA agree that some of their machines might easily have been mistaken for flying saucers (but probably not for flying shields seen by ancient Romans!). All of this has become so well known that it is often used in the plots of movies and television programs. (This information and much more is available on Wikipedia and various other websites.)

Believers in the Area 51 legend base much of their belief on the writings and TV interviews of Bob Lazar, who claimed in 1989 that he had worked at Papoose Lake with alien spacecraft. Lazar went on to describe how element 115 serves as the nuclear power source for the UFOs, which also used the power to produce anti-gravity effects.[2] Lazar claimed to have been given introductory briefings that described how the extraterrestrial beings have been visiting this planet for 10,000 years. The UFOs, he reported, came from the star system Zeta Reticuli 1 (which we'll discuss in Chapter 6 in relation to the Betty and Barney Hill case; suffice it to say, the Zeta Reticuli story is now being seriously questioned).

Lazar claimed to have degrees from the California Institute of Technology as well as the Massachusetts Institute of Technology. At that point, the Los Angeles Times and other news agencies began to look into Lazar's background. No connection with Caltech or MIT could be verified, and it was found that Lazar had a record of bankruptcy and felony pandering. Of course, most of us don't put much stock in Lazar's claims, but as is typical, he has written a book, and he has had a following.

To me, none of the information about Area 51, not to mention the claims of Bob Lazar, alters my conviction that the vast majority of UFO sightings and encounters cannot be explained as secret weapons or government projects.

Another Kind of Government Conspiracy

In the third volume of his trilogy, Jacques Vallée makes a strong case for another kind of conspiracy: a conspiracy to utilize or even create UFO events to mislead or test the public or government-service people. In the Prologue, I noted that Vallée can make a good case that the Rendlesham Forest sightings were staged by a government intelligence agency (Vallée, 2008 c., pp. 158–60), although he does not insist on this interpretation. For me, at least, the strongest part of Vallée's case is his report of a televised interview with Larry Warren, who had been in the security forces at Bentwaters, near the forest. Warren relates that some forty people were assembled at the site with cameras, lights, and other equipment—but no weapons. A dense fog was there, but the UFO did not appear until all the witnesses were assembled (a version that does not agree with other reports, as related in the Prologue). Vallée thinks that the fog could have easily been produced by those who were carrying out the experiment, and even the UFO could have been a fake: a sort of official hoax! The point was to test the responses of the witnesses—many of whom had the responsibility to guard against enemy attack—possibly even from an extraterrestrial UFO!

That is only one of several situations that Vallée (2008 c.) describes in considerable detail—more detail than is appropriate for this book. Vallée tells the Area 51/Lazar story in the context of Lazar being duped by others so that he will tell his tale and thus further muddy the waters.

Vallée is not the only one to suggest that government intelligence agencies are using UFO sightings and stories, such as Roswell and Area 51, to distract serious researchers. James Carrion (2009) gave an interesting talk at the 2009 MUFON Symposium in Denver, Colorado, in which he analyzed several events going back to before the Kenneth Arnold 1947 sighting that ignited the public interest in "flying saucers." Apparently, the government was happy to let our Cold War enemies, the Soviets (and possibly others), think that we might be the developers of the UFOs that were being reported. Regardless of what really happened at Roswell, for example, comments by Air Force personnel at the time strongly suggest that our government was happy to let the public—and other countries—spend much time thinking about secret weapons, invasions from outer space, and related ideas. Why not?

Another long-running conspiracy controversy concerns the Majestic 12. In December 1984 a roll of undeveloped film was received by a Los Angeles television producer, Jaime Shandera. The film contained eight pages of documents (some of which are reproduced in Friedman, 2008, Chapter 11), supposedly written in 1952. One document establishes a group of twelve high-level people under Vannevar Bush, to be called "Majestic 12," who were to investigate the UFO information. There is a letter addressed to the newly elected President Eisenhower, informing him of the remains of the Roswell crashed saucer and mentioning the bodies that were found. If this is a valid document it, of course, blows the top off of any effort to claim that the government knows nothing about flying saucers! But is it a valid document?

The story of the arguments one way or the other is far too long for this Uintah Basin book, but the fact that Stan Friedman spends forty pages defending these documents in his 2008 book certainly illustrates that the arguments are still raging. These arguments concern the kinds of type-writer used to produce the documents, whether the "secret" stamps are valid, and numerous other details. Friedman has concluded that the original documents are indeed valid, although several other related documents are "emulations"; that is, fakes. His arguments are intricate.

Jacques Vallée (1991, 2008 c., Chapter 2) disputes these arguments and suggests that the whole business might have been part of a government disinformation scheme. His arguments are also intricate. Reading these two extended discussions makes me glad that I was not involved in UFO research during the time that all this argument was really raging!

A small part of my conversion to the government-knows-all hypothesis came in a late phone call just as I returned from the MUFON symposium in August, 2009. The call was from Jean Livingston Kamal, who had worked with me in the early 1960s. She told me about her life during the 1950s before she came to work with me. Her husband was an Air Force intelligence officer, first assigned to the Holloman, New Mexico, base. He was sworn to secrecy and never confided to her what he was doing, but as time passed, he became more and more stressed, apparently by his work. He began to drink heavily, and he had a nervous breakdown. At one point, after collapsing from too much alcohol, he muttered to Jean that "UFOs are real!" The stresses led to the breakup of their marriage. Was he working on UFOs at a highly secret level—deeper than projects Sign, Grudge, or Blue Book? One evidence in favor of that idea is that he often traveled to Wright-Patterson Air Force Base in Ohio, which, it is now known, has been the central location for Air Force studies of UFOs.

The Bottle Hollow UFO and Choppers

Recently Junior Hicks encountered an event that happened only a few months ago, just before Thanksgiving 2009. If this story can be accepted, and that must always be questioned when there is a single witness of a truly far-out and spectacular event, it should certainly answer the question of whether there is still UFO activity in the Basin and of whether the government knows anything about UFOs!

Junior was doing some electrical work for Ron Cuch, who lives on the road to Randlett, about a mile and a half south of the turnoff to the skinwalker ranch. Cuch supervises the Ute Tribe Alcohol and Drug Rehabilitation Center at Fort Duchesne. The center is located east of and close to the Bottle Hollow Reservoir (which is about one square mile in surface area). Junior is still known as the Uintah Basin ufologist, so Cuch volunteered his account while Junior was working for him. Cuch gave us permission to use his name and publish his account, as recorded by Junior Hicks on December 3, 2009.

Ron mentioned that he was doing a night shift at the center on the night of November 23rd or 24th. As Ron was doing his rounds outside of the building about 5:00 AM, he heard a loud noise coming from the east. He looked up and saw a UFO coming toward him at a low altitude. It was a double convex shape, which looked about the size of a full moon, coming directly overhead. It had lights pulsating red, green, and orange around the rim or middle. The object was moving quite fast, to the west. Right behind the UFO were three military Black Hawk helicopters. Behind the three choppers came two black, delta-shaped, jet fighters.

The UFO dived into Bottle Hollow Lake. The three choppers then started to circle the lake; the jets swooped low over the lake, and continued to the west. The choppers circled the lake for a short time and then also left the area to the west. The UFO then shot straight up out of the water and disappeared in the sky.

That certainly seems to implicate the government in the UFO business! But there is also a tiny possibility, Junior tells me—based on talks with a Black Hawk pilot—that the UFO itself was a government vehicle! See how confusing ufology can be?

Notes

1. After writing these paragraphs, my wife, Mary, and I went to dinner with our neighbors, Raymond and Marg Alvey. Because Ray had been an Army Air Force pilot in World War II and then an air traffic controller at the Salt Lake

Airport for many years, I couldn't help mentioning what I had been reading about Area 51. He was well aware of the restricted air space and the role of the Groom Lake base in developing such special aircraft as the Blackbird and the U2. He also said that he could remember "perhaps a dozen" UFO signals on their traffic-control radars, and in one case an aircraft was scrambled to pursue the UFO. The pilot saw the UFO but could not approach it—it thus was a UFO with both radar and visual sightings.

2. In 2004, a team of physicists from the Joint Institute of Nuclear Research in Dubna, Russia, and the Lawrence Livermore National Laboratory in California reported synthesis of four atoms of element 115 (temporarily named ununpentium) by bombarding americium-243 with calcium-48 ions. The element 115 atoms decayed in about 100 milliseconds. Since then, a few dozen more atoms have been created, but it has so far not been possible to study the chemistry of element 115, let alone its use in a UFO propulsion system!

6

Psychology and the UFO

It would be comforting to many people if we could assign the UFOs to the minds of their observers. Perhaps the UFOs are psychological projections of some kind, concocted in the minds of mentally ill individuals in the same way dreams are produced during normal sleep. Or maybe we are dealing with mass hallucinations—if there is such a thing. Could the witnesses be suffering from some kind of self-hypnotism? Or perhaps they were drunk or high on drugs.

The trouble with these explanations is that none of them begins to hold up under scrutiny. We have repeatedly emphasized that UFO witnesses are a cross section of the population as a whole; they do not include even an unusually high percentage of mentally disturbed persons. On the other hand, studies have been made of mentally disturbed individuals to see if they have an unusually high incidence of UFO stories to tell (Schwarz, 1969). As it turns out, they do not. Although some UFO accounts may well have been generated by mental illness, we must reject this concept as an explanation for the vast majority of UFO sightings. The idea that alcohol or drugs might be responsible is equally difficult to fit with the facts. If a man was drunk when he saw a UFO, he probably wouldn't tell anybody about it! I've never heard of a UFO sighting by someone who was drunk. And numerous sightings were reported before hallucinogenic drugs were available.

Explanations based upon dreams, mass hallucinations, self-hypnotism, or other forms of psychological projection don't fare much better—although we'll return to this topic below in one special application. Although there are exceptions, frequently the circumstances surrounding a sighting make such explanations extremely unlikely, although they cannot be totally ruled out because we know so little about such things. An honest-to-goodness mass hallucination is probably about as foreign to modern science as the UFOs themselves. Could the 70,000 witnesses at Fatima have been mass-hypnotized? Besides, how could such explanations fit when photographs are taken or the object is followed on radar? If a witness can project with his mind an object that can be picked up on radar, then we certainly have a great deal to learn about the operation of the mind.

The idea that UFOs might be "after-images" in the eye produced by looking at a bright light has been suggested. It should be quite apparent from the accounts already presented that this is a totally inadequate explanation.

The Psychology of UFO Watching

So the way out of the UFO enigma is not via a psychologist's theories. No psychologist who has studied the UFO evidence suggests this. Yet the importance of psychology to scientific UFO study should not be minimized. Since, as we have seen, the UFO investigator is nearly always dependent upon the accounts of witnesses, the psychological responses of both the witness and the interviewer will always play a role. To properly evaluate UFO reports, ufologists cannot ignore the psychology of observation, reporting, interpretation, and interviewing.

Excitement is undoubtedly one of the most important factors in UFO observation. Watching what could be a galactic spaceship must be rather exciting. We have seen this in the Uintah Basin accounts. But does excitement make one a better or a worse witness? If excitement reaches panic, it probably would not improve one's observing abilities. Under extreme anxiety the witness might see things that aren't there. Usually, however, excitement improves the witness's capabilities for observation. One pays attention! Adrenalin as well as sensual acuities are markedly increased. We all know that memory is markedly improved under conditions of stress or under conditions greatly different from the ordinary. Virtually all Americans who are old enough can remember where they were, what they were doing, their own emotional reactions, and probably such insignificant things as the status of the weather on the day that President Kennedy was assassinated or the twin towers were attacked. With this in mind, I am not greatly surprised at the detail remembered by a witness decades after an encounter with a UFO. Brief and unreal as it was, I still vividly remember my observation of the planet Venus for those few seconds in Germany. I was excited! I paid attention!

What about distortion? How well does a witness observe, and how well can one communicate to an interviewer? Surely this is one of the weak points in the scientific study of UFOs. The differing accounts given by different witnesses of a single sighting illustrate the point well. The accounts of Leland Mecham and Dee Hullinger in the Uintah Basin provide one such example. They are not quite mutually exclusive, but they differ in detail. The stories below of Marjorie Beal and her daughter provide another excellent case study. There is no doubt that different individuals see and remember things differently—and possess varying abilities to describe what is in their minds. Abilities of both observation and description can be greatly improved by training, but how many trained UFO witnesses are there?

Probably the most important complication in observation is the strong tendency to interject an interpretation. We see and remember what we expect to see—or what we want to see. This is the principle of the Rorschach ink-blot test. And the principle should be familiar to all of us from our everyday lives. The eye and the mind are not merely recorders, like a camera.

As a matter of fact, this is one of the most amazing aspects of the mind. When you look at a rectangular tabletop, the picture projected on the retinas of your eyes and transmitted to the brain might be anything from a square to a rectangle to a trapezoid, and it may be any size from a figure covering nearly the entire retina to a minute figure covering only a few cells of the retina. But in all of these cases the mind sees essentially the same thing: a rectangular tabletop of a given size. Corrections are made quite unconsciously for distance and angle of viewing although the apparent differences in shape and size are there if you think about them—but normally you don't. Such compensation for angle and distance requires a frame of reference. We see the tabletop correctly because we see it in its expected setting. When distorted rooms are constructed (as in an amusement park funhouse), familiar objects take on quite unexpected appearances. These are the principles that make optical illusions possible.

The application to UFO watching should be quite apparent. By definition, the UFO is an unfamiliar object—yet we see things only in the context of familiarity. Often the frames of reference are minimal during a sighting: It may be night, or the object may appear against a clear blue sky, with no dependable distance cues. A trained observer is always aware of these limitations, but the typical UFO watcher may not be. He tries mightily to interpret what is being seen: to bring it into a familiar context (e.g., "It is as big as a basketball.")—even though he has no idea whatsoever how big it really is. Or perhaps a witness injects into the middle of his story the idea that it must have been a secret government project. Mere correlations are thought to be evidences of cause and effect. For example, one says an object must have reacted to one's thoughts because a sudden idea happens at the same time the light changes or the object accelerates. We human beings, who are the only animals capable of understanding, have a terrible craving to understand. It takes a supreme act of conscious will to be truly objective, to try to record what we are actually seeing without trying to account for it.

So we should expect UFO accounts to contain distortions. When a witness says that an object was the size of a football, we should listen carefully but remain appropriately skeptical. But should we reject an entire story out of hand because of the possibility of psychological distortions? To do so would be folly. Experience has now clearly shown that people are basically good observers, in spite of the frequent distortions and interpretations of detail. In Chapter 3, I told the story of the weather kite described near Fort Collins, Colorado. The witnesses were convinced they were seeing a UFO, but they described a square weather kite. And "Mable" was emotional and excited by her UFO, but she was still able to give a clear description of Venus (and the way it looked in unfocused binoculars).

One frustrating aspect of UFO investigation concerns the difficulties of communication between a witness and her or his interviewer. Although the witness will usually have a fairly accurate mental picture of the event, it may be virtually impossible to convey this picture from the witness's mind to the mind of the interviewer. To some extent this must always be true, and occasionally it can become exceptionally frustrating. What, for example, did Thyrena Daniels really see? Even if the picture is clear in her mind, the picture in my mind or Junior's mind might be significantly different. Or how about the "tube" hanging from the UFO seen by Morlin Buchanan and Richard Faucett? It reminded them of a tornado funnel, but for some reason I can't rest very securely with that description. It was beyond their experience to begin with and totally beyond mine. This being the case, how can I imagine it? We've all had the experience of seeing pictures of some distant place (New York, Rome, or the African Veldt). Then when we get there, regardless of how many pictures we've seen, we are surprised at the appearance of things. Nothing quite replaces experience. If we could take the reel from Joe Ann Harris's mind and play it back, the chances are good that we would be most amazed at the actual reality of her experience in spite of her careful description of it.

And we are always concerned with the problem of memory. Does the witness remember what was actually seen, or has some slightly distorted picture become fixed in his mind?

The Sociology of UFO Watching: Group Dynamics

Sociology is the psychology of groups, and it certainly must be important in the UFO phenomenon. For example, some interesting studies have been made in the field of group dynamics. They might have bearing on such UFO sightings as the Almira Barauna sightings and photographs, as related in the Prologue and Chapter 3. The Brazilian navy ship was leaving the Isle of Trindade, when, in the most widely accepted version of the story, sailors at opposite ends of the ship simultaneously shouted that they had sighted an approaching object. About one hundred sailors saw the object, and Barauna photographed it. The film was developed below deck within the hour, and the sailors who had seen the object identified it on the negative (although the image was very small, and identification was not easy; see Fig. 3-1).

That's the way one version of the story goes. Another version says that Barauna faked the pictures, and that he was assisted by two friends who shouted that they saw the UFO when it was not really there (Menzel and Boyd, 1963).[1] The group dynamics question is: Could a few witnesses fraudulently claiming to see a UFO convince others that they, the other witnesses, had also seen it?

A series of classical experiments relating to these questions were carried out by Solomon F. Asch (1952, 1962). In the basic experiment, a single subject (the minority of one) was confronted by a unanimous majority of six others. The six were instructed ahead of time as to how they should answer, but in no case did the subject suspect this. The test was to match a standard line with one of three lines presented on a card. The two non-matching lines deviated from the standard by a very noticeable amount, so that when control tests were made by silently writing the answers, virtually no errors appeared. In the test, the seating arrangement assured that each of the six would announce his answer in turn, and then the subject would announce his. After two "straight" card presentations, the majority announced a choice that was clearly an error—but all of the six agreed without hesitation.

The responses of the individual subjects were highly interesting and also highly varied. Sometimes the subject would defy the group, in a few cases on each of twelve wrong answers. On the other end of the scale, some subjects were almost completely swayed by the majority answers. The subjects were always badly disturbed by their experiences, and the ones who defied the majority sometimes seemed to be the most upset of all. In an interview that always followed, the experimental set-up was explained to the subject. Independent subjects typically reported that they felt great pressure to agree with the group, some of them nearly capitulating. Some of the subjects who agreed with the majority did so even though they were fully aware that the lines, as they saw them, did not match. They felt there must be some kind of illusion that they were not experiencing, and they "did not want to upset the experiment"—whereas they seemed equally aware that not telling the truth would surely upset any good experiment. In a few cases, the compulsion to agree with the group was so great that the subject honestly felt, after hearing the judgments of his peers, that the short or long line matched the standard. When shown the lines again during the interview, he could hardly believe that he had previously given the answers that he did. When a witness sees something that isn't there, it is clearly of considerable interest from the standpoint of UFO watching.

Experimental conditions were varied, using different-sized groups with only one subject. There was virtually no effect when the subject was confronted by only one other person, yet a majority of two began to cause wavering in some subjects, and a majority of three was as effective as larger groups. When the minority of one was instructed to give wrong answers, and the majority were uninstructed subjects, the wrong answers provided by the one man never influenced the others but were greeted by joking and laughter. When a second "subject" occurred in the group (either as an uninstructed subject or one instructed always to give the right answers), there was a marked effect upon the subject who gave the final answer. With the support of one other human being, he tended much more to give correct answers in spite of the majority opinion—although when deserted halfway through by his "companion" who began to agree with the majority, the subject reverted back to the behavior typical of a minority of one. (Statistically, as many capitulated to the majority as in previous tests.)

These experiments imply that if an individual is sufficiently suggestible, when confronted by a unanimous majority of fraudulent UFO witnesses, he might himself become a convinced witness. It is difficult, however, to think of UFO cases in which this situation might occur. What about the Trindade photos? Most of the above results suggest that the hoax would not succeed. Barauna and his friends constituted a clear minority of strangers. As they shouted UFO and took their fake photos, wouldn't they simply be laughed at by the majority on the ship? Or is it invalid to compare this situation with the above experimental results? Perhaps the sailors all wanted to see a UFO so badly that they capitulated to the apparent authority of the visiting dignitaries. This seems unlikely, since some of the best corroborating witnesses were officers of considerable authority and experience in observation.

Two Related Psychological Studies

While I was writing the first edition of this book, I became aware of two studies that might have an application to UFO watching. They were published in the mid to late 1960s. Psychology is not my field, and in no way have I kept up my research on the two topics that I described in the first edition. But even after all these years, they are at least worth examining briefly here.

The first topic involved rumor formation. I was skiing at Alta and found myself on a lift with Jan Brunvand (of urban legend fame). We skied together the rest of the day. I told him of my UFO activities, and he told me about a book by Tamotsu Shibutani (1966), who proposed that rumors are not a demonstration of a human pathological condition (as seems to be widely assumed) but rather a form of improvised news that appears when formal news channels fail. I thought that the word-of-mouth testimony of UFO events might be related to how rumors form, so I bought the book and studied it with some care. Shibutani concluded that the greater the failure of the usual channels of news (or mistrust of them due to censorship or something similar), the more men and women attempt to pool their intellectual resources to obtain information. As a result, rumors form. These often deviate widely from the truth (which may simply be unobtainable), but they are always within a framework of what seems reasonable to the participants. Shibutani emphasizes that people are not gullible, although the rumors may make them appear so to a more objective observer under different and less trying circumstances. To be accepted, rumors must reflect the prevailing mood. People do become more suggestible when they are excited; at the same time, however, they become more alert and capable of concentrated thought. Their suggestibility relates to their desire for news and inability to find it. During rumor formation, the participants pay particular attention to those who apparently have special competence, and surprising as it may seem, once a rumor has been formed, it becomes relatively stable and not subject to the distortions so important during the early stages of its formation. After acceptance by the majority, there is considerable pressure applied to anyone who fails to accept the rumor—as in the experiments described above, the dissenter experiences much inner turmoil and desire to go along with the majority.

Most of this probably has little to do with the ufology discussed in this book, although there are obvious parallels with the psychology of observation discussed above. A UFO witness is driven by a compulsion to understand what he sees or has seen, and in this state he is open to suggestions from anyone who apparently has competence. Ufologists often tell how UFO witnesses plead for some explanation of what they saw. In this book, however, we have dealt with UFO reports rather than rumors. The psychology of rumor formation probably has its best application to ufology in the many conspiracy theories that abound, which we discussed in Chapters 4 and 5. Consider also the efforts at explanation given by witnesses, especially the idea that UFOs are secret government machines.

The second topic that caught my attention back then considered a rather simple question: Is any special segment of the population more or less likely to see and to report UFOs? A 1966 Gallup Poll found that 5 percent of the United States population claim to have seen a UFO (see Condon, 1968, p. 214).[2] The poll found that sighters do not differ from non-sighters with respect to education, region of the country, age, or sex. Donald I. Warren (1970), in one of the few articles on UFOs in the literature of the scientific establishment, studied the poll population with respect to a criterion called status inconsistency. A status inconsistent individual is one whose income, education, and occupation (the indicative sociological status levels used in his study) are not at levels consistent with each other in terms of the norms of our society. For example, a low income, low education, day laborer is status consistent, but a high income, low education, dye maker is status inconsistent (income out of line).

Warren found that white status-inconsistent males of moderate income were sixteen times as likely to report a UFO sighting as comparable white-consistent males. Low income with moderate to high education or occupational status produced a high level of sightings. The best educated saw the most UFOs! Furthermore, the status inconsistents were far more likely to interpret the UFO as an extraterrestrial machine. (All such answers in this poll came from status inconsistents—the status consistent males suggested weather balloons or something of that nature). Status inconsistents in other categories (including women, but not blacks) were also more likely to report UFOs, although somewhat less than moderate-income, white males.

So what does it mean? Warren suggests that status inconsistents are status frustrated and that their marginal condition leads to "withdrawal, defeatism, and retreat from the larger society . . . . The UFOs provide, therefore, a form of escape into unrealized and perhaps unrealizable consistent situations . . . . What makes such phenomena amenable to association with status inconsistency is the possibility of change that it offers. It presents the opportunity to escape the system without threatening one's gains in the immediate social environment defined by the political-economic structure." The clear implication is that UFO sightings, or at least their interpretations as extraterrestrial machines, are generated in the status-frustrated minds of their beholders.

But we must be careful. It seems to me that seeing, reporting, and interpreting UFOs as spaceships is far removed from escapism. Doing these things nearly always leaves one open to ridicule and pressure that increase feelings of social alienation. Thus I suspect that status inconsistents report UFOs because they are used to alienation and thus have more courage to "buck the establishment" than their more complacent counterparts. Junior Hicks confirmed my intuitive feelings that there are various degrees of status inconsistency among the Basin sighters, but that many highly stable individuals had good sightings. Junior also suggests that he may have selected for stability in his witnesses. If a reporter were known to be "a little far out," Junior just wouldn't get around to interviewing him.

I have long had the impression that scientists who study UFOs may be status inconsistent. Not that their inconsistency derives from levels of income, education, or occupation; rather, they may have religious convictions not accepted by the majority of their colleagues, or their research field may be somewhat on the fringes (e.g., a psychologist studying extrasensory perception).

As a matter of fact, studying UFOs might tend to make one status inconsistent. J. Allen Hynek was probably highly status consistent when he was originally asked by the Air Force to consult with them on UFOs. After twenty years of doing so, he was clearly on the fringes of establishment science. But that's where the action is! There is a real danger of losing touch with reality, as Warren's study shows—to be positive, for example, that Venus is a spaceship. Yet to make important forward strides in science (or in society as a whole), it is often necessary to challenge the established system, to question and to doubt complacently accepted ideas. Progress may depend upon status frustration. (At least that is what we status inconsistent UFO researchers tell ourselves.)

What about the Abductions?

If you start delving into the UFO literature of today, it doesn't take long to see that reported abductions have become a very important part of the phenomenon. By now thousands of women and a few men have reported strange experiences in which an alien shows up in their bedroom in the middle of the night, paralyzes them, floats them out to the spaceship parked in the backyard, performs medical procedures often related to the sex organs, and then returns them to bed. Perhaps the first book to tell such a story is Whitley Strieber's *Communion*, published in 1987. There were others. Budd Hopkins (1987) tells a book-long, intricate story about "Kathie," who was abducted once or twice and then visited again when the aliens introduced her to her young daughter, a hybrid between Kathie and some kind of alien. The implication was that Kathie was artificially inseminated, but the fetus was taken from her in another abduction and developed under some kind of artificial conditions—or in the womb of a female alien! Hopkins is convinced that our visitors are here to perform genetic experiments on mankind. This kind of story shows up again and again in today's ufology.

As a biologist, however, I find the cross-breeding stories especially disturbing. And Budd Hopkins' Kathie was not the first. You'll remember that Antonio Villas Boas in 1957 claimed to have been abducted into a craft and seduced by a beautiful space lady, who indicated that she was going into the sky somewhere to have Antonio's baby (story in the Prologue and below).

If it is even remotely possible for any of the UFO occupants to interbreed with us, the implications are profound. Our closest known relative is the chimpanzee. Human genomes have nearly 99 percent of their nucleotide sequences in common with chimpanzees, and evolutionists tell us that the most recent common ancestor of humans and chimpanzees lived about six million years ago (Pollard, 2009). If we can form hybrids with the UFO aliens but not with chimpanzees, we must have an even more recent common ancestor with them!

These stories of human-alien hybrids force me into creating my own just-suppose stories. One story is that Budd Hopkins and others were writing fiction instead of reporting facts as they claim. Yet these authors sometimes provide impressive evidence that this is not the case—that the alleged abductees existed and believed their stories themselves. Or is it possible that we and the aliens do share a relatively recent common ancestor? Or are the aliens putting these strange memories into the minds of those they abduct, maybe just to confuse us? Or are these false memories that form in the mind like a dream does? (I've had some very intricate dream stories and I'll bet you have too!)

There is one very good reason to be skeptical of many of these abduction stories: They were obtained well after the reported events from witnesses who had no conscious memory of the events but reported their stories under hypnosis, which is why we discuss this story in this chapter on psychology. A couple of decades ago, it was assumed without much direct study that hypnosis was a wonderful way to recover lost memories. At that time, many cases of "forgotten" child abuse, typically of girls by their fathers, came to light as psychotherapists "counseled" grown women under hypnosis. These cases often led to great disruption in families, including divorce, and sometimes prison terms for the alleged abuser. Finally, scientists got around to studying the validity of "recovered memories" gained via hypnosis. It became clear that hypnosis is a very dangerous way to attempt to regain lost memories. A human mind under hypnosis has no compulsion to tell the truth. Rather, such a mind is in a highly suggestible state. When told to recount an event (i.e., tell a story), the mind can respond by coming up with an intricate series of events, and typically, these events seem designed to please the psychotherapist—or the ufologist who is looking for more evidence to support the idea of UFO abductions. Furthermore, it is virtually impossible for the ufologist to conceal personal desires and UFO convictions. Typically, the hypnosis wouldn't be going on if it weren't for the possibility that there is a UFO connection to some strange feelings in the witness. In some respects, the abduction stories from numerous witnesses have much in common: Most seem to fit the currently popular scenario of such abductions. But detailed examination reveals that there are numerous highly important details that vary among abductee accounts.

One thing is very clear: Once the "memories" have been brought out under hypnosis, they become a very conscious part of the total memory of the witness. In controlled experiments, it has been shown that false memories can be implanted under hypnosis, and once they are there, the subject has no doubt about their validity. All of this is well documented in a book by Susan A. Clancy (2005). She is a total skeptic about UFOs in general. It doesn't occur to her that there might be UFO phenomena that have nothing to do with aliens from other solar systems, and since relativity theory clearly tells us that they can't get here in any kind of time significant to their home planet or to ours, they must not exist. (True, for the travelers going near the speed of light, the time would seem much shorter, as we note in Chapter 7.) In spite of her UFO skepticism, her book is a fine summary of false-memory research (her speciality) and the difficulties of believing that abduction stories told under hypnosis can be relied upon. Jacques Vallee (2008 b., Chapter 11) also has a nice summary of the difficulties encountered when hypnotism is used by UFO researchers.

Vallee concludes, and so do I, that genuine abductions might well have occurred, and there are cases that strongly support this conclusion. But we are entitled to be highly skeptical of stories that are pulled from the subject's mind by hypnosis—even if the abduction took place. It was the loss-of-time, hypnosis experience of Betty and Barney Hill that seems to have brought the entire abduction phenomenon to the attention of the public. We'll examine that story next. Then I'll present two missing-time stories from my own records—one from the Uintah Basin—in which no hypnosis is present in either case, followed by three stories in which the abduction was reported not long after it occurred and was a vivid part of the witnesses' memory, not brought to the surface by hypnosis. Finally, I'll relate an experience that I found very humbling, forcing me to decide between simple logic (Occam's razor) and the convictions of two very solid witnesses.

Missing Time

Betty and Barney Hill's Interrupted Journey. Nearly everyone has heard of the Betty and Barney Hill case (Fuller, 1966). Betty and Barney watched a UFO on their way back from Montreal through northern New Hampshire. It first approached at a great distance, but finally it came in close, at which time the Hills got out and Barney had a close look with binoculars at the huge object with its strange occupants staring back at them through windows in the UFO. Then, what seemed to them to be a few moments later, they found themselves some thirty-five miles down the road, and upon consulting their watches, discovered that about two hours had elapsed. After two subsequent years of increasing physical difficulties, especially on the part of Barney, and numerous nightmares and other mental symptoms, they consulted Dr. Benjamin Simon, a psychotherapist in Boston. Under hypnosis, they recalled the UFO encounter and told what had happened during the elapsed time period. According to their story, they were taken aboard the craft by the UFO occupants. They were physically examined and interviewed at length. Many of the questions and the answers seem interestingly naive. Certainly they make little sense in terms of our theory of long-term exploration of our planet by extraterrestrial machines.

Again, it is not easy to assess the validity of the Betty and Barney Hill story. They might have made the story up subconsciously in response to the hypnotist's request for information about what transpired during the elapsed time. Many of the details of the story were similar to dreams experienced by Betty and related to Barney. Dr. Simon never accepted their story.

In her account, Betty tells that after the physical examination, she was left alone with the leader. At this point she had recovered from the fright that she had experienced in the initial abduction, and then she asked for proof of some kind that she has been on the spaceship. She found a book with strange vertical writing, and at first the leader agreed to let her take it with her—but later he took it back. At about this point, she asked the leader where he came from. He asked what she knew about the universe, and she admitted that she knew very little except for a few things she had learned while she was in graduate school about the solar system and that there were a great many stars. She had heard the famous astronomer Harlow Shapley talk, and she had seen photographs he had taken of millions and millions of stars in the universe. The leader went across the room and opened something in the wall not quite like a drawer. He pulled out a map and asked Betty if she had ever seen one like it before. She walked up and looked at it closely. It was three dimensional and gave her the impression that she was looking out a window:

> And it was a map—it was an oblong map. It wasn't square. It was a lot wider than it was long. And there were all these dots on it. And they were scattered all over it. Some were little, just pinpoints. And others were as big as a nickel. And there were lines, they were on some of the dots, there were curved lines going from one dot to another. And there was this one big circle, and it had a lot of lines coming out from it. A lot of lines going to another circle quite close, but not as big. And these were heavy lines. And I asked him what they meant. And he said that the heavy lines were trade routes. And the other lines, the solid lines were places they went occasionally, and he said the broken lines were expeditions . . . . So I asked him where was his home port, and he said, "where are you on the map?" I looked and laughed and said, "I don't know." So he said, "If you don't know where you are, then there isn't any point of my telling where I am from." Then he put the map—the map rolled up, and he put it back in the space in the wall and closed it. I felt very stupid because I did not know where the Earth was on the map. I asked him would he open up the map again and show me where the Earth was, and he again laughed. (Fuller, 1966, p. 175.)

During a later session of hypnosis, Betty again remembered the Star Map. She said she could see it so clearly in her mind, that she could almost draw it. Dr. Simon gave her a post-hypnotic suggestion to draw the map sometime during the next week when the vision of it again came clearly into her mind. She did this, and her drawing is shown in Fig. 6-1.

Marjorie Fish, of Oak Harbor, Ohio, an elementary schoolteacher with wide interests, especially in exobiology, read Fuller's book in 1966 and got to thinking about this map. It was obvious that the distribution of stars as drawn by Betty Hill didn't resemble anything visible in our skies. But why should the map be drawn from the vantage point of Earth? If the Hill's story were true, the UFO drivers must have been from somewhere else in the universe—and their map would probably be drawn from some

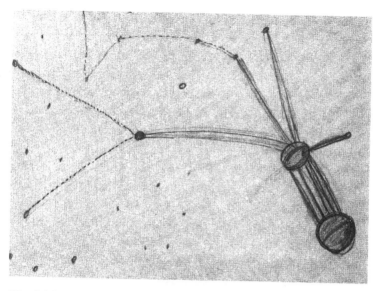

Fig. 6-1 *Betty Hill's star map (Fuller, 1966 b.).*

vantage point familiar to them.

Marjorie Fish went to work with a 1962 Yale Star Catalogue. Her first model (built by stringing large beads on a grid of strings) included 259 star systems and had no resemblance to Betty's map. Then she eliminated from her consideration stars whose planets (if any) probably would not support life as we know it. These included stars that varied in intensity, double star systems, and extremely large and extremely small stars (giants and dwarfs). She used only the rather medium stars in the so-called "main sequence" (stars not unlike our sun). She would consider the closest star to the sun, and the star or stars closest to it, and so on. Finally getting help from Dr. Walter Mitchel, an astronomer at Ohio State University, her later models began to show resemblances to Betty's map, but a good match didn't appear until she refined her data with the help of the Gliese Star Catalogue published in 1969—about five years after Betty drew her map. Fish's final map placed the two stars, Zeta Reticuli 1 & 2, at the front of her map, matching the two large stars, connected by many lines, supposedly representing frequent trade routes. Thus, the Zeta Reticulis were said to be the home solar systems of Betty and Barney Hill's starship hosts.

Some of us were impressed by the apparent match, but Menzel and Taves (1977) argued that the match could easily be coincidental. I obtained the star data from Dr. David Saunders (an original member of the Condon

Committee) and constructed a model using his data. A photo of my model was included in the first edition of this book. But in the ensuing years since the Gliese Star Catalogue was published, much more accurate measurements have been made of the stars that appeared to match Betty's map. Some of them proved to be much farther away than was originally thought, so that now Marjorie Fish's stars do not form anything like a match with Betty's map. But of course new maps are being generated to match Betty's map (Pearse, 2009).

Stolen Time by a Huge UFO Above the Road. On September 9, 2009, Junior Hicks, James Carrion (Director of MUFON), and I interviewed Marjorie Beal, an eighty-four-year-old woman who has lived in her present house (or one very close to it) on an out-of-the-way highway for many decades, including about 1966 when she had the experience that she describes. Marge was a very literate witness who told an impressive story that required little editing on my part. The first part of the interview tells the story clearly:

> **Marjorie Beal:** My daughter Rebecca was an honor student, and we went over to Union High School [in Roosevelt] for the banquet. And another daughter, Diane, and a son Burton were taking care of the small children at home. We figured we would be home about 11:00 and no later than that. So we left town, came out along Highway 40,

Fig. 6-2 (A) *Marjorie Beal (1997) and* (B) *Rebecca Crandall (2009).*

and we both remarked that there wasn't any traffic, especially after we left the Ioka turn [but] we didn't think too much about it. We went up the hill and across what we call the Mortinson Bench, and when we got over to where Keith Mortinson lives right on the edge of the hill, all of a sudden here was this flying saucer out in front of us. We both sort of gasped, you know, and the next thing I knew, I felt like I was waking up from something—like I had been asleep—and I was realizing there was something out there, and I looked at it, and it had a dome shape and windows all around here with lights on. I kept looking at those to see if there was anyone in there that I could see. And then there was this [round bottom (recording not clear)] that came down all the way around, and under that was this bright light that shone down on the ground. And I was trying to get my bearings because I felt like I wasn't all there or something. And I looked out the window of the car on the left, over into Keith Mortinson's yard, clear into his yard, and bushes against his house—and I could see not just the leaves but the stems in those bushes, and weeds and things growing up, and down in the barrow pit weeds and everything, and of course the edge of the road had gravel, and I could see each tiny little piece of gravel and then onto the asphalt were these little tiny pieces of gravel, and that light was so bright that you could see that, but it didn't hurt my eyes or anything. Finally, I said "I've got to touch ground; I've got to touch ground!" And Becky said "No mom, no mom!" But I did. I stepped out of the car, just leaned on the open door and just watched it and looked at it, and I could feel the Earth under me, so I felt . . . I sat down back in the car, and I said I guessed we had better get home. And I went to turn my key on, and the key was still on; the car was stopped. I don't remember putting on the brakes or anything that way, but the motor was stopped, but the key was still on. And I thought "Oh boy!" Well, I turned it back, and turned it on and the car started. And we started off the edge of the hill here. . . . The car didn't go anywhere, you know. And as we started off, that [UFO] thing went that way and then off to the east, and we didn't see it. Then we went down and across that next little bench, and over a hill, and at the bottom of the road that goes up to Boreham Lake over here and the canal, and as we passed the canal, I pulled over and stopped, and we both got out of the car, and it shot to the east again, and we were kind of relieved again so we drove through Myton and up around the road, and I said "Oh, I'm so glad that thing's gone," and Rebecca said "Mom, take a look," and it was off to the right of us following right along, and we came up just the same way you did on top of the hill and down to this next little house and pulled in, and Diane came running out, and she was crying and was upset. She said "Where have you been? And what has happened?" And I said, "Well, we're just coming home." We were so shocked or whatever that we didn't say anything to her about it. She said "I looked for you about eleven o'clock," and she said "It's two thirty in the morning." So I said, we'd better get to bed, so she went in—Becky had already gone in—so the next morning, she [Diane] said "You look like you've seen a ghost." She said "I want to know what happened," so we told her the story.

Here, as in so many other interviews, Marge digressed to other sightings she'd experienced or had heard about. Earlier, she had said that they were watching the moon rise in the east as they left the banquet (in 1966), but that it was well overhead, almost in the west, when they arrived home. The moon was full on May 4, 1966. If the banquet let out about 9:00 PM, and the moon was just rising, it would have been a few days after May 4, which agrees with Rebecca's memory of the date.

Marge told us that she had never been hypnotized so that she could remember what happened during the lost time—nor had Rebecca. "I don't know what happened during that time, because it just felt like I was waking up finally, realizing it was out there. And I had been somewhere, or something. It was really an odd feeling. Then I started studying and realizing. . . . It was just right in front of us, just hovering right there in the road way. It must have been quite close because the bright lights came right down. No farther than 100 feet." Marge's final comment seems highly relevant to me: "And I never remember being afraid. I was curious but never afraid."

On October 6, 2009, my wife, Mary, and I visited with Rebecca Jensen Crandall in Peoa for over an hour. She told her story before I gave her a copy of her mother's interview to read, which she did only after Mary and I left. In a later call to her, she was troubled by her memories that differed from her mother's, although the basic memory of the experience is closely similar for both mother and daughter. There are a number of interesting differences—as one might expect after 43 years! I was amazed that the memories of the object remained so vivid and similar in each other's minds. The differences nicely illustrate what I've been saying about imperfect memories and perhaps even imperfect initial perceptions. Two people might well see the same thing differently. Incidently, there is no way to know which one, mother or daughter, was right about the factual details that differ. Luckily, in this case the details of exact place and time are unimportant; the two most impressive memories are of the object and the loss of time—and both witnesses agree nicely on those things.

Both remember driving home after the dinner (which was only for students—Rebecca's mother came to pick her up), and both emphasized the lack of traffic. Both remember topping the Mortinson Ridge, but Marge's memory is that the event was experienced next to the Mortinson residence, while Rebecca feels certain that they had gone down off the ridge a mile or so. Both saw the huge, double-convex object with moving lights around the middle hovering very close and over the highway. Marge said the object was "as big as a house," but Rebecca would only say that it was "huge." Rebecca's memory places the object to the left about 30 degrees; that is, east of the highway although they were parked on the right shoulder—and she thinks it might have been 200–300 feet away but no farther than 500 feet (based on her experience with installing fences on a ranch in Wyoming). Marge remembers "waking up" and getting out of the car, whereas Rebecca had no sense of lost time until she got home. But Rebecca remembers her mother getting out of the car as soon as it stopped. Rebecca doesn't remember opening her car door, but she remembers the brilliant light (but not its source) and the distinct, tiny rocks with their shadows on the side of the highway; so she thinks she must have opened her door. Rebecca clearly remembers the object following them along Highway 40 until they got to the road that turns off the highway toward where they lived. Rebecca felt peaceful, and she considered that the UFO had followed them home to see that they got there safely! Their memories of the times differ a bit; Rebecca had the times moved up a bit compared with Marge, but both remember how upset Rebecca's brother and sister were to see them coming home when they did—as they were themselves shocked at the time loss! And they both remember not talking about the experience until the next morning.

There were other interesting details in Rebecca's story:

> All of a sudden, my mom said, "Oh, my God!" and that's totally not my mother! [At that point, mother put her hand over her heart.] And there was just this huge flying saucer, UFO, hanging in the sky. . . . I mean it was just hanging there, and she pulled over and stopped the car. I remember saying "Mom, don't!" But she opened the door and she got out of the car, but it was so quiet! . . . And I could hear, as mother got out of the car, her feet crunching among the rocks along the road— just so loud. But there were no—I don't remember other sounds but for the noises that we made . . . But this UFO, it was huge, I couldn't give you any idea how big it was other than it was enormous.

To me, the most striking discrepancy in the two accounts is the locations of where the car was parked. As I have reread the two accounts, I've cooked up a just-suppose story. There is no way to know whether it might be true, but see what you think.

It is very difficult to imagine that an abduction did not take place. As Rebecca noted, if they were sitting there in the car on Highway 40 asleep for two hours, someone would have stopped to see if anything was wrong. So I am essentially forced to accept the idea that there was an abduction, and if there was an abduction, clearly the UFO drivers messed with their memories, because they remember no such abduction. So it seems obvious that they would indeed have different memories. Say the UFO used its electromagnetic interference apparatus (reported in many UFO cases) to stop the car, without turning off the key—which Marjorie remembers vividly. Rebecca had no way to know whether the key was off or on because she was not driving, but she does remember utter silence; that is, no motor running. Say the car was stopped next to the Mortinson place, as Marjorie remembers. She was zapped by the memory suppressor but commanded to get out of the car, which she did and remembers doing, although this could have happened before the abduction instead of after, as she seems to remember. Rebecca thinks she must have opened the door, but she doesn't remember doing so (possibly due to the memory zapper again). Now comes the real what-if part: What if both were levitated up into the UFO, and the car was levitated somewhere so it wouldn't be sitting there on Highway 40 while the wise man in the UFO was implanting thoughts of peace into mom and daughter? And of course the UFO had to move so it wouldn't be seen by other cars, which inevitably had to come along that busy highway even if there was a (UFO-controlled?) stretch of no traffic. When the instruction period was over, the car was brought back, but it was set down a mile or so along the road, where Rebecca remembers it to be! Remember that the memory zapping of Rebecca was seamless; she had no memory of any time loss. Marjorie's zapping was not quite so seamless because she remembers "waking up" or something. But she didn't pay attention to where she was because she was amazed by the car not running but the key being turned on! And the UFO, having brought them back, stayed around to see that all was okay. (I think I'll take up writing science fiction.)

Most impressive to me, as we discussed with Rebecca at length, was their peaceful reaction to an experience that has terrified many others. What insight into the phenomenon does that provide? It is in sharp contrast to the next account, which I include here mostly because it does show that sharp contrast. Larry Sorenson was almost paralyzed with fear although he doesn't remember the UFO being very close (admittedly, it could have come much closer at any moment):

Detained on the Nevada Desert. I had told Mr. Jay Hall, a Utah State University extension agent in Millard and Fillmore Counties (southwestern Utah) about my interest in UFOs. A few weeks later he told me that he had taken a very unusual call one evening (August 29, 1968) on the sheriff's phone in Delta, where he shares an office. The man was emotionally upset, and he seemed to be unable to account for one or two hours of time. I recorded a telephone interview with Larry Sorenson, of Sacramento, California, but I'm going to summarize his story here, along with part of the interview:

Larry was driving in the evening between Ely, Nevada, and Delta, Utah, when he noticed a bright light way off in the distance. It was white and looked like a star, but then it turned red. Already, Larry "was pretty frightened." He considered turning back but then decided not to. He said he "figured [he] was imagining something." Then his truck "completely went dead and came to a stop." Nothing happened when he tried to start it. He was so shaken at this point that later he couldn't remember whether or not he turned the lights off, but he got out and looked around; "it was pitch black." Then the object moved directly overhead, and "it flashed from red to green and back to red and back to green, and it went white at one time, but principally it was flashing red to green all the time it went over the top of me. And, of course, I was pretty . . . out of my mind at the time. Couldn't figure what in the heck was going on. I thought I was seeing things. I stood there, not doing a thing, trying to start my truck up or anything. I was sort of, so to speak, frozen." When the object finally left, and he could start his truck, he noticed another car way ahead; its lights came on about the same time his did. He tried to stop the car as it approached, but it sped on by. "He was going pretty fast. About as fast as I was after I shuddered and started going to pieces. But at the time, like I said, I was pretty shaken up, and I look back upon it now, and it's certainly something that did happen. I can't explain it." He couldn't see any shape to the object, only a light and that was well above him in the sky. There was no sound.

> Between Ely and Delta is a distance of about one hundred and fifty miles, and it took me about four hours to go from one point to the other. And I was averaging sixty to eighty miles all the way. That's

straight road out there. . . . Well, when I finally got the truck going and was on my way again, I traveled about seventy-five miles more before I came into Delta. But, you see, four hours elapsed. . . . Looking back, I can't remember of having lost any sense of time [and] I wasn't stopped for over a half hour all the time this thing was going on. . . . [The trip] would only be two hours. It took me quite a bit longer. Whenever I talk about it now, I get goose flesh just thinking about it. . . . To be truthful with you, to be frank, I was scared out of my wits.

Larry suffered no physical symptoms, but it was a frightening emotional experience for him—quite contrary to the experiences of Marge and Rebecca.

No Missing Time

I'm more impressed when the evidence for abductions does not involve hypnosis—which is not to say that true things cannot be extracted by hypnosis. The problem is that there are so many pitfalls with hypnosis that information obtained that way cannot be relied upon. So let's briefly consider three classic cases in which the abductees told their stories not long after the abduction allegedly took place so that hypnosis was not involved. There are cases much more recent than these (Vallée, 2008 b.), but these are sufficient to make the point. Note that a skeptic cannot reject these cases on the basis of problems with hypnosis. Indeed, the only logical rejection is that the "abductee" perpetrated a hoax—and that's what skeptics do suggest.

Antonio Villas-Boas and the Space Lady. Antonio was plowing his field in Brazil one night when his tractor was stopped by a large UFO that landed nearby. (For details of this case, see Lorenzens, 1967; Rutkowski, 2008; Wikipedia.) Three small humanoids (shorter than five feet), wearing some kind of tight-fitting costume that included a helmet and mask covering all but their eyes, captured Antonio and after some struggle took him into the spacecraft, where two others were waiting. After several rituals that included taking samples of blood, removing Antonio's clothes, and rubbing his body with a liquid of some kind, he was ushered into a room in the spacecraft. There, while he was left to his own thoughts, the room began to fill with a smoke that made him ill (a disinfectant?), after which a space lady entered. She proved to be as naked as Antonio himself. The hair on her head was long and white but her underarm and pubic hair were bright red. A normal sex act followed and was repeated once. Antonio claims that the liquid rubbed on his body must have been an aphrodisiac that lowered his will beyond the power to resist!

Obviously, Villas-Boas may have been indulging in sexual fantasy or an erotic dream plot to produce his story. There are reasons, however, to indicate that he could have been telling the truth. For example, for several months following the incident, he suffered from strange sores on his body that could be neither diagnosed nor cured (an interplanetary form of venereal disease?). Vallée (1969, 2008) points out that these sexual shenanigans are all highly reminiscent of the fairy faith, as well as the angels and demons of Renaissance times.

In the middle ages, according to a number of mythological and legendary traditions, an incubus (plural incubi) was a demon in male form supposed to lie upon sleepers, especially women, in order to have sexual intercourse with them. Its female counterpart was the succubus. As with the UFO encounters, many proposals were suggested to account for reported cases. Sexual dreams and fantasies were of course among them, but some historians take some reports seriously.

Fire in the Sky: The Travis Walton Case. This is another well-known story (see its Wikipedia entry). It was told in a book (Walton, 1997) and made into a movie: *Fire in the Sky*. On Wednesday, November 5, 1975, near sunset, a crew contracted by the Forest Service to thin scrub brush from forest land near Turkey Springs, Arizona, was driving in a truck off the mountain. Mike Rogers had hired six others, including Travis Walton, all from Snowflake, Arizona. As they approached a clearing, they saw a UFO hovering over it. Walton jumped out of the truck and ran under the UFO, which shot out a beam of blue-green light that knocked him onto the ground. Rogers was understandably frightened and accelerated the truck away from the site. After calming down, they went back to find Walton— who was nowhere to be found. An extensive search was instigated, but by Saturday there was still no sign of Walton, and the police began to suspect not only a hoax but that there could even be a homicide: Travis might have been killed and the story made up to cover the crime. On Monday, a polygraph test was administered to each of the seven crew members. Questions included whether they knew where Walton was, whether they knew of his being murdered, and whether they had actually seen a UFO. All but one of the crew passed the test. They denied knowing where Walton was, claiming that they had indeed seen a UFO. The one who did not finish the test later explained that he had concealed a criminal record and was afraid that the test might reveal his lie. But he stuck with the others on the important questions.

Just before midnight on Monday, Walton's brother-in-law, Grant Neff, received a phone call: "This is Travis. I'm at a phone booth at the Heber [near Snowflake] gas station, and I need help. Come and get me." At first, Neff thought it was a prank call, but he became convinced that it was indeed Travis, so he and Walton's brother, Duane, went to pick up Travis. He was weak and very upset. Unfortunately for development of the case, his return was not reported until Tuesday afternoon, and in the meantime, Duane had taken Travis to Phoenix for an examination by a doctor—but the doctor turned out to be a hypnotherapist recommended by a UFO group! Coral Lorenzen of APRO called the Waltons, and by Tuesday afternoon, Travis had been examined by a general practitioner. Then the *National Enquirer* complicated the picture by arranging with the Lorenzens to pay all expenses in return for exclusive rights to the story. (The Lorenzens had no good way to fund an extensive investigation.) An interesting part of the physical examination was that a urine sample, taken immediately after Walton's return, showed no ketones (acetone and related molecules), which appear after fasting in response to the breakdown of fats. Does this support a hoax, or does it suggest that Travis was treated someway during his abduction such that the normal formation of ketones did not occur? Or that he was not starved?

Travis claimed that he remembered only about two hours of the five days that he was missing. He tells of three small, humanoid "greys" with huge eyes and large, bald heads. There were also nearly normal humans although their eyes were a bit larger than usual and bright golden in color. James Harder later hypnotized Travis, but no new memories were brought to light. Travis also took a polygraph test not long after his return, but he was still very nervous and failed the test. Some months later, he took two more tests which apparently showed that he was telling the truth. When the movie was released, tests were also taken by Travis, Mike Rogers, and one other crew member; all were declared to be telling the truth.

Obviously, the case has been shrouded in controversy from the beginning. Still, it is interesting and unique in several ways. For one thing, there were six witnesses who claimed to see the abduction itself—at least the "capture" of Travis Walton. As far as I can learn, none of the seven people involved has ever admitted that the group perpetrated a hoax. Further-more, an independent witness came forth to claim that he had seen a UFO with a blue beam of light in the right place and the right time to be related to the Walton sighting. Again, a polygraph test was administered, and again the witness was apparently telling the truth.

One of the early debunkers was Town Marshall Sanford Flake of Snowflake, who was convinced that the crew carried out a hoax. He tried to catch them in the hoax even before Travis reappeared. From May 30 to June 1, 1977, a year and a half after Travis's abduction, I was in Snowflake speaking for three days at a Brigham Young University Education Week. We on the tour spent an evening at Sanford Flake's home, and he told us of how he was still convinced that the whole thing was a hoax. Although I had other things keeping me busy (including a "Planet Venus UFO Sight-ing!"), I was able to interview Mike Rogers as well as Travis Walton. I could detect no indication of a hoax in their stories—but who was I, a practicing plant physiologist, to detect truth and lies by talking with a wit-ness? It is still an interesting case.

Mississippi Fishermen. Another widely publicized incident occurred in Pascagoula, Mississippi (see Wikipedia entry). Two men, Charles Hickson, forty-five, and Calvin Parker, eighteen, were fishing on an old abandoned iron pier at the Schaupeter Shipyard on the Pascagoula River between 9:00 PM and 10:00 PM on October 11, 1973. Suddenly a flying object descended about forty feet behind them in an open area, where it hovered about two feet off the ground. It was sixteen to eighteen feet long with a trapdoor in the back, out of which three "creatures" emerged. They were about five feet tall, pale gray in color, and had wrinkled "skin." Their heads came directly down to their shoulders, and their arms ended in claw-like appendages with two digits, about the size of a normal hand. As they moved, they moved above the ground, never touching it and never separat-ing their legs as in a normal walking manner. They had two small cone-shaped "ears," slits where the eyes should have been, a small, sharp nose, and a hole below that. They had only a single leg—or two legs were fused together. (In view of the description of the creatures, the possibility that they were robots has been considered.)

One of them made a humming noise, and they began to approach the two men. Hickson said he thought of jumping into the river but was paralyzed by fear. Parker lost consciousness, and one of the creatures grabbed him with his pincerlike hands and floated him into the ship, where Hickson also was taken. Upon entry into the ship, the two men were separated. Parker remained unconscious, but Hickson noted what detail was available. He said that with the creature's touch, he experienced a complete cessation of all feeling.

The area into which the two men were taken was completely bare, well-lit, but with no indication where the light came from. Neither of the men ever touched the ship itself but were suspended in air while an instrument of some kind, which Hickson described as resembling a huge eye, moved along their horizontal bodies as if observing or photographing them.

Hickson estimated that they were in the ship about fifteen to twenty minutes, after which they were "floated" outside and returned to their original location. The three creatures then re-entered the object, but neither Hickson nor Parker saw the object leave. The two debated for about an hour as to whether to report the experience. They finally called the sheriff's office and went down to make a statement.

The account was picked up by numerous newspapers and broadcasting stations. APRO arranged to send James Harder and J. Allen Hynek to Pascagoula to interview the two witnesses. In company with a number of other people, Dr. Harder interviewed and hypnotized the two men. Little was learned, however, because as they were regressed to more vividly remember their experience, they became terrified and came out of hypnosis. Harder, Hynek, and the others were convinced that the men could not have simulated their feelings of terror while under hypnosis. A tape recorder was left on accidentally while everyone was out of the room except the two men, and their debates about whether they would be believed or ridiculed and their discussions of the experience were extremely convincing to those who heard the tapes. Although the appearance of the "creatures" and other elements of the experience are almost without precedent, the case is convincing in many ways, and we must consider the possibility that it really happened as the witnesses tell it. Hickson had been in frightening situations during the Korean war, but Parker had no such experience. Perhaps that is why Parker was so terrified; he was later hospitalized for an "emotional breakdown."

Naturally, Philip Klass called the story a hoax—no other explanation would even come close. In addition to some insignificant discrepancies, the best argument against the validity of the event is that there were two twenty-four-hour toll booths in full view of the landing site, and neither operator saw anything that night. Also, the site was in range of security cameras from nearby Ingalls Shipyard, and the cameras also showed nothing that night. However, many years later one witness, at least, told about his sighting of a UFO in that area on that evening.

A Sobering Story: UFO or Hot-Air Bag?

On January, 1974, I had an experience that made me carefully re-evaluate all of my thoughts about the role of psychology in ufology. I see things now with a slightly different perspective. It's an important perspective, one that you should have too.

In 1974, I was on leave, working at the Atomic Energy Commission Headquarters in Germantown, Maryland, about twenty-five miles north of Washington, D.C. (The next year, the commission became the Department of Energy: DOE.) I returned to Utah State University at the end of August. On January 23, Virginia Lott, a contract assistant in our division, came into my office all excited about an experience she had had the night before. She, my office mate, Frank Brooks, and I had discussed the UFO problem several times. One or two days before in one of those discussions, she had said that she would give just about anything if she could really see a UFO. As she ran into my office on the morning of January 23, she said that she had indeed finally seen her UFO. She quickly told me her story, and then I switched on the dictaphone and asked her to tell it again. Here's the full interview:

> **Virginia Lott:** It was January 22, 1974, about 8:10 in the evening, and I was driving on Randolph Road towards Georgia Avenue [in Wheaton, Maryland]; my daughter, Virginia Lott Jr. [age nineteen], was sitting in the seat next to me. We were across the street from the Randolph Hills Nursing Home when my daughter very excitedly said to me, "Mother, mother look at this—what is it, what is it?" and I said, "Junior, I can't look now, I'm driving." She said, "You've got to see this, you've got to see this—I've never seen anything like it before— mother, you've got to see this no matter what happens. It's hovering!" So I glanced out of the window real quickly, and I saw this weird light. It reminded me of the reddish and yellow effect that you get when you look at a flame. It was on the top of a large, shadowylike object that was hovering about fifteen to twenty feet off the ground in the middle of a large schoolyard.
>
> **FBS:** And which you had the impression had the shape of an egg?
>
> **Virginia:** Yes, uh-huh, definitely the shape of an egg. Um, and the

top part (the light) looked like a half of a full moon, about that size, with the object below much larger. So we went around the block to try to get closer to the object, and my daughter kept an eye on it as we went around the corner. As we pulled into the back of the schoolyard, the lights from my car illuminated the schoolyard, and immediately this object took off so fast it just—well I can't think of words to describe the speed with which it took off—it seemed to be ten to fifteen miles on down the road in a matter of thirty seconds.

FBS: And you didn't lose sight of it during the time it was . . .

Virginia: No, my daughter had her eye on the light all the way around until we got behind to the schoolyard, and then as it took off we had our eyes on the light constantly. We decided we should try to follow the light, so we pulled out of the schoolyard, but by the time we got around, we had lost sight of it. It either disappeared or we couldn't find it.

FBS: You can locate the original position very accurately because first you saw it out of the right window and then you went around the block and pulled into the schoolyard and saw it out of the windshield in front of you, so it couldn't possibly have been at some great distance and just seemed close.

Virginia: No. No. It was right there at the schoolyard. In fact, if I hadn't have had to come to work today, I'd be over to the schoolyard right now looking around.

FBS: Which is where you should be!

Virginia: I know, but I would have to take leave.

FBS: You had trouble describing the light. You think it reminded you of a flame, but it did not have a flame shape?

Virginia: No. Definitely not. It had a sharp edge and didn't change in shape. It was a reddish and yellowish type thing that seemed to be flickering; and still, flickering is not the right word to use. Have you ever been to a show at Shady Grove or some place, and the star or the girls in the chorus would be dressed in dresses that might have sort of like sequins or silver or something worked into the material, and as the person moves, there is a shimmering (sort of), a motion to the color as it moves? This is the impression I got of this light.

FBS: An undulating, shimmering flicker?

Virginia: Right. We could hear no sound, although of course we were inside the car with the engine running. I wish we had had the radio on to see if there might have been interference or static.

I found this story most exciting. Surely, it was one of the best that I had ever encountered. There was no question about the location of the light. The two Virginias had seen it first to the south and then around the block (actually, around the corner), to the north. It had to be hovering above that schoolyard. The big black object was certainly an ominous and exciting element in the story. And the rapid departure to the northwest surely seemed to put the object into the category of strange and unexplainable things. A perfectly fine UFO.

Virginia and I went back to the school ground during the lunch hour. We hunted around but couldn't find anything important. Then at 8:00 PM that evening I was parked behind the school where Virginia had parked when she saw the object depart. I intended to knock on doors and ask if anyone had observed TV or radio interference at about 8:10 PM on the previous evening. I couldn't suppress considerable excitement. After all, UFOs have been known to appear at the same place twenty-four hours after a sighting. I decided to wander around a bit before knocking on doors.

I noticed some high school-aged boys and girls at the rear of the circular schoolhouse. It occurred to me that they might have some information, so I strolled over to see what they could tell me. They were constructing hot air balloons. They did this by building a cross with soda straws, tying together a bunch of birthday candles, and placing these at the center of the cross. Then the bottom of a polyethylene plastic bag, obtained from the nearby dry cleaners, was fitted over the crossed straws. When the candles were lit, they made a good-sized flame inside of the transparent, shimmering plastic bag, soon heating the air in the bag enough to lift the whole contraption gently into the air. It would float slowly higher until it was caught by a breeze, when it would move almost horizontally with the speed of the breeze.

Naturally, I asked: "Were you guys by any chance making hot air balloons last night?" Well yes, they were. They began making their balloons on the night of Virginia's sighting a little after 7:00 PM, and five or six balloons were launched during the course of the evening. They weren't watching the clock, so one can't be positive, but considering the time that they started and the time it takes to put one together, it was perfectly reasonable to imagine that a balloon had been launched at about 8:10 PM.

They had launched the balloons from the front of the school. I watched them launch a couple of these bags, and their appearance seemed to match perfectly Virginia's description of the flamelike light. It was the transparent (slightly translucent) plastic that provided the shimmering effect and the sharp edge. After rising slowly, the balloons moved with the prevailing breeze to the rear, where they hovered over the schoolyard exactly where the two Virginias saw their UFO. Then the balloons would rise slowly until they were caught by the wind blowing over the top of the schoolhouse, at which time they moved off rapidly in a northwest direction toward Rockville—exactly the direction taken by Virginia's UFO.

How about the really rapid departure of the object? It seems quite reasonable that the object appeared to leave much faster than it actually did. Virginia and her daughter thought they were seeing a large UFO. They thought that it moved a matter of miles in 30 seconds or so. Here again is the problem of depth perception. If an object moves only a few hundred feet, but the witness thinks it is moving several miles, it will appear to move with a high velocity. Furthermore, as the candles began to burn out, they would grow dimmer, accentuating the illusion of a speedy departure.

But how about the big black object? Was this generated in the minds of Virginia and her daughter by their high interest in UFOs and their desire to see one? Frank Brooks suggested that there might have been some kind of shadow produced by the bundle of candles, black smoke, or something that would account for their thinking they saw an object. Maybe so, but this is difficult to evaluate. Clearly if Virginia and her daughter imagined the object, this is of extreme interest to UFO investigators. How many other big black shapes might have been imagined when they weren't really there?

The next morning when Virginia came to work, I told her about the hot-air bags. She was a bit crestfallen, as one might expect. Nevertheless, she tentatively accepted my explanation, because so many details seemed to fit so well. I asked her to return to the area under similar conditions. A few days later she made the trip, after which she came into my office, looked me straight in the eye, and told me I was out of my mind! She said that there was simply no way that she could possibly have imagined the big black object. She knew the case was overwhelmingly detailed against her, but she had decided not to yield an inch. She saw the object, and that was that.

What could I do about that? Obviously, the next best thing to do would be to talk with her daughter. I had instructed Virginia not to discuss the sighting with her daughter, and as the days and finally weeks slipped by, she carefully avoided doing so. Virginia Lott Jr., worked and went to college, but finally on February 21, I did get to talk with her while Virginia Sr.

took down the conversation in shorthand. The daughter's story is virtually identical to her mother's account. There is much emphasis on the big, egg-shaped, football-on-its-side black object. After hearing her version of the story. I then told her my experience with the high school students making hot-air balloons.

Virginia Jr.: I don't think that was it. I don't think it would have actually hovered in one place.

FBS: They did rise slowly and then get above the school where the wind caught them, moving them rapidly toward Rockville. That is what the students told me, and without my asking.

Virginia Jr.: I don't think the wind could make a plastic bag go as fast as this went. It wasn't that windy; I don't believe that. There is just no way. Even if you accept the theory that the plastic bag could hover like that, it couldn't possibly go off that quickly. I didn't think it was an anything. I didn't have a preconceived idea of what it was going to be. I just made an observation.

FBS: You might have had an unconscious preconceived idea.

Virginia Jr.: Well, of course. But I can't believe your theory.

FBS: Imagine if you were in my place, you would have to think it was 99.44 percent likely that it was the gas bag. Otherwise, it would be fantastic.

Virginia Jr.: It could have been a flying saucer stopping by to see what was going on!

So there you have it. Both Virginias stuck by their original story. They saw a light that matches exactly the appearance of a plastic, candle-powered hot-air bag, but they insisted that they saw a large black object beneath that light. They were fully aware of the case against their story, but they wouldn't yield an inch. They were likewise fully aware that their position was an extremely insecure one: that a large UFO hovered in an area where gas bags were being released and even turned on a light on top that exactly resembled the gas bags (just so the observational abilities of Virginia and Virginia would subsequently be questioned!). Yet the Virginias are so convinced by their experience that they maintain that the unlikely event is indeed the one that happened, while the likely one (that they misinterpreted a hot-air balloon) did not. But as an objective scientist, I have to go with the likely event. That's called Occam's razor, attributed to 14th-century English logician and Franciscan friar, William of Ockham. It says that when there are two explanations for a phenomenon, the simplest is

likely to be the true one. Virginia and her daughter forgave me for applying Occam's razor, but I don't believe it was easy for them. (Incidentally,
don't judge the two ladies too harshly for being stubborn in the light of
overwhelming evidence—unless you have had a closely similar experience
and reacted differently.)

What is the lesson in all this? There is the extremely slight possibility that the story indicates how diabolically clever our visitors are. Much
more probably, the story indicates that one must be extremely careful in
evaluating UFO accounts. This looked like one of the best I had personally encountered, yet it turned out to have an ordinary explanation. Does
this mean that one might also find an explanation for the stories of Joe
Ann Harris, Dean Powell, Thyrena Daniels, and hundreds of others? (The
UFO debunker will shout: "Yes! That is what it means!")

As I drove back from my interview with the hot-air balloon makers,
I had to seriously ask myself this question. I have decided that it does
not mean that all sightings have some "natural" explanation. Although I
am now faced with the precedent of having found an explanation for an
excellent case for which no explanation seemed apparent, it still seems
inconceivable that this could one day happen with all the Uintah Basin
sightings. The objects were too large, too close, too brilliant, too rapid, and
sometimes hummed or buzzed. Certainly they were not all hot-air bags!

But we must be aware that a witness can probably imagine important
details that aren't there—and that two witnesses can even imagine the
same detail—probably when this is mentioned by the first witness before
the second witness has a chance to look, as in the case of Virginia and
Virginia. Their story illustrates the observation that witnesses are good
observers but that they do try to interpret. If the object was a hot-air bag,
the Virginias did an excellent job of describing its light and its movement,
but their interpretation apparently involved conjuring up in the mind's eye
a big black object that wasn't really there (unless the shadow phenomenon
is the explanation).

My friend, Bert G. Drake, who was my graduate student and then
worked at the Smithsonian Radiation Biology Laboratory, called my
attention to another phenomenon in which observers see something that
isn't really there. Every year, dozens of things, animals, and people are shot
at by deer hunters who think they are shooting at deer. In Colorado, a
hunter actually shot two teenagers who were riding motorbikes along a
road! In Idaho, a hunter shot a little girl waiting for a school bus. Bert

tells of a case he heard about when he first went to Colorado in 1958. An experienced local resident was hunting elk. He saw a small herd go into a grove of Aspens. He tethered his horse to a bush and circled the aspen grove. Finally, he came all the way around the grove and shot his saddled horse! So there is no doubt that when a person is properly excited, he can see things that aren't there or misinterpret what is there.

Notes

1. Menzel and Boyd (1963, p. 215) discuss the Barauna photos at length. They imply that the photos might have been a simple double exposure, but this is impossible because the object appears darker than the overcast sky, and a double exposure could only produce a lighter image against the sky (i.e., on the negative, the sky is very dark; any object added to such a dark negative can only make it darker—lighter on the print). Menzel and Boyd claim that only Barauna's friends claimed to see the object, but other sources confirm that there were a large number of witnesses. Menzel and Boyd's claim seems to be based on interviews some months after the event, by which time the Brazilian navy had been pushing the idea that the photos were a hoax (meaning that personnel could have been commanded to deny being witnesses). There are many websites that consider the case; for example, the following is a careful analysis of the photos: http://www.martinshough.com/aerialphenomena/trindade/intermask.htm

2. In a little-reported poll taken in early September, 1996, the Gallup Organization asked 1,000 U.S. adults about their belief in UFOs and life in outer space. The poll indicated that belief in the reality of UFOs remains about where it has been for the last two decades—around 50 percent. Also significant is the finding that 71 percent of those polled believe the U.S. government knows more about UFOs than it has disclosed. Here is a summary of some findings related to the subject of UFOs. The results are based on telephone interviews conducted September 3 through 5, 1996 with 1,000 U.S. adults aged 18 and up. On this basis, Gallup states with 95 percent confidence that the margin of sampling error is ±3 percentage points.

   + Question: Have you heard or read about UFOs?
     Yes: 87 percent — No: 13 percent
   + Question: Have you, yourself, ever seen anything you thought was a UFO?
     Yes: 12 percent — No: 87 percent — No opinion: 1 percent. This number has varied only slightly over the years. In 1990, 14 percent said yes; in 1973, 11 percent said yes.
   + Question: In your opinion, are UFOs something real, or just people's imaginations?
     Real: 48 percent — Imagination: 31 percent — No opinion: 21 percent.
   + Question: Do you think that UFOs have ever visited the earth in some form, or not?

Yes: 45 percent — No: 39 percent — No opinion: 16 percent. This question had not been asked on previous polls. It obviously implies, though it does not specifically state, that "UFO" is equivalent to "extraterrestrial spacecraft." The previous question about the reality of UFOs does not necessarily carry the same implication.

7

The UFOs as
Explorers from Distant Worlds

Are we alone in the universe? Or are there planets orbiting distant suns where proteins and nucleic acids have come into being and cooperated to form cells, tissues, organs, and organisms; where plantlike creatures absorb their luminary's light energy for photosynthesis; and where animal beings consume these organisms to obtain the energy needed for movement—and perhaps for thought, for happiness and misery, love and hate, compassion and aggression? By now, no one much doubts that there has to be other intelligent beings in the universe—just because the universe is so large, and we are here, proving that intelligence can exist! But do the planets of Tau Ceti or Zeta Reticuli or some other cosmic orb support a race of intelligent beings who have learned to travel through the vastness of the galactic expanse? Is it possible they have managed to encapsulate themselves in life-support systems inside shiny spaceships that are propelled by hyper-drives capable of rushing through space with nearly the speed of photons themselves—or faster, perhaps, by some ultraphysics not yet known to us? Have these beings with their marvelous vehicles—and their unthinkable purposes and psychological-sociological-ecological abilities—been entering our atmosphere on many occasions and for many years to be seen only by some of us?

These are the questions that have long sparked the interest, even the consuming passion, of many UFO researchers. These are the things implied by the much simpler question: Are the UFOs extraterrestrial machines controlled by intelligent beings, explorers from distant worlds?

For many decades, many ufologists—and much of the public at large—have answered yes. The nuts-and-bolts, or space-ships-from-other-worlds hypothesis has predominated in the minds of many people. This is the ET hypothesis. Stanton Friedman (2008, 2009), for example, has been a vocal proponent of this idea for several decades (vocal enough to make a living by lecturing on the subject!).

Some musings about the spaceship hypothesis are presented in this chapter—along with some UFO accounts that make it difficult for me to accept the nuts-and-bolts explanations. It is the strangeness that has come to bother me. Some other strange events are presented in the following chapter about the skinwalker ranch. In this and the next chapter I will present these events and then I'll do my speculating in the Epilogue.

To Prove or to Disprove

In principle, it should not be difficult to prove the reality of the UFOs. We only need to catch one and take it to our laboratories for study. But as we've seen, such proof has not been forthcoming—or if it has, we ordinary citizens have not been informed about it. Most of the mainstream scientific comments on UFOs have been aimed at debunking them. Yet a little philosophical reflection will indicate that this approach is doomed to failure. Probably the only really valid way to disprove that the UFOs are extraterrestrial machines would be to *demonstrate* this in each and every UFO sighting. We have seen that in many cases it is possible to prove that a UFO is not an extraterrestrial machine (e.g., it is identified as the planet Venus or a weather balloon), but it is equally apparent that this is not possible in all cases if only because data are incomplete.

The first alternative to proving that all UFOs are not extraterrestrial machines is to prove that most are not, and then to infer that since most are not, probably all are not. It should be quite apparent that this approach is not logically valid. It is an example of induction proper. Remember the white crow: If all the crows we examine are black, we cannot logically conclude that all crows are black, simply because we haven't examined all crows—a white one may yet appear! Proving that 99.9 percent of all UFO cases do not involve extraterrestrial machines still isn't sufficient. Of the millions of sightings, only one needs to involve an extraterrestrial machine to provide us with a point of real interest.

Another problem with applying an inductive or statistical approach to

UFOs is that the cases that are clearly explained might not be representative of all UFO sightings. Clearly, they are not. Just because many witnesses have mistaken the planet Venus for a UFO, we cannot conclude that a saucer-shaped object fifty feet in diameter with windows and landing gear that put down in someone's backyard was really Venus. The important thing about many unexplained sightings is that they have so little in common with those that can be explained—which is why they are unexplained.

The Impossibility Theory

How about proving that UFOs cannot be extraterrestrial machines? This second approach is also full of logical pitfalls, although it is an approach that has often been taken. Obviously, it assumes that we know enough about the operation of the physical universe to say in every case what is possible and what is not. For example, William Markowitz (1967) argued in *Science* that UFOs could not be extraterrestrial since interstellar rockets are impractical. He said that the energy requirements for inter-stellar travel necessitate a rocket of such huge dimensions or with expulsion of material at such high temperatures (85,000 degrees Celsius) that no resemblance to the commonly reported UFOs could be imagined. He described the Apollo Saturn 500-F space vehicle used to launch our moon rockets and went on to calculate the ratio of the initial to the final mass and the time required for various interplanetary and interstellar trips based on known propulsion systems. Then he told of his troubles in finding reliable reports of UFOs landing and taking off, apparently assuming that every UFO takeoff would represent a departure for the home planet; that is, that all UFOs must be interstellar spacecraft. He then pointed out that UFO takeoffs do not resemble a launch from Cape Kennedy. (There actually is some resemblance in Kent Denver's account, #6 in Table 1!) He further mentioned that it would be foolish to expend such efforts on interstellar travel, only to arrive at the new planet and then not make contact with its inhabitants. He dismissed "metaphysics" (i.e., physical laws that we do not understand but that could allow interstellar travel).

This article was so patently naive about UFOs and its arguments so unconvincing, that it is amazing that the article was ever published in *Science*. Philip H. Abelson, the editor of *Science*, was an outspoken opponent of UFOs as extraterrestrial machines. J. Allen Hynek, after eighteen years of UFO investigation, was probably the most competent scientist in the

United States to write on this topic, but Abelson only reluctantly accepted his carefully prepared letter to the editor (Hynek, 1966), suggesting that UFOs might be worthy of scientific study.

By an interesting coincidence, on the very day (October 21, 1969) that I was reworking these pages in the original manuscript, Markowitz was on our campus presenting a Sigma Xi National Lecture entitled, "UFO Mania." He discussed most of the arguments summarized here plus some added approaches. For example, he stated that not only was interstellar travel in reasonable time an impossibility, but UFOs were not worthy of scientific study because alchemists wasted time searching for the philosopher's stone or the elixir of life, and other people have spent time building perpetual motion machines. He then talked at length about how scientists really are open-minded, willing to investigate anything, always motivated by free and open inquiry. Yet at the end of the lecture, he refused to "argue" with anybody (that is, answer any question that intimated a viewpoint opposite to his own), and he stated that he had never personally investigated a UFO sighting, nor would he ever do so (which sounds a trifle like an astronomer who refuses to look through a telescope). He also said he would never believe the extraterrestrial hypothesis until he was personally confronted with an extraterrestrial being. A most interesting, open-minded scientific attitude. Yet this is the approach that convinces many scientists that UFOs have no reality, and that we shouldn't waste our time studying them. In her book, Susan Clancy (2005), the expert on false memories, dismisses UFOs based on the impossibility argument.

Is interstellar travel really impossible? To make such a negative statement (formulate a so-called impotence principle), it would be necessary to provide rather rigorous proof. Remember that it took centuries to demonstrate to everyone's satisfaction that it is impossible to square the circle, trisect an angle with compass and straight edge, or build a perpetual motion machine (in modern context, to break the second law of thermodynamics). Hence it appears a bit presumptuous to make such an all-inclusive negative statement in relation to space travel. After all, our first real step into space was taken less than two decades before Markowitz's talk, and Einstein's relativity, which limits the absolute velocity of any object in the universe to some speed less than that of light, has only been considered by a handful of scientists for a little over a century. (One continues to hear reports of exceptions.)

Anti-gravity devices could account for some UFO behavior, but then they seem fantastic. Yet we don't know what gravity is, so it is somewhat difficult to disprove anti-gravity devices. Much of Markowitz's argument is based on the laws of inertia, but we don't understand the physical basis of inertia; we merely apply empirical equations that describe our experiences. What unknown energy sources could be tapped in the space between the stars? How about the "dark energy" that current cosmologists are so interested in but that wasn't known in 1969? It is a little premature to state the impotence principle that interstellar travel is impossible. We recognize that impotence principles exist, that some things in the universe are impossible. But we should also recognize that at this stage of our development, we have only been able to state a very few such principles with any degree of certainty.

Yet one aspect of the impossibility argument remains impressive: UFOs do appear to do impossible things. Although this is no more logically valid than saying that interstellar travel is impossible, it provides a real stumbling block for the scientist who would investigate UFOs. Numerous impressive examples are provided in the Uintah Basin sightings. Not only do the UFOs hover with no sign of spinning helicopter propellers, but they move in the atmosphere at extreme velocities without a sonic boom and without burning up with frictional heat. They accelerate from a standstill to these velocities in a fraction of a second, even though the forces of acceleration that would be generated would disintegrate any man-made vehicle—and its occupants!

In the March–April 1973 APRO Bulletin, James Harder told of his analysis of an interesting photograph. The witness, Mr. C. Dwight Ghormley, saw a large "tank" about three quarters of a mile from the road near Sedona, Arizona. Because it appeared to be in an inaccessible spot, he decided to stop and photograph it. After snapping the picture, he noticed that the object was gone, leaving nothing but a cloud of smoke or dust behind. The photograph showed only a long, broken streak of light. The owner of the photography shop that developed the film noticed this and brought it to the attention of APRO. Harder assumed that Mr. Ghormley had photographed the object as it took off, in which case the streak of light would represent the distance it traveled while the camera shutter was open—about one sixtieth of a second! Knowing the distances involved, the characteristics of the camera, and so forth, Harder could calculate the speed the object was able to achieve from a standstill. This proved to be around 16,000 miles per hour!

Still, we can't say that it's impossible. We can even imagine how it might be done. All that's required, perhaps, is an understanding and a control of gravity. Forces of acceleration can tear apart our contemporary machines because they are applied to one part of the machine and transferred to the other parts through stresses and strains in the material. The wheels drive an automobile, or the jet engine an airplane, and the forces must be transferred through the strength of the material from the axles to the rest of the automobile, or through the body and wings to the rest of the airplane. The acceleration is transferred to the passenger through the seat. Say that we could apply some kind of artificial gravitational field to a vehicle. If the source of the field were to the front of the vehicle, each individual atom in the vehicle and its occupants would be accelerated equally, and the vehicle would move ahead in such a manner that a passenger inside would not even be aware of being accelerated—as in free fall. If the strong gravitational field should suddenly be reversed so that its source came from behind the vehicle, the vehicle would stop and move off in the reverse direction, again with no stresses or strains in the vehicle and with the passenger not being aware of any acceleration, let alone change of direction. A gravitational field equivalent to that produced by the Earth at its surface would accelerate our vehicle only about thirty two feet per second (the acceleration observed in free fall). But if the gravitational field could be increased to values hundreds of thousands of times that produced by the Earth at its surface, then the reported behavior of UFOs might be accounted for.

There is only one difficulty: We haven't the slightest idea how we could produce such a field, let alone control its direction in relation to a craft. I have wondered about another possibility. Say that the gravitational forces produced by all the matter in the universe are extremely high, but that they come equally from all directions so that the only gravitational force of any real importance to us is that produced by the Earth. If this were the case, then it wouldn't be necessary to produce high gravitational fields, only to shield from them. When the UFO wanted to accelerate in one direction, it would shield out the forces of gravity coming from the opposite direction. Thus the forces coming from the desired direction would be extremely high and would move the vehicle in the manner described above. Of course we also haven't the faintest idea how one might go about shielding from gravitational fields, but intuitively it seems to me that this might be easier than producing them.

Many such speculations—just-suppose stories—have been presented.

For example, Eugene Burt (1970) described diamagnetism, a little known phenomenon that just might be applied in a UFO propulsion system. A much more detailed analysis was published posthumously by the daughter of Paul Hill (1995). Hill worked at NASA for many years and became a sort of an unofficial "clearing house" for UFO reports. NASA was officially not interested in UFOs, that job belonged to the Air Force, but NASA kept getting reports anyway, and these were given to Hill because he became known as a hobby ufologist (much as Junior Hicks became known in the Uintah Basin). Hill eventually collected many of the best reports including well-known cases and others that were less well known. His training in physics was put to good use as he did much mathematical study of certain cases, preparing detailed drawings to go with his calculations. Hill claims that extensions of our current technology would be sufficient to account for UFO propulsion systems. His ideas are based on control of the gravitational field as discussed above. There is one way to test his ideas: build the systems he proposes! This has not been done, at least not to public knowledge, and if it ever is done, it will revolutionize our technology. In the meantime, we must consider Paul Hill's calculations as another example of a just-suppose story, albeit a very carefully devised one, based on current knowledge of physics.

I just purchased (but have not yet read) a similar book that describes a gravity control propulsion system: *UFOs and Anti-Gravity: Piece for a Jig-Saw*, by Leonard G. Cramp (1966 and 1996). My UFO-hunter friend, Elaine Douglass, tells me that Cramp has some ideas that even surpass those of Hill.

Incidently, the UFOs might indeed apply one or more of these postulated propulsion methods, whether the UFOs come either from other solar systems or from other dimensions—or both.

Lack of Formal Contact

An impressive and frequently cited argument against the UFOs as extraterrestrial machines concerns their social behavior. After all, it is said, if we were to achieve interstellar travel and discover another planet supporting intelligent beings, wouldn't we want to land and get acquainted? If the UFOs are driven by explorers from another world, certainly one of the most baffling aspects of the enigma is the lack of formal contact. All right, so there are hundreds of Adamskis, Raëls, and Billy Meiers claiming contact, but why doesn't a UFO land on the White House lawn and send its pilot to the nearest White House policeman to utter in the expected metallic voice: "Take me to your leader!"? Why haven't "they" established an embassy at the United Nations?

With a little effort I can do a pretty good job of talking my way out of this argument. For one thing, it is quite impossible for us to be certain that we can guess the motives of an extraterrestrial intelligence. One can imagine any number of reasons why they might not want to establish formal contact. Perhaps they want to conquer us for our natural resources, in which case there is no reason to be friends—but then why have they observed us for so long? Perhaps we are an ecological experiment, established by them some 6,000 years ago—or millions of years ago as the Raëlians claim. This would at least explain why most witnesses of UFO occupants tell us that they are humanoid in appearance. We might have begun as a colony of outcasts, placed here under primitive conditions to see how long it would be before we developed a technology on our own. Civilization had been in such an advanced state for so many millions of years on the home planet that such an experiment into origins seemed appropriate. This, of course, would account for some religious events. The Mother Civilization might have intervened occasionally in "supernatural" ways, subsequently studying the effects of such interventions.[1]

Stan Friedman (2008) points out over and over in his book that humans have always been engaged in tribal warfare. This would be obvious to any extraterrestrial intelligences observing our planet over any extended interval of time, especially since technology entered the warfare. And if extraterrestrial intelligences watch the same nightly news that I watch, it becomes overwhelmingly apparent that humans also kill each other one at a time or molest weaker individuals; in many ways, it is an evil world. Why should a superior intelligence want to be friends with us as a society? But that intelligence might well contact individuals, even if only to plant false notions in humanity to support the debunkers.

We could multiply these science fiction tales at length, but suffice it to say that the extraterrestrials might simply have their own reasons for not wanting to make formal contact, and that we, in this stage of our development, simply cannot fathom those reasons. Or, as noted above, we might have many suggestions about their purposes but no way to know which of our ideas might be the correct one—if there is only one purpose, and there might be many.

Strangeness

Unfortunately, I am no longer convinced by my clever arguments designed to fortify the idea that the UFOs are visitors from other worlds. True, we can't prove that it is impossible for them to get here, we can't claim to know all the laws of physics, nor can we know how extraterrestrial visitors might act. But the accumulation of stories about the behavior of UFOs and their occupants has taken me away from the nuts-and-bolts hypothesis. The fact of the matter is, the lack of formal contact is only one small aspect of the strange behavior associated with UFOs and their occupants. Jacques Vallée is certainly the best known proponent of the idea that the UFO phenomenon has much in common with the fairy faith and with the angels and demons of many religions. As noted in the Prologue, I was troubled by the strangeness of UFO behavior at the time the first edition of this book was published, and during the next five to six years I gravitated more and more toward explanations based on my own religion. I was also influenced by Vallée's (1969) book, *Passport to Magonia*, which made me aware of the relationship of UFOs to historical legends (although as far as I can remember, I was already uncertain when I read the book; so it was not exactly a turning point). I've just finished reading Vallée's more recent trilogy (1988, 1990, & 1991; republished in 2008): *Dimensions*; *Confrontations*; and *Revelations*. I stand in awe of the research that Vallée has accomplished, very much of it by direct study in the field and by close contact with the witnesses. Most of the research in these books is his own—as it should be. Among many other things, Vallée not only updates his research on medieval legends (*Dimensions*), but he carefully documents cases (*Confrontations*), mostly in Brazil, that involved hostile actions from the UFOs against witnesses—or even bystanders!—sometimes even resulting in death, which is also a part of the medieval legends.

If one is going to be open-minded enough to consider the possibility that UFO witnesses are telling the truth (although somewhat distorted), then one must be prepared to examine the evidence connected with the stories of fairies, angels, and demons. The evidence is clearly similar in both cases, so what do we do about that? We could reject all of the UFO stories along with the fairies, angels, and demons—or we can accept them all together. Vallée has argued that there is logical inconsistency in accepting the one and rejecting the other. It is a hard paradox. (We might get out of it by arguing that the evidence relating to fairies and so forth is not as good as that relating to UFOs.)

Even if we reject the fairies, angels, and demons, we are left with a vast residual of UFO stories that make little sense in terms of our explorers-from-another-solar-system idea. Remember, for example, the story of Antonio Villas Boas, who in 1957 was taken aboard a UFO and seduced by a naked space lady (Chapter 6). Granted, a highly superior intelligence might not survey a new planet in quite the manner that we would at this stage of our civilization, but would any intelligence, anywhere, ever do many of the things that UFOs and their occupants are reported to do? Following are three examples noted in the first edition.[2] They still send chills up my spine when I read them. I've added another story, this one from the Uintah Basin. This last encounter took place in 1968 but only recently came to the attention of Junior Hicks and me. The story has two elements that are completely new to me, although I must admit that there is much UFO literature that I have not read. In Chapter 8, we'll consider some more recent strangeness that occurred on a ranch right in the middle of the Uintah Basin. After reading about these things, you tell me if they sound like expeditions from some planet around Tau Ceti carefully exploring our Earth!

The Creatures at Kelly-Hopkinsville

There are numerous strange reports involving totally alien beings. Some of these reports can be studied in books by Vallée (1962, 1969, 2008 a., b., and c.), Sanderson (1967), Rutkowski (2008), and others. The creatures at Kelly are representative of this class. After a UFO landed at a farm house about halfway between Kelly and Hopkinsville in Kentucky, these small (about 3½ feet tall), silvery creatures, with arms twice as long as their legs and large luminescent eyes, surrounded a house filled with frightened occupants. They seemed to retreat from the bright light but clambered all over the house and nearby trees. The frightened people shot at them, causing them to tumble through the air—but failing to kill them. One shot was point blank through a window screen, where the creature was peering inside. When struck with a bullet, the creatures would gently float to the ground after a tumble or two in the air. They plagued the house for three hours, after which the family got in the car and drove to the sheriff's office. In spite of its strangeness, this is a good story because it was thoroughly investigated immediately following the event, and because several witnesses were involved. The sheriff and others who did the investigating were thoroughly convinced by the condition of the witnesses (as well as by bullet holes in the screens) that what was reported must have actually occurred. Sceptics suggested that the people were drunk or hallucinating but the sheriff denied it. After investigation, one debunker suggested that the people were shooting at monkeys escaped from a nearby zoo; another careful debunker became convinced that the people were shooting at owls—so why didn't anyone find dead monkeys or owls all over the place? Virtually no ufologist likes this case, but we seem to be stuck with it.

The Miracle of Fatima

For details concerning this case, you'll have to consider some of the other literature (e.g., Vallée, 1965, 2008 a.; Walsh, 1947, and many volumes of Catholic literature), but consider the following greatly abbreviated story:

For six months beginning in May of 1917, three children near Fatima, Portugal, claimed to be visited on the thirteenth of each month by an apparition that identified itself as the Virgin Mary. The transparent little blue lady with her hands in an attitude of prayer was seen by Lucia de Santos (age ten), Jacinta (age nine), and Francisco (age seven), but she was heard only by the two girls. She gave them messages quite appropriate to Catholics in the Portugal of 1917. Each time she appeared, a larger crowd of people was on hand, but only the children were able to see her. Finally she said that on October 13, a sign would be given that would convince everybody. It is estimated that some 70,000 people were waiting for the sign, milling around in a muddy field during a light rain storm. Suddenly the clouds parted, the rain stopped, and the "sun" came through the clouds—that is, it flew through the clouds, being not really a fiery ball too brilliant to look at, but rather a flattened disc shining like a pearl. It maneuvered around in the sky for a few minutes while all of the witnesses looked on—including some who were as far away as fifteen miles, having been unable to make the pilgrimage to Fatima itself. Finally, it became a brilliant, blood-red color, not unlike numerous red spheres described in the Uintah Basin. It began to move rapidly toward the crowd below, appearing much larger and more fiery at each instant. The crowd, dried by the heat given off from the object, fell on their knees and cried for mercy, convinced that this was the end of the world. At the last moment, the Fatima sun halted its terrifying descent and retreated back through the clouds from whence it came. It was never seen again.

So, you might say, the case is somewhat bizarre and certainly well witnessed, but it is not greatly unlike hundreds of other fiery-ball UFO stories reported from all over the world. But what about the role of the children? How could they see the lovely apparition (who was indirectly responsible for all the other witnesses being there) when no one else could see her? And why was little Francisco unable to hear the words of the lady from space although he could see her lips move? Most perplexing is why the entire event should occur exactly within the context of the Catholic faith as it existed in Portugal in 1917 (but not in other parts of the world, such as South America, where similar miraculous events have been reported, but in a different context).

The skeptics must confront this event with its tens of thousands of witnesses. Joe Nickell (2009) presents a skeptic's version of the events. Some of his comments are rather convincing: Lucia had a history of creating fantasies to attract the attention of others, and she was clearly the dominant figure among the three children. The three prophecies, called secrets: were the end of World War I, the imminent death of the two youngest children, and a third rambling prophecy not made public until 2000. These were not recorded by Lucia until many years after the first two had come to pass—although it is possible that they were made known verbally before that. In any case, Nickell's analysis makes some sense except for the thousands of people who witnessed the "Fatima sun," some of them kilometers away and thus not being influenced by the mood of the huge crowd. Here, he can only conjure some just-suppose stories. He points out that no other observers in other lands saw the sun dance, but why should that surprise us? We ufologists don't think that the sun danced; it was the huge disc that came through the clouds. In my mind the event remains intriguing and challenging to sanity as well as to science.

Aimé Michel's Report of a Miraculous UFO

I would like to present a story that first came to my attention while I was preparing the final version of the first edition of this book. I decided against including the story at that time, mostly because I had only heard a verbal account and therefore couldn't check the details, but partially also because the story seemed so incredible that I was reluctant to present it. The French ufologist, Aimé Michel (Fig. 7-1), visited me at my home in Logan in the spring of 1972, while on a tour through the United States. I

Fig. 7-1 *Aimé Michel. I took this portrait in the spring of 1972.*

drove him to the airport in Salt Lake City when he left, and during perhaps the last twenty miles of the drive, he told me the story. It made chills go up and down my spine at the time and continued to do so when I read his carefully written accounts in the *Flying Saucer Review*, published in England. (Aimé Michel, 1969, Special Issue No. 3, September, "UFO Percipients," *Flying Saucer Review*; and *Flying Saucer Review*, November–December, 1971, No. 17 (6): 3–9; Vallée, 2008 b., has also interviewed "Dr. X" and his account is the most detailed that I've seen.)

Michel states that this case was the most thoroughly investigated and the best case of any that have come to the attention of French investigators during the previous twenty-five years. The witness was extremely competent, and an analysis of the details he presented brought out factors of the sighting that the witness himself could not have known without the analysis. The witness was a friend of Michel's, and other people were involved in the sighting and subsequent investigation: the witness's son and his wife were involved immediately after the sighting, and a number of other investigators joined a few days later.

I have already mentioned Michel's 1958 book in the preceding pages, since I still consider it to be one of the best written accounts of UFO investigation I have read. On two occasions I visited Michel in Paris and corresponded with him through the 1970s. He is a UFO investigator with a truly scientific approach to the problem—and he also became a friend. With the added testimony of Jacques Vallée, the story must be taken seriously. This is important because the story has elements of strangeness exceeding any serious account I have encountered. Here it is:

The witness holds an important official position in a town in the southeast of France and insists for this reason upon remaining anonymous. He has a doctoral degree in one of the fields of biology. During the Algerian War, he was caught in a mine blast (May 13, 1958), and after several months of recuperation was left with a hemiparesis on the whole of his right side. He could not stand on his right foot unassisted, and he lost much of the use of his right arm, making it nearly impossible for him to play the piano, which he had formerly done very well.

On October 29, 1968, as he was chopping a stump on his property, he slipped causing the stump to strike the front edge of his left tibia, which produced a superficial wound and a broken vein that led to enough swelling to deform the trouser leg and to cause intense pain. In spite of antibiotics and drugs administered to reduce the inflammation, the wound was extremely painful and the swelling extensive. This was his condition on the night of November first just before the sighting.

Sometime before four in the morning of November 2, the doctor's fourteen-month-old child called out, expressing the onomatopoetic sounds by which he designated everything shining—a sort of rho! rho! The doctor arose (though his wife remained asleep), filled the empty feeding bottle, and gave it to the baby. The baby was pointing at the window where periodic flashes of light showed around the edges of the shutters. The doctor, preoccupied with the pain in his leg, paid little attention to this phenomenon. He heard a shutter banging on an upstairs window and, after painfully making his way up the stairs, got his first look at the countryside. It was being illuminated by flashes of pale light about the color and intensity of the full moon. The wind was blowing and a storm was brewing, so he at first thought of lightning, but the flashes were coming at intervals of about a second, in a manner quite atypical of lightning. He could not see the source of the light from that window, so he returned to the kitchen, poured himself half a glass of cold water from the refrigerator (indicating how low his level of excitement remained at this point!), and then made his way onto the terrace. The clock in the kitchen read 3:55 AM.

As he stepped on to the terrace, he finally saw the source of the flashing light: It was coming from two luminous objects hovering at some distance to his right. The objects had the double convex form reported by several Uintah Basin witnesses. The top half was a luminous silvery white, but not as brilliant as the full moon; the bottom half was a deep sunset red, brighter at the top than at the bottom. Two "antennas" extended out horizontally, one from each edge of each object. A third on each object was located at top center and was perfectly vertical. Figure 7-2 shows tracings I made from the doctor's drawings as published in Aimé Michel's *Flying Saucer Review* article.

A vertical, cylindrical, white shaft of light came from the lower center point of each object. It illuminated the thin mist hanging in the valley below his home. As soon as the doctor stepped on to his terrace and noticed the objects, they began to move to the left and toward him. In a moment or two, the points where the two light beams struck the ground could be seen at the top of a small hill. From then on as the objects flashed on and off with their one-second periodicity, illuminating the surrounding countryside (up to a distance of a few kilometers), with the weak white light, the doctor was forming almost photographic images in his memory. Later, when Michel investigated, the doctor could draw the objects on photographs taken from his terrace, indicating at each point in time their size and the positions of the beams of light on the ground directly below. White light also emanated from around the antennas, and the doctor had the impression that these objects were "sucking in the atmospheric electricity and that I could see it entering through the antennas and then exploding between the two

Fig. 7-2 *Tracings of some of the drawings of Dr. X. The objects appeared to move up slightly at first and then from right to left as they approached.*

objects, the whole thing producing one single glow of light." It was this glow that lit up the countryside more than the narrow vertical beams.

The objects continued to make their broad sweep to the left, at the same time approaching each other. As they nearly touched, light seemed to jump between the approaching antennas. It was bright, but not so brilliant that the doctor could not observe it directly (e.g., the way one can observe a fluorescent lamp). When the objects were nearly in front of the house, an amazing thing happened. They continued to come together until they actually touched and then began to interpenetrate each other. This continued for a moment or two until the interpenetration was complete, and only one object, identical in its structure to the previous two was visible.

Such a phenomenon is of course beyond any kind of physics known to us. I have wondered if it might not have been an illusion in which one object moved directly behind the other. The beams of light on the ground had blended together at this point, but this could have been arranged without the objects themselves blending together. The witness feels quite positive that he actually saw them interpenetrate each other. I am personally willing to imagine that one might have gone behind the other with some kind of optical manipulation—a pattern of light on the surface of the front object—so that the interpenetration was only a totally convincing illusion. Or we might fall back on the idea of projected holographic images, which would interpenetrate nicely. Anyway, compared with subsequent events, the interpenetration may not appear quite so strange after all.

Just before the interpenetration, the flashing lights on the antennas ceased, and the countryside became dark again. (The vertical beams of light illuminated it only for a short distance.) After the two objects became one, this object swung closer to the witness. When it was directly in front of his house (on a line at right angles to the face of the house), it began to move directly toward the doctor. As it approached, it appeared to grow in size until it was enormous. At its closest approach, the doctor was able to accurately estimate its size in relation to the houses and trees below. Michel later measured the diameter at about sixty-five meters (about two hundred feet, exclusive of the antennas, which were estimated at about seventeen meters each, equal to the thickness of the object at its center).

At this point, the doctor, who was first astonished and then perplexed, began to experience considerable fear. With the object so close, he was able to observe it in detail. He could see a protrusion on the bottom, from which the beam of light was being emitted. The bottom half had sections, and there was a dark line that appeared to move from the middle toward the bottom, much as interference lines sometimes drift across an old television screen. This phenomenon held him transfixed, so that he was unable to run inside and get his movie or still camera.

The object remained stationary for what seemed like a long interval of time, and then suddenly the doctor noticed the beam of light moving toward him. This was not because the object was moving, but because it began to tip or rotate on an axis through the two protruding antennae, so that the top antenna was moving away from him, and the bottom was tipping up toward him. Finally, the object must have tipped almost ninety degrees, for the light beam illuminated the doctor and presumably all of the front of his house. He instinctively raised his arms to cover his face.

All of a sudden there was a sort of "bang"—the first sound during the entire encounter. Then, according to the witness, the object dematerialized, leaving nothing behind but its cloudy, whitish, fleecy shape, which at once disintegrated and was borne away eastward by the wind. A very luminous, fine, white thread shot out vertically in a fraction of a second toward the sky and vanished there into a small white shining dot, which then vanished with the sound of an explosion like an aerial bomb on the 4th of July.

The doctor experienced considerable shock. He went indoors and noted that it was 4:05 AM. He got a note pad and wrote down the details of his sighting along with sketches (thereby qualifying himself as one of the best UFO witnesses on record). He woke up his wife and told her all that he had seen. Both were deeply moved. Suddenly she cried, "Your leg!" The doctor, who was walking to and fro talking excitedly, had lost his limp. He pulled up his pajama trouser leg, and the wound was healed, both the swelling and the pain completely gone. They did not return. Michel visited five days later and was able to ascertain the facts in relation to the healing of the wound, not only from the doctor and his wife, but from others, including the doctor's physician.

The doctor fell asleep and remained in a sound sleep until two o'clock the following afternoon (his wife awoke at ten that morning). When he awoke, he remembered nothing of his experience until he suffered a fall on the living room stairs, which produced a bump on his head and the full memory of the previous night's events!

For a few days, the doctor experienced further shock, and this produced certain physical symptoms of illness. During this time, he became aware that the symptoms of his Algerian War wound seemed to no longer be with him. Finally, as the symptoms of shock disappeared, it became apparent that this was indeed true. And once again he was able to perform expertly on the piano. On November 8, Michel visited and began his investigation. Various experts were called in to help. On the same day, the doctor began to have cramps and pains in his stomach. On November 17, he felt an itching and pricking around the navel, and a red, cutaneous pigmentation of striated appearance began to develop. This pigmentation formed the shape of a perfect isosceles triangle, seventeen centimeters on the base and fourteen to fifteen centimeters along the sides. The pains, itching and prickling disappeared suddenly, never to return. A psychosomatic explanation was put forth by Michel (who didn't believe it himself) but had to be discarded when the same triangle appeared on the stomach of the witnesses's fourteen-month-old son. The two markings were identical.

There are many more details relating to the investigation and the doctor's life following the sighting. It became apparent to all of their friends that the doctor and his wife had undergone a striking personality change (reported by Michel in his second *Flying Saucer Review* article). The triangular markings disappeared and reappeared on many occasions during the ensuing two years (usually at intervals of about three weeks). On one occasion, Michel was visiting the doctor and jokingly asked about the condition of his stomach. He answered that nothing was there and then pulled up his shirt to demonstrate—exhibiting the triangle, which had reappeared without his knowing it! The next morning, they called the grandparents who were taking care of the child. The grandmother was quite distraught, telling them of the strange marking on the child's stomach. (She had not heard of these events.)

The doctor has had numerous strange experiences—or so he reports. Some of these are telepathic and others resemble poltergeist phenomena. The lights remain on after the switches are turned off, for example, and the doctor reports that he has experienced levitation on a few occasions. Indeed, the things he now reports would certainly tend to discredit him as a witness. This is a phenomenon not atypical in the UFO business. For example, Kenneth Arnold, the man whose reports of the Mt. Rainier sighting got everyone so excited back in 1947, ended up writing totally incredible books about how UFOs are really living organisms. One can't help but think of the discussion a few pages back about how the extraterrestrials might try to discredit themselves by communications through the contactees. Certainly the story here could now be viewed in the same manner. Yet the initial story seemed straightforward to Michel, and there was the business of the healing. As in so many other cases, Michel and others who have investigated the story seem almost compelled to believe it—even though it clearly cannot be proven.

There is an aspect of Michel's story that brings us back to the Uintah Basin sightings. From the moment the doctor stepped on to his terrace, the objects behaved as though each action was directed toward him. Michel's analysis indicated, for example, that after a brief moment or two before their interpenetration, the two objects were at exactly the same distance from the doctor—a situation not readily apparent from the position of the lights on the very broken terrain below the terrace. Of course the doctor's being spotlighted by the beam and the subsequent miracles of healing lead to the same conclusion. It seems clear that the fascinating display with its interpenetration, healing beam, dematerialization, and conclusion with a brilliant bang high in the sky were intended for the doctor's avid consumption.

Were the extraterrestrials demonstrating some kind of fantastic technology in which two objects can occupy the same space at the same time (in different space-time continua?) and disappear by sudden teleportation or time travel to some other universe? Or was it a technology of projected three-dimensional holographs, so that the doctor saw only light images but thought he was seeing material objects? Or was it all somehow projected directly into the doctor's mind? Was the healing some fantastic rearrangement of molecules and cells by an electromagnetic beam? Or was it just another demonstration of the amazing power of the human subconscious mind to heal the body when the mind is suitably stimulated?

These explanations seem utterly far out and difficult to accept, but the idea that the doctor was witnessing scout-ships from another planetary system here on a simple expedition of exploration is certainly much less acceptable. And the same conclusion seems inevitable after an examination of the Uintah Basin sightings. The objects want to be seen in their strange performances by a few witnesses who will probably not be believed. But why?

Russ Perry and Alicia's Pursuing UFO

Shortly before my visit to the Uintah Basin in September, 2009, Junior Hicks received a letter from Russ Perry, who owns Perry Motors in

Fig. 7-3 (A) *Russ Perry with* **(B)** *his green UFO (AlienDave's, actually) on the screen of his laptop computer, which was present during the interview (2009).*

Vernal. Perry told about an experience he had as long ago as 1968. Junior, James Carrion (director of MUFON, who accompanied me on my trip to the Basin), and I drove to Vernal to see Russ. He had told very few people about his experience because they nearly all suggested that he was crazy! But, as he says in one part of our interview, he longed to have someone listen to his story sympathetically without saying he was nuts. Junior, James, and I did just that. We ended up with a long interview, which I have tried to shorten considerably.

We sat in his office, where he had a laptop computer on his desk, with a photo on the screen of a UFO he had found on the Internet (Fig. 7-3). It was triangular, mostly yellow, flat on the bottom, not as tall as it was wide, with a green, blurry border. There were short star trails on the black background. Russ had found it on the website of AlienDave, a Utah UFO hunter. Russ was amazed to see the picture, which was very much like the UFO that chased Russ so long ago. We discussed the photo for a while and then Russ told us what had happened:

> **Russ Perry:** Well, it's not much different from the story I told [in the letter sent to Junior], and it boils down to: I had a date with this gal . . . for the Sweetheart Ball, which means it had to have been very close to Valentine's Day; I'm pretty sure it was 1968, . . . depending on when I graduated, which was '69, but I still think it was '68. . . . This was when all this crazy stuff was going on, and some of it was real, and a lot of it was kids with road flares and garbage bags or dry-cleaner bags with candles. . . . There had been for a couple of years a lot of sightings over by the Ute Hill and along Lapoint Road, and lots and lots of talk. So anyway, it was on everybody's mind. I picked her up and was just kind of driving around wasting time waiting for the dance to start, out west of town, and Alicia seen this light in the sky. It didn't really look any different than Venus; just a big old bright light up there in the sky. She said, "Hey, maybe that's a flying saucer!" I said, "Na, that's a planet or a bright star or something like that." . . . And then I got the bright idea: "Well, okay, yeah, let's go chase flying saucers." You know how you are when you're sixteen years old. So that sounded like a really good idea. We were up about Fifth South out there where the stop light is out there by Kentucky Fried Chicken—one of those roads up there; turned and went up there towards the cemetery.
>
> By the time we got up there by the Ute Hill and the cemetery you could tell that it wasn't a planet; there was something up there. And as you leave town on the Lapoint highway there's a big old yellow hill

[Fig. 7-4], and now they've built some houses on top of there. Anyway, we pulled up to the intersection and took a left turn and headed down towards Lapoint [about 18 miles west and a little south of Vernal], and not very far from there is a place where the Highline Canal goes under the highway and a little road that follows the canal, and there were two or three cars parked there alongside the highway. This thing was hovering up above the yellow hill . . . Let's say the yellow hill might be 500 feet high at the very most, and this thing was about twice as high up, and this side. . . . between the hill and the highway. So we stopped, and we get out, and here's these kids all standing there, and everybody's going, "Wow! Look at that!" It's this triangular thing that looked like that [picture on computer monitor].

We might have been there for two or three minutes or so or maybe longer than that, and all of a sudden this big green light comes down out of the corner of it and just lights up that yellow hill with this eerie weird-looking green beam of light. And we're all going, "What's this?" Lot of hollering and yelling and stuff going on. It left that light on that hillside maybe ten seconds—maybe not that long: five to ten seconds. Then it went out. We're all standing there saying, "Wow, what's going on?" And a couple of minutes later, same story! Lights it up again. Then it would go out, then it would do it again. And it did that maybe half a dozen times. And then it just started moving off to the west.

Then here's old Warren Caldwell; he's in this old beat-up Mustang that barely runs because he'd been working on it in shop class, and he's

Fig. 7-4 *Yellow hill by the road going west from Vernal to Lapoint, Utah (2009).*

got it all messed up. He had a couple of Roosevelt girls with him, and they jumped in the Mustang, and they take off, and here's Randy Poulson and Ted Mecham in this old Willy's Jeep that's good for about forty [mph]. I've got a brand new Pontiac Bonneville, a 428, my mom's new model. You know it was running good! So anyway, I just went around them and kicked it up as fast as it would go, 80 in places, and we were keeping up with it; I was following it! We're going out around like this [drawing map], and it's just making a straight shot towards Lapoint, but you know, I'm pushing that thing as hard as I dared, and keeping up. So, when we got to Lapoint, this thing kind of went out there and hovered over the fields north of Lapoint. . . . We were just sitting there looking at it, you know. By then it would have been about eight o'clock, plenty dark, that time of year. We sat there and looked at it five or ten minutes and got ourselves good and scared and decided, "Well, let's go back to the dance and tell everybody about it." It was more like we both had kind of had as much adventure as we really wanted—time to go back!

So on the way back, we're just driving along. I was not in any big hurry . . . . I was going a lot slower than I was on the way out there. As you get a little bit more than halfway back, you come around a corner—you're coming from the west and you're coming around that corner to the north, and it then makes an S-turn back east again, and as you come around that corner to the east, you go up this big long straight hill. And just as we're coming around those S-turns there, Alicia says to me, "Russ, that's thing's not getting any farther away!" And I says, "What?" And she says, "I think it's following us."

"Yeah, right!" And I turned around like this and looked out the back window, and there it is! I'm going up that big long hill, and I had this bright idea—like you do when you are really smart. I say let's trick 'em! So we get up to the top of the hill, and I put it up in park and turned off the lights. No sooner than I did that—I'm looking out the back window again—and it's just like this thing is coming down out of the sky. But it's not coming straight; it's doing this [zig-zag, falling leaf motion], and it's getting bigger and bigger coming in to the back window. So Alicia starts screaming, and I'd probably guess that I did too, I don't know. "Let's get out of here." I turned back around, and pull it back into drive, and I turned on the lights, and I mashed down on it, and I mean we ought to be rippin' and going. You remember what those big old V8s used to sound like when you opened them up and those carburetors—428 cubes in the four barrel, and it's screaming, and we're not going anywhere. We've got a flying saucer right on our butt, and we're going forty, and it never varied. It didn't matter if I let off the gas or put it clear to the floor or whatever, it never changed from forty—not thirty nine or . . . .

I was in a mass panic by then. And I'm looking to see if it was in first drive, and I thought the brake must be on, but . . . it wasn't. And I'm trying to figure out why this car isn't going any faster than it is. It was really roaring.

I asked Russ about his sense of speed in relation to his surroundings—fence lines.

We're doing forty! I wasn't doing 120 and thinking I was doing 40; this baby was going 40 miles an hour! Just as slow as can be. It was like something was just holding me there! And that engine was going 120. I'm absolutely certain of it. It was really holding us back. [It was an automatic transmission, so that was slipping.] Just like somebody had a cable on the back of me!

Junior: In your estimation, how close did that spacecraft get?

Russ: I'll bet it was like a hundred yards. I don't know. It was not down to the ground level; it was still up above. But a hundred yards, probably—200 maybe?

But then, we come around the corner. That's where it gets really weird. (You read the letter.) So we get to where we could see the yellow hill again, and that sucker is just glowing green all by itself. There is no beam on it. It was the whole hillside just sitting there glowing green. I let off the gas then. I was completely over stimulated by then. And I remember, I'm driving by this thing looking out the window, and I remember saying, "Wow! Look at that! What the hell's going on?" And I just kept driving; it wasn't like I was going to stop. I wasn't hurrying any more either. I'm just cruising along.

When we get back down to the intersection, there's a guy in a truck that pulled up from the road that goes up towards Dry Fork sitting there at the stop sign waiting for me to come by. When I saw him, I gassed it and pulled in there on an angle and just cut him off. Alicia and I both jumped out of the car; it worked like a champ then. . . . We jumped out of the car, and we're both just babbling: "Flying saucer! Green mountain!" You know. I mean we were overloaded. I got him out of his truck to show him the green mountain and stuff, and I say, "It's right up there." At the time there were these big silver-leaf maples or cottonwood trees on the corner there, so we had to kind of walk out into the middle of the intersection, and all this time I'm saying it's this big green . . . and blah, blah, blah. So we walked out there, and I say

"It's right up there," and I point out like that, and it's still there—but it's orange, just as orange as it can be. By then I've really had it! I remember I turned around and looked at him and said: "Well, it was green a minute ago." And this guy is one of those guys that—you know how some guys kind of go through life kind of half steamed. He was one of those guys. He lived right there on the corner. He sat and listened to us for a while. He says: "I live right here on this road, and we've all seen this." He said: "If you tell people, they'll think you're crazy. And I advise you not to tell anybody because they'll think you're crazy." And he just walks back to his truck and drives off to town. And I'm standing there thinking, *Wait a second. There's a flying saucer up there. It's been following me all the way from Lapoint, and you're driving away!*

So there's me and Alicia, out in the middle of the highway again, looking at this orange light. The mountain wasn't green anymore. What the heck happened? I don't even know. But in the amount of time, a minute or maybe two or three, or whatever it was, that when I went past that green mountain, pulled down here, and we walked out there and took a look, it wasn't green anymore. And I just looked at Alicia, and I says: "Let's go back to the dance and tell everybody, even though he told us not to because they are going to think you're crazy." Sure enough. We walk into the dance. It's probably nine o'clock by then, and we start telling all our friends about it, and they jump in their cars, and we all go back out there and it's gone. Then it's, "What you been smoking and drinking? Blah, blah, blah," you know. All of that kind of stuff.

To tell you the truth, it's really refreshing to have somebody come and listen to it because, for all these years, nobody ever believed it, you know? There might be one or two, but for the most part everybody thinks, *Yeah, that's a great story Russ. How did you come up with that one?* And it's like you really, really want someone to believe you, you know? Strange, huh? Now, I don't think any [missing] time went by. I don't think we actually got stopped or anything like that . . . there's lots of questions like, "What was it? Where's it from?" It had to be intelligently operated. And you say, "Did I really see that? Did that really happen? Could I have just imagined all that? Turned Venus into a great big, old fanciful story like that?" And then you go, "Oh, yeah, except there was the green mountain and the forty-mile-an hour thing . . . the guy with the truck." Then the other question was, "What were they doing? Who's doing it?" So what do you think?

James Carrion: That was an interesting time. That whole time frame, '66 to '68, there was a whole lot of activity all over the United

States, where UFOs were chasing cars and cars were chasing UFOs. There was a famous case in Ohio where deputy sheriffs chased a UFO over eighty-something miles.

FBS: So that puts you right in line with a lot of other people. A big UFO followed Thyrena Daniels from Vernal to Roosevelt. That was one year before. We have other cases of car-following.

Junior: It's still going on.

FBS: You're a good storyteller. I thank you for that interview.

Russ: You're welcome, Frank! I know that we have incredible technology in our Air Force, but I don't think we have that kind of technology. [Russ went on to speculate about future space travel and what he should have done that night. All of which is typical of so many witnesses.]

James: What about Alicia?

Russ: She married a guy about twice our age, moved to Kansas City or something like that. About 15 years later she came in here for an oil change. First thing we did, we looked at each other and we both said: "We really saw that, didn't we?" That was it! There wasn't much to say, and I have no idea what became of her since. . . . Ted Mecham died. Warren Caldwell died. I never did know the girls who were in the car with him. Randy Poulson lives in Rock Springs, and I haven't seen him since high school either. We did talk with the others for a while after the event. Then it all kind of went away.

We talked for quite awhile, although we drifted away from Russ's experience with the pursuing UFO and the green mountain. Russ was well versed in UFO lore; he had clearly read a number of books about the topic—including *The Utah UFO Display*. He had been impressed by the Leland Mecham/Dee Hullinger case in which a huge object hovered over a desolate area over a mile away, shining some kind of light to the ground, which caused red dust to boil up halfway to the UFO. Come to think of it, to illustrate strangeness, that case and several others recounted in Chapter 1 might well have been saved for this chapter. The truncated red beam of light that shows up in several of Junior's cases is another example. Tony Zufelt's "train windows" are certainly strange. Dick Hackford's "automatic shift" blows the mind if his recall can be trusted. The Ouija board announcement to the children of the Clyde McDonald family must take the phenomenon out of the realm of explorers visiting us from other worlds.

Now let's see about the strange goings-on at the skinwalker ranch, right in the heart of the Uintah Basin.

Notes

1. In the 1960s and 1970s, the most vocal proponent of the idea that ancient man was visited by extraterrestrials was Eric von Däniken (1972). His first book, *Chariots of the Gods?: Unsolved Mysteries of the Past*, was published several years ago, but a TV special titled *In Search of Ancient Astronauts* was shown several times during 1973; and a movie *Chariots of the Gods* premiered in neighborhood theaters beginning in March 1974. His thesis was that ancient engineering works such as the pyramids, the stone heads on Easter Island, "landing strips" in South America, and so forth, testify that early man was visited by extraterrestrial astronauts who provided the technology to accomplish these works—and may also have given primitive man his foundations for a belief in deity. Early peoples might have thought their visitors were angels or gods. Van Däniken has been roundly criticized by many archeologists, and his books are loaded with pseudoscience and wild speculations. Yet the idea that ancient man was visited by residents of other worlds is interesting and worthy of study. (In Chapter 4, we briefly outlined the Raëlian movement, which also claims that ancient astronauts from other worlds guided evolution and eventually the development of civilization on our planet—as well as accounting for modern religions.)

2. The first three stories are documented in much more detail in Vallée's trilogy (2008), and Wikipedia has long articles on each of them.

8

The Skinwalker Ranch

In June of 1996, a story appeared in the *Deseret News*, Salt Lake City's second largest newspaper. This told about unusual UFO and other paranormal activities that were going on at a 480-acre ranch about four miles south and west of Fort Duchesne in the Uintah Basin. According to the article, Tom and Ellen Gorman bought the ranch in the spring of 1994. The Gormans, who left a ranch in New Mexico, were caught up in the beauty of the ranch, although it was run down and needed much work. The property had been empty for almost seven years. "The elderly previous owners had virtually abandoned it. The owners were a prosperous family who now resided in Salt Lake City, and they visited their property a couple of times a year . . . . The previous owners had bought the property in the 1950s but now seemed glad to unload it." The Gormans were surprised by deadbolt locks both inside and outside of the doors. Even the windows were bolted. There were huge metal rings at both ends of the house, where large dogs had been chained. There was a strange clause in the real-estate contract that there was to be no digging on the ranch without notification of the previous owners. That seemed to be "a meaningless clause crafted by elderly eccentrics." As should be evident if you've been reading this book up to here, there have been UFOs and other strange events going on in the Uintah Basin for many years, but "the greatest concentration of high strangeness has always taken place at what became the Gormans' 480-acre ranch." This family was soon caught up in all this UFO activity on the ranch, and the stresses became so severe that they finally "decided to go public in 1996. Gorman reported some of the details to reporter Zack Van Eyck of the *Deseret News*." By then, the Gormans were eager to sell the ranch and get out.

Who wouldn't be? The Gorman's experiences included strange beings such as a huge wolf that mangled a calf's head and whose tracks stopped abruptly in soft ground; a running cow whose tracks also ended abruptly, this time in snow; a huge black object that hovered over the ranch; orange structures in the western sky through which objects seemed to pass into some world beyond the sky; mutilations of several very expensive cattle; and a blue orb that apparently incinerated three prize dogs that chased it into the woods. The dogs were the final straw.

Robert Bigelow, a Las Vegas millionaire, got wind of these unearthly things. Bigelow had been interested in UFOs since he was young and had set up an organization to study the phenomena: The National Institute for Discovery Science (NIDS). He was able to fund serious study of UFOs and related manifestations. Bigelow bought the ranch in August, 1996, and NIDS moved in to set up instrumentation and begin serious study. Shortly after Bigelow bought the ranch, Gorman was hired to take care of it, although he lived some 25 miles away.

The NIDS team saw moving lights that qualified as UFOs, and they experienced some strange events such as the wiring of three surveillance cameras being mysteriously ripped out. Even after Bigelow bought the ranch, however, the really strange events were experienced only by Tom and sometimes his wife. For example, within about 40 minutes, a calf was horribly mutilated. Then, while the Gormans were not far away, four huge, prize bulls were somehow transferred to a small trailer, and a huge, red beast chased horses in a corral and then disappeared into thin air as Tom watched!

The above is a very brief summary from *The Hunt for the Skinwalker: Science Confronts the Unexplained at a Remote Ranch in Utah*, by Colm A. Kelleher, Ph.D., and George Knapp, published in 2005. Kelleher was (and is) the leader of the NIDS group that studied the strange activity on the ranch. The book has been very successful and is known to most UFO buffs, especially in Utah.

The Challenge to Science and to Sanity

Kelleher's and Knapp's book is very important to the Uintah Basin UFO situation for at least two reasons, which we can consider as questions:

1. Is the skinwalker ranch (as everyone now calls it) really the center of UFO activity in the Uintah Basin, and has this been true for at least the last six or seven decades or perhaps even back to Native American times? This is important, because it is important to ask if such an area as the Uintah Basin can have a "center of UFO activity." Furthermore, the practical result of this idea being accepted by the UFO community—which it certainly is, in Utah, at least—is that people think they can go to the ranch or nearby, especially at night, and watch the UFOs flit around above the ranch! I've met people who have driven out to the ranch after dark from the Salt Lake City area (about a 2.5-hour drive), keeping watch until morning.[1] Having never seen a really good UFO myself, it would be nice if I could go somewhere to see a UFO that is guaranteed to be there! Is the skinwalker ranch such a place?

2. Does the UFO phenomenon in the Uintah Basin include what are called paranormal events such as the strange beasts, poltergeist phenomena, and wormhole passages into other "dimensions" or distant worlds? We've noted that virtually all of the UFO experiences that Junior Hicks collected and that we've presented in this book come close to fitting the ET hypothesis. They match the science-fiction ideas of space ships that have traveled here from other worlds: advanced craft with futuristic shapes like double convex, convex planer, or huge balls able to shine red all over. However, it should be clear from this book that I'm highly suspicious of a simple ET hypothesis.

The *Skinwalker* stories introduce a whole new element into Uintah Basin sightings. Strange animals (skinwalkers), spectacular mutilations, poltergeist events, flying orbs able to taunt dogs and then destroy them (so much for the friendly space visitors), and beasts that vanish into thin air, just don't sound like your Black Eagles Space Patrol from Zeta Reticuli.

As if extraterrestrial intelligences coming from afar aren't a big enough challenge to science, how can science handle the poltergeists, portals, and solid objects and creatures that disappear into the void? So far, science has met the challenge only by suggesting that all such things must be products of twisted minds because they are simply "impossible." Most scientists say the fact that over half the population takes them seriously only shows how stupid the public can be. Come on, science—you can do better than that! Start considering the possibility that the universe isn't as cut-and-dried as you thought it was. You may not understand it now, but you never will if you refuse to examine the phenomenon.

I don't really think that those who take such witnesses' accounts seriously have lost their sanity, but in a figurative way, I ask myself if I am crazy for thinking that the universe might be as strange as the *Skinwalker* stories imply.

I think all of this is important. Much as it pains the skeptics, these events deserve an honest and open consideration, not just a preconceived debunking, based on very little evidence. Presumably, you have been considering the "ordinary" Basin accounts and interviews we have been presenting, as well as the "typical" classic accounts. (Of course, Kelly/Hopkinsville, Villas Boas, and Dr. X—none of which took place in the Uintah Basin—are far from typical.) Even Russ Perry's strange story of speed control can be thought of as an ET event. Now it is time to look at the markedly stranger things presented in *Skinwalker*.

Five Sources to Evaluate Skinwalker

Except for some stories Junior Hicks picked up during the 1990s, until recently all I had to go on about the ranch was the book, *Hunt for the Skinwalker*. But because of the importance of what it says, we must ask how close it comes to matching the facts—how accurately it portrays the events. I've now had the opportunity to talk with some of the original sources—to see what it might be like to be an investigative reporter! There were five of these sources:

1. The *Deseret News* articles by Zack Van Eyck. There were follow-up articles, the first one telling about Bigelow's purchase of the ranch. These articles contain interesting material, and many of the stories that Van Eyck presents about the ranch are also in *Skinwalker*. (There are also internet stories that I'll ignore here.)

2. *Hunt for the Skinwalker*. In addition to the summary that begins

this chapter, we'll have frequent occasion to refer to this book.

3. Contact with Garth Myers, brother of Kenneth Myers who lived with his wife Edith on the ranch for almost sixty years; Garth negotiated the sale of the ranch to the Gormans. Garth was close to his brother and his sister-in-law, and as executor of Kenneth and Edith's estate after they passed away, he is well acquainted with the history of the ranch.

4. Extended discussions with "Tom Gorman," as he is known in *Skinwalker*. Most of the stories in the book are about the Gormans, the pseudonym used by Keller and Knapp in *Skinwalker*. Although their real name is well known throughout the Basin and by virtually all UFO buffs who are interested in the ranch, the Gormans prefer to remain anonymous in this book, and I will respect their wishes. Hence, at this point, I'm going to drop the name Gorman and refer to those who lived on the ranch during the period discussed in *Skinwalker* simply as "the witnesses." It is important to remember that the first half and the main theme of *Skinwalker* is their story and not that of Kelleher and Knapp. Furthermore, the witness told me that he knew nothing about the book until it appeared in print! That is an important point to keep in mind. It is also important to realize that, when their stories came out (first in the *Deseret News*), they were subject to much pressure, sometimes more direct than just ridicule (as Junior Hicks testifies). They finally decided to leave the area. Hence, I can understand why they do not want their names used in this book. The witness also understands why I must tell his story if I'm going to consider UFO phenomena in the Uintah Basin of Utah, but the version in this chapter must be based mostly on *Skinwalker*. It is important to note that Van Eyck's articles support the skinwalker stories, although they were reported before NIDS took over the ranch.

5. Accounts from Junior Hicks and some neighbors to the ranch. Two neighbor accounts are presented at the end of this chapter. We have their permission to use their interviews (which they have read) and their real names. My collaborator, Junior Hicks, has been visiting the ranch virtually from the time the witness family bought it, and he is thus able to confirm that he heard most of the accounts shortly after the events happened.

Garth Myers' Version of the History

By an amazing coincidence, I found myself in contact with Garth Myers.[2] It turned out that Myers lived only a few blocks from my home, and after talking with him on the phone, I recorded my first interview with him on September 3, 2009. In our first telephone conversation, Myers cleared up a few things and told me the location of the ranch. After the interview, there were follow-up visits as we got to know each other. Here is a summary of the ranch's history from our interviews.

Garth's brother and sister-in-law, Kenneth John Myers and Edith Childs, had purchased the ranch around 1933 (not in the 1950s). Garth, who was eighty-eight-years old at the time of my interview, was much younger than his brother; he had actually worked on the ranch for three summers as a teenager. Kenneth and Edith began with about 160 acres and accumulated other parcels until they had formed the 480-acre ranch, living in quite primitive conditions at first but improving things through the years. They had one child who died in infancy before they moved to the ranch. There were no other children. Kenneth died in 1987 at age eighty-six, but his widow continued to live on the ranch for five years, until she was taken to a rest home. For two years the ranch was vacant but always leased out to other ranchers to farm and run cattle, even before Kenneth died. Then when Edith died on March 3, 1994, the ranch reverted to Garth Myers and his sisters, Helen M. Baxter and LaPriel Poulson. Less than three months later, Garth, as executor of the Kenneth and Edith Myers estate, negotiated sale of the ranch to the witness family. But after nearly two years, they ran into difficulties, losing several prize cattle, as recorded in *Skinwalker*. (This was when Junior Hicks first visited the ranch, witnessing some of the cattle mutilations and other phenomena; Junior had not visited the ranch when it belonged to the Myers.) But by then the UFO rumors were circulating wildly, especially after the two articles about the ranch in the *Deseret News*. Along came Bob Bigelow and the ranch was sold to him.

What about the important statement that "the greatest concentration of high strangeness has always taken place at what became the [skinwalker] 480-acre ranch"? Garth Myers vigorously denies it! Here are the important parts of the interview that I recorded:

> **Garth:** I can tell you right off that my brother died in April of 1987. My sister-in-law lived alone there until about 1992. She died in March 1994. And I can tell you unequivocally that up to 1992 there had never been and there never were any signs of that [UFO and similar activity].

Now, the ranch was vacant for about two years after she [entered a rest home]. I went to it occasionally just to check the house. Then we sold it to [the witness] about six months after she died [actually, about three months]. I don't know what happened while it was vacant, but I don't think anything went on. There was nothing, unequivocally, absolutely nothing, that went on while she and my brother lived there. She lived there alone from 1987 to 1992, five years. And part of the time she had a dog. Before my former brother died; he had a dog that got caught in a trap and had one hind leg partially amputated. He lived for about three years, and then she was alone without a dog. . . .

FBS: I think that they make a statement in the book that things had been going on since way back to the Indians, and so on.

Garth: See, this is [the witness]. That's the story he made. But it's not the right story!

FBS: That's why I'm here to talk to you, because you are somebody who knows.

Garth: . . . The next thing I knew I get this information that there were UFOs, and he was scared to death, and then this man in Las Vegas phoned in and was going to buy it. . . .

All I know is, about a month or six weeks after he bought it, Bigelow called me on the phone and wondered why we hadn't told anybody about the UFOs. I told him they didn't get there until [the witness] got there, and he said "UFOs were coming there and you had dogs keeping the people away." And I said all they had at most were two dogs, and the last time my sister-in-law lived there five years with a three-legged dog and part of the time with no dog at all, and there were no UFOs. And he said "Oh, you're not telling me the truth." I said, "If you don't believe it, I guess we don't need to talk any more," and that was about it. So, after about six months I got another call from somebody, and they kind of told the same story. The last caller was maybe five or six years ago—don't know who. He said he wanted to have lunch with me. I said "On one condition: That you'll show me the ranch." He said: "Can't do it." I said: "Okay, I guess no lunch." That's the last I've heard. You probably have the articles in the *Deseret News*.

At this point, I told him about my scientific interest in UFOs, that I was a professor emeritus at Utah State University, and a bit more of my history. I told him that I don't "believe" in UFOs; I investigate UFOs. I told him that I was working on *The Utah UFO Display*, originally published in 1974. I said, "I must have a chapter on the ranch, so that makes this interview very valuable to me, because I can say there is another side to it that isn't known."

Garth replied, "My brother had 480 acres, if I remember. My brother bought that ranch in about 1933. Just a little house, an outdoor privy, and no water, electricity, telephone. They had to haul water from Fort Duchesne. They were essentially hermits. They only established relationships with two people in Randlett, but other than that, they had no communication with their neighbors. Hard worker, honest, hard man to work for. I worked for him awhile."

Garth Myers practiced with his M.D. in pediatric neurology. He spent much of his career at the LDS Primary Children's Hospital but also worked for the State Department of Health. In his discussions with me, it became clear that, like most educated people with a scientific background (and no real knowledge of the extent and evidence of the UFO accounts), Garth simply rejects any idea that there might be some reality to the UFO phenomenon. I told him a few Uintah Basin stories, but he said: "That's fine. As long as you know they are just stories!" This being the case, in all honesty we must consider the possibility that Kenneth and Edith Myers were experiencing UFO visits on their ranch, but knowing that their brother was such a skeptic, they decided not to share this information with him. Remember, however, that he was there himself (as a teenager) for three summers without seeing any UFOs. Yes, that was long ago, but the *Skinwalker* statement says the UFO activity goes back even to the time of the Native Americans.

In a telephone conversation on September 5, 2009 (sadly, not recorded!), I asked him if it were possible that his brother and sister-in-law didn't tell him about UFO activity they were experiencing. This he vehemently denied. He said he was very close to his brother (in spite of the age difference), knowing every detail of their lives. After his brother died, he kept in very close touch with his sister-in-law—many visits and close emotional ties as he worried about her living there alone. He feels totally confident that his brother and sister-in-law would have told him about any strange activity, especially under the circumstances. Nevertheless, the point is so important that we'll return to it several times in this chapter. Did the Myers couple have a secret life that was not known even to their brother? There are those who keep making that suggestion.

Later, I called Garth Myers from the Uintah Basin to ask him a few more questions.

First is the matter of locks inside and outside the house when the witness bought it. Garth has said that this simply was not true. When he visited the ranch, it took one key to enter the home, and if that key didn't work, a sharp kick on the door would let him in! There was no profusion of locks. (The witness, however, told me that there were small sliding locks on cupboards inside.)

Second is the matter of no digging being allowed on the ranch. That rumor might have been fortified by Charles Winn, who said he was digging something for Kenneth Myers with his backhoe when Kenneth told him for sure not to dig in a certain area. That doesn't sound very sinister. If I owned a ranch, I might not want someone with a backhoe to dig in certain places. So what? Garth said that the only stipulation in the real estate contract was that the previous owners retained the oil rights to the property! Since oil has become important in the Basin, such a stipulation is common when a ranch is sold. So the real-estate contract stipulated that if the new owners dug for oil, they must notify the previous owners. Does this sound like "a meaningless clause crafted by elderly eccentrics"?

Further, as noted in my interview with Garth, he denied that his brother had ever used large guard dogs. The widow Edith had only the one three-legged dog, and he died a couple of years before Edith left the ranch for the rest home. And what about the following statement in *Skinwalker* with its ominous implication?: "The previous owners had bought the property in the 1950s but now seemed glad to unload it." Does it sound ominous that an elderly brother and his two sisters might like to unload a ranch that they had no way of keeping up? When the witness wanted to buy the ranch, it offered Garth and his sisters a chance to settle Kenneth and Edith's estate.

But doubts persisted, so as the three of us—Junior, James Carrion, and I—made our Uintah Basin visits, we considered the question over and over, discussing it among ourselves and with many of those whom we interviewed: Was the Myers ranch plagued with UFO activity for over half a century while the Myers established their ranch? Junior had only one story to support this: He seemed to remember that a clerk at a drugstore told him that Edith Myers had UFO stories to tell. But that is very tenuous evidence. Memories long after the fact, especially of such trivialities as a brief conversation while counting out the change, tend to be distorted— and perhaps influenced by the extensive publicity that followed the *Deseret News* articles and then publication of *Skinwalker*.

We had a long conversation with John Garcia (called Mr. Gonzalez in *Skinwalker*), whose ranch adjoined the Myers/(*Skinwalker*) ranch on the east, and with Charles Winn, whose ranch adjoined it on the northwest. Each rancher had some wonderful UFO stories to tell, as I'll relate at the end of this chapter, but again and again we asked if this activity occurred while the Myers were living on the property. Time and again they would search back in their memories and come up blank as to activity on the ranch before the Myers left. Garcia's account, the one related below, did go back to the Myers' time, but he didn't think the Myers were aware of his sighting. Except for Garcia's account and various cattle mutilations, most of the Garcia and Winn stories were generated by experiences after Robert Bigelow bought the ranch. The cattle mutilations were confirmed by Pete Pickup, who had been a deputy sheriff and a tribal policeman starting during the Myers' occupancy. He had investigated at least a dozen cattle mutilations at various ranches, going back to the 1970s, and he was employed by NIDS and Bob Bigelow, but he could not confirm UFO activity prior to the witness's purchase of the ranch.

So according to Garth Myers, and there certainly is good reason to think that he should know the basic facts about the history of the ranch, and with the backing of Junior's memory plus the comments of John Garcia and Charles Winn, the *Skinwalker* version of the ranch's history is badly distorted.[3]

Examining the Skinwalker Ranch History

Let's revisit and correct the *Skinwalker* version of the ranch history: The ranch was not empty and virtually abandoned for seven years; Edith Myers was living there for the first five of those years, and other ranchers were working the property from before Kenneth Myers died until the ranch was sold to the witnesses. Surely, the ranch needed work, but it was never abandoned. The elderly owners of the ranch did reside in Salt Lake City at the time the ranch was sold, but those owners were Garth Myers and his sisters—not the couple who had lived on the ranch for almost sixty years (since 1933—not just since the 1950s). Obviously, the owners wanted to sell the ranch—not because of UFO activity (which they didn't accept anyway)—but because they wanted to liquidate their inherited estate. Although there were dogs on the property at one point, Garth denies there were large guard dogs. Garth also denies that the house had multiple, large door locks. And the strange no-digging clause turned out not to be so strange and meaningless: It was a commonly used clause to protect oil rights.

From the standpoint of the history of UFOs in the Uintah Basin, the key sentence in *Skinwalker* is "the greatest concentration of high strangeness has always taken place at what became the Gormans 480-acre ranch." The truth of that statement constitutes our first question, at the beginning of this section. The ranch as a center of UFO activity is certainly contrary to Garth Myers' knowledge. Could Kenneth and Edith Myers have kept such "high strangeness" from their brother Garth for nearly sixty years? He certainly doesn't think so—and remember that he even worked three summers there as a teenager without seeing any UFOs.

At this point, then, our (necessarily tentative) answer to the first question is no, the skinwalker ranch has not always been the center of UFO activity in the Uintah Basin. The answer is only tentative because we cannot enter the minds of the long departed Kenneth and Edith Myers, but the evidence certainly suggests that with all the UFO activity going on in the Basin for over half a century, there is no reason to think that it was centered on the Myers' ranch.

Nevertheless, a debunker like the late Philip Klass would pounce on the discrepancies between *Skinwalker* and Garth Myers to discredit all the other stories in *Skinwalker*. But there is more to this tale, and I'm not ready to discredit the stories.

The Witness's Version of His Skinwalker Experiences

For the most part, the principal witnesses who experienced the most spectacular events related in *Skinwalker* are the rancher (Gorman), his wife, and their two children. (As noted, the NIDS investigators do have some accounts of their own.) When I first read *Skinwalker*, I found the stories to be very exciting, and I assumed that the authors had interviewed the witnesses extensively to get the stories right. Although the book is written in the first person with Colm Kelleher as the speaker, rumor has it that George Knapp (a television journalist) did much of the actual writing, so I assumed that Knapp had many in-depth interviews with the witness while writing the book. Clearly, the original information about their experiences had to come from the family itself, so it was easy to assume that the history in *Skinwalker* with its discrepancies also came from the family and that they must have embellished it a great deal.

The more that I thought about it, the clearer it became that I could

not write this chapter based only on the skinwalker book with its historical problems. The really spectacular stories were those of the witnesses,
not Kelleher and Knapp, and here I was, telling the story of the witnesses'
experiences based only on Kelleher and Knapp's version. If there were
historical errors, as Garth Myers insists, the reported experiences might
also have distortions. Did the witnesses make up the stories to interest
Robert Bigelow so they could sell the ranch? Since Garth Myers rejects the
whole UFO business out of hand to begin with, he strongly implied that
he thought that is probably what happened—but I have a different take on
Uintah Basin UFOs.

There was only one thing to do: contact the witness. But how? He
and his family had experienced much harassment because of their stories,
and for that and other reasons they had left the Basin for parts unknown.
I wanted to talk with him but I didn't know how to go about it. Then my
friend Ted Bonnitt came up with a forwarding address! In late November
I wrote a letter to the witness, hoping the address was valid, telling him
about my contacts with Garth Myers and my growing doubts about various aspects of *Skinwalker*. I gave him my phone number, and on December
3, 2009, he called! We had a long conversation and planned to meet face-
to-face as soon as could be arranged. There were other long phone conversations, but to an extent they emphasized the witness's reluctance to be
involved with this book in any way.

A couple of significant facts came out of our phone conversations,
however: As noted, the witness didn't even know a book was being written
about his family's experiences until *Skinwalker* was published! And he had
never met George Knapp, although they had talked on the phone (but not
about the book). How's that for careful research! Apparently, the authors
thought that their memories plus notes and log entries of the stories were
sufficient. The witness emphatically did not think so! He said that many
things in their book only resembled a true accounting of his experiences.[4]

The witness basically supports Garth Myers' version of the history of
the ranch. So where did the exaggerated version—the ranch as center of
UFO activity—come from? This was a version that Bigelow learned early,
as indicated by his calling Garth Myers a liar when Garth would not confirm it. Although I have some suspicions, I don't know where the embellished story originally came from. (I'm assured that it did not come from
Zack Van Eyck, the *Deseret News* reporter.)

The activity seemed to begin when the witnesses moved onto the ranch. Hence, the challenge to science begs the question: Are the reports of the strange happenings on the skinwalker ranch close to what actually took place? Thank goodness we have the witness himself to comment on this question. In my conversations with him, I became convinced that the events did take place—even if the *Skinwalker* details are not always correct. As to their validity, these experiences are in the same category as other Basin stories told by witnesses—but the ranch accounts tend to be much more bizarre than anything else reported in the Basin. The witness is very reluctant to comment on anything in this chapter, however, so except for a couple of points, the stories that follow are condensed from *Skinwalker* and not from accounts given by the witness to me.

As to the basic validity of the events, I am also confirmed in my thinking that they did occur because of my collaborator Junior Hick's involvement. He met the witness shortly after the family moved onto the ranch, and Junior was told about some strange experiences. Indeed, as we'll note, Junior was shown the evidence of some of the things that had occurred. In September of 1997 and by another surprising coincidence, I encountered Junior in Columbus, Ohio, where he was visiting a daughter and where Mary and I were serving an LDS mission. Junior spent an hour or two telling us about the ranch activity. Having left the UFO field at that point, I was only mildly interested, but I vaguely remember that Junior related many of the events described below. (For some reason, I especially remember the orbs.) This meeting with Junior was during NIDS's active involvement at the ranch, which began in August 1996. But remember that Van Eyck's record of the events was published before NIDS's involvement.

And what about the Native American stories? Junior has heard many Native American stories, and much of the area around the ranch is Native American Reservation. But the stories Junior has heard do not apply to most of the ranch—although he tells me that the ridge that forms the north boundary of the ranch does hold special significance for Native Americans. They refuse to go there.

Parcels of private land are situated in various locations on the Reservation, and there are certainly many Native Americans living not far away from the ranch, who have related UFO stories to Junior and to me—as we saw in Chapter 1.

As to the uniqueness of the *Skinwalker Ranch* events, the witness says he has heard similar bizarre stories from other people in the Basin. Remember that the accounts so far in this book are based almost entirely on the files of Junior Hicks, and there is no way to be sure that witnesses of more paranormal events simply did not pass their stories on to Junior—until the present, that is. Junior now has some skinwalker stories. The importance of the ranch witness's testimony is that it is known and published (in however an imperfect form). So it becomes necessary for us to integrate the strange events into our thinking about the phenomenon as it manifested itself in the Uintah Basin. Let's take a little closer look at some of the strange occurrences on the *Skinwalker Ranch* as presented in *Hunt for the Skinwalker*.

Skinwalkers and the "Wolf"

Speaking of Native Americans, the skinwalker title is based on Native American legends that are shared by most tribes. Let's take a brief look at these legends (partially based on *Skinwalker* and partially based on Wikipedia, which also has articles on the ranch):

Native American tribes of the Southwest have their various versions of the skinwalker legend, but in all those cultures, the skinwalker is a being of pure evil, a witch (usually male) who can take on the appearance of any animal, and with the appearance (the "skin"), also the attributes of that species but intensified. A skinwalker wolf, for example, can run as fast as an automobile—but upright on its hind legs! Skinwalkers are capable of mind control. As a skinwalker, the Native American witch reaches the highest pinnacle he can achieve, gaining these supernatural powers. In view of the UFO phenomenon, it seems that a skinwalker could also be an extraterrestrial entity, but that's not part of the Native American legend, which says that skinwalkers are humans who take on supernatural abilities. With all their reported capabilities, however, it seems to me that alien visitors could take on the attributes of skinwalkers. How could you tell who was human and who was alien? So I'll refer to the strange beasts as skinwalkers, even though they could be of alien or extraterrestrial origin.

Junior Hicks has about a dozen recent stories of skinwalkers seen by Caucasians in the Basin. One story tells of a wolf walking across a road, along a fence, and back—all the way upright on its hind legs! Unfortunately, when I visited the Basin in September 2009, Junior could not arrange interviews with his skinwalker witnesses.

Colm Kelleher and/or George Knapp are excellent writers. Knapp is a Las Vegas TV personality with much writing experience, and Kelleher has also written at least one best seller, *Brain Trust*. His PhD from the University of Dublin at Trinity College was in biochemistry. Perhaps their literary backgrounds help explain why *Skinwalker* is such a page-turner. Their first chapter, about what seems to me to be an "alien skinwalker," is absolutely riveting. It is presented as the first strange experience of the family after moving onto the ranch—and yes, I must conclude that the story reads so well because the authors inserted details such as what was said, each little action, and the emotions experienced by the family, things that could only be guessed long after the fact. And the family was not consulted! Such artistic license, however, surely makes for exciting reading!

The story is strange indeed. The witness family, including the two children and the witness's father, saw this huge animal approaching from a distance. It looked like a wolf, but it was much too big—at least three times the size of a normal wolf. The animal came right up to the family, where they petted it and were entranced. Suddenly, the wolf darted to the corral where a calf had its head and neck through the bars. The beast clamped the calf's head in its jaws and tried to pull it through the bars. The witness and his father kicked and beat on the animal with no effect. Finally, a powerful handgun was retrieved from the truck, and the witness put a bullet into the wolf's chest—still with absolutely no effect! No blood, no apparent discomfort! The witness pumped two more slugs into the animal, and it finally released the calf—but stood a few feet away, quite unconcerned. The witness's son ran to the homestead and brought back a thirty-aught-six rifle. After two shots with the wolf about forty feet away, a chunk of flesh fell out of the shoulder where the bullet exited. The witness and his son chased the wolf, first into a grove of cottonwoods and then russian olives. A recent rain had made the ground soft, and the wolf's tracks were easily visible—until, about sixty yards away from the river, the tracks simply stopped. There was no sign of the wolf, which had apparently disappeared into thin air. The wounded calf, the stinking piece of flesh that had been dislodged by the bullet, and the strange tracks remained as tangible evidence of the witness's experience—evidence that the wolf was not some kind of hallucination or spirit being. But there was no way to explain the experience. The only way out was simply to try to forget it. (In response to my questions, the witness would only tell me that much of this story is based on hearsay; he would not elaborate beyond that. Nor did Van Eyck mention it in his articles.)

During the coming days, there were other huge wolves seen by the witness's wife. When she complained to the tribal police, she was told that the last wolf in the area was killed in 1929. It would be years before off-spring of the wolves released into Yellowstone Park in 1995 made it to northern Utah.

The Skinwalker Ranch UFOs
and Other Experiences

There were night sightings of a huge (larger than several football fields), black "aircraft" that silently hovered over the ranch, accompanied by bright spots of light dancing on the snow. On separate occasions, both witnesses saw these crafts. The obvious explanation was that they were some kind of government project—except the silence and the hovering made that seem unlikely.

Most common were the strange and truly bizarre orange structures that would appear in the western sky, often well after sunset. Each of the family members saw these things dozens of times. They appeared to be about a mile away. The witness watched through binoculars and a rifle scope. He would steady these instruments on a four-foot tree stump in the yard. Sometimes the thing appeared flattened and elongated, but other times it was perfectly round and as large as a full moon. Sometimes the witness would see blue sky through the object, as though he were looking into another world where the sun had not yet set: another dimension or a parallel universe? Other times he would see a black object emerge from the orange hole, moving at high speed. Driving away from his ranch, he noticed that it became less visible until it appeared only as an orange cloud—or it completely disappeared. Turning around and driving back to his place, the object would appear and become more distinct. It was as if he were look-ing through a cylinder or tunnel that was aimed directly at his ranch, with sides that were perfectly camouflaged to match the sky. His neighbors, typically a mile or so away, would not be able to see the phenomenon. (The witness and I discussed this phenomenon at some length.)

There is a story of a prize cow that disappeared in a blinding snow storm. The witness hunted until he found very clear tracks in the snow. He followed them through brush, noting that the cow had started to run at high speed—until the tracks suddenly stopped in the middle of a clear-ing as though the thousand-pound cow had been lifted into the air by a helicopter. But at a dead run? It didn't make sense—unless the cow ran through one of those portals into another dimension! In any case, the witness never saw the cow again. (Van Eyck also told this story in 1996.)

Then the cattle mutilations began. The witness's son was chasing a calf in a heavy rain storm when he saw an unhappy but healthy cow stuck in a canal. About twenty minutes later, after returning the calf to its mother, he went to help the cow out of the canal. The cow was dead, but its rectum had been removed as though with some kind of surgical saw, and there was a hole in the animal about six inches in diameter. The cows insides had also been cleanly and precisely removed. How could it have happened in a mere twenty minutes, in the day time, and during a storm?

We noted in Chapter 3 that the Basin mutilations followed the pattern of thousands of such mutilations that had occurred all over the western United States and Canada, and to a lesser extent all over the world. Sometimes the mutilations involved the sex organs, the mouth, the ears, or some other part, but always the cuts were clean and there was no blood. (We mentioned Snippy the Horse in Chapter 3, but cattle were the most frequent victims of mutilation. Also in Chapter 3, I presented veterinarian Dr. Daniel Dennis's skeptical views of mutilations.)

The mutilations probably reached their peak in the 1970s, both on a national level and also in the Uintah Basin, but no one has ever seen a mutilation in progress, and the whole phenomenon remains a great mystery. Is it part of the UFO experience? No one knows for sure, but it became a very important event on the *Skinwalker Ranch* and seemed to be associated with UFOs. The witness lost several very expensive animals. Three just disappeared while others were found mutilated. Although his neighbors might not have seen the orange "portal," they were certainly not immune to the lost cattle. John Garcia had several such stories to tell, including one of a calf found by a pool with all the flesh removed. The skeleton was white with no teeth marks and lay in an undisturbed state, every bone in place. Garcia took photos because the sight was so unusual.

During all of these events, stresses were also increasing in the family because poltergeist phenomena were taking place in the house and even outside. The witness's wife would set a pan down on the sink, turn around to pick it up, and it would be gone. She would later find it in the freezer! The witness lost a post-hole digger, which made him quite angry. Later he found the seventy-pound tool suspended high in a tree. Their first thought was someone, perhaps one of their children, was playing pranks. But the phenomena became so prevalent and the children denied any connection so soundly that it became one more stressor to drive the witnesses away from their dream ranch—and make them question their sanity!

Then there were the orbs. One evening, the witness and his wife saw a bright blue orb or sphere, about three times the size of a baseball, drifting among the trees and around their cattle and horses, which remained strangely calm. The orb gave off enough blue light that the cattle were illuminated. It came up close to the witnesses, about twenty feet away and fifteen feet above the ground, where they could see it clearly. It looked as if it were made of glass, with a swirling blue liquid inside. The witness's wife reached for her flashlight, and the orb sped away into the trees, where it maneuvered under apparently intelligent control. Later, they saw it out of their window. During the close encounter, both the witness and his wife were so gripped by fear that they later said that the orb must have exercised control over their minds! Yet the orbs became a common sight on the ranch, with many appearances.

The final straw involved one of those orbs. One evening the witnesses were watching the orange thing in the western sky when, out of the corner of their eye, they saw one of those blue orbs. It again came close, but the witness made the mistake of releasing his three barking and well-trained dogs, which were a special pride to him. The dogs chased after the orb, which descended from its ten-foot altitude close enough to earth for the dogs to jump and lunge at it. It seemed to tease them, moving away just as the dogs' jaws almost made contact. The orb made its way toward a grove of trees, moving into the trees without touching as much as a branch, and with the dogs barking right behind. Soon the barks turned to yelps of extreme pain, and then there was silence. The witness was not about to go into those trees after what had happened, but the next morning, after making his way through the thick vegetation, he came upon a clearing. Leaves on the trees were dry or burned. There was a powerfully unpleasant odor, and there were three large circles of brown, dried-out grass. In the center of each circle was a greasy, dark mess—apparently what was left of the dogs! The witnesses had a family conference and decided to sell the ranch.

This story gains credibility because Junior Hicks visited the ranch, heard the account of what had happened, and saw the circles of dead grass with their piles of "grease" in the center. (His memory is of only two dogs and circles, but to me the witness confirmed three dogs.) Furthermore, Charles Winn's grandson told us about seeing an orb moving close to Winn's house, as we'll see in an interview near the end of this chapter.

Such orbs are part of the UFO literature from all over the world. Quite recently, I was contacted through email by Richard F. Colagiovanni who had been a student of mine at Utah State University back in my UFO-hunting days. I had forgotten both the student and the story he had told me, but it had bothered him enough that after forty years he wanted to tell me again. In 1964, he was with a companion, Dave DeCrosta, near Cranston, Rhode Island, in a wooded area shooting BB gun pellets made of copper-coated steel. These pellets made sudden, right-angle turns in their two-hundred-foot-per-second trajectories, moving in any direction, apparently in response to a strong magnetic field! There were no power lines or other possible sources of magnetism. Then along came a bright, metallic sphere or orb about the size of a tennis ball, also doing right-angle turns. It had a bright, semi-glowing, silver/platinum appearance. It disappeared into the ground, leaving no mark at its entry point!

Robert Bigelow and NIDS Take Over the Ranch

In the autumn of 1996, the NIDS team, headed by Colm Kelleher, arrived at Bob Bigelow's new ranch. Garth Myers and his sisters got their money, and the witnesses were glad to be off the property, but the witness felt like something had defeated him, and he wanted to see it through. So when Bigelow offered to hire him to take care of the ranch, he accepted, although he had bought a small ranch twenty-five or possibly more like fifteen miles away and thus had a long commute.

The NIDS team did their homework before starting the project in earnest. They studied my book, *The Utah UFO Display*, to gain background about activity in the Basin (judging by the nice things that they say about the book in *Skinwalker*). They recorded hours of interviews with neighbors including "Mr. Gonzales" (who, based on the stories he told them, was clearly John Garcia—see below). They hired some of the local people, including Pete Pickup, the former deputy sheriff and tribal policeman. Junior Hicks was used as a major resource, just as he and I had worked together for my book. I envy the quantity of information they must have accumulated—although if I had all that information, this book could grow to encyclopedic size! (A NIDS analysis of Junior's files is in Chapter 2.)

There was much discussion about the approach that NIDS should take. This must have involved the high-level advisory board that had been assembled, which included some astronauts as well as an author whom I have quoted in this book. Junior Hicks attended at least one dinner with the board, accompanied to Las Vegas by John Garcia in a Bigelow private jet.[5]

Should they keep a low profile or go for broke with all the scientific instruments they could assemble? The witness, as well as Junior Hicks and several others, strongly urged the low-profile approach—perhaps a headquarters in Roosevelt with quiet visits and observations from afar. Surely the intelligence behind the activity was capable of knowing what the NIDS team was doing and responding accordingly. But the temptation to scientifically monitor a center of UFO activity was too strong. Rarely had a group of ufologists had the resources that were available thanks to Robert Bigelow. So a rolling laboratory and headquarters was moved onto the property, and towers were built to position cameras and other sensing equipment. Here was a chance finally to get solid data such as spectra of the strange lights that had been seen, not to mention high-quality photographs and video.

After a few months of careful monitoring, however, with many private-jet trips back and forth from a home base in Las Vegas, not much had happened. Kelleher and Knapp in *Skinwalker* admit that those who urged a more guarded approach might well have been right. (Could that be why they would not allow James Carrion or me to visit the ranch in September, 2009?[6] Probably. By early 2010 even Junior Hicks was denied visitation rights!) Still, in spite of the decrease in activity after the investigation began in earnest, there were a few events that seemed to validate what the witness had told them. Fairly early in the project, lights were seen that were definitely unidentified, thus qualifying as UFOs. But photos showed no detail, and other data had little value. The NIDS team was able to investigate some cattle mutilations, and the witness told of events that he'd experienced when he visited the ranch and the NIDS team was not present, but those reports just added to the stories that were already known.

My long-held, totally unscientific gut feeling is that the intelligence behind the UFO enigma is on display; it wants to be seen by many people—who will only be believed by a few others. It wants to influence the thinking of many of us, but it wants no formal contact nor tangible proof that would convince the skeptics. And its intelligence is great enough that it can control the situation so that we know only what it wants us to know. But I'm getting ahead of myself. I'll explain my philosophy in the Epilogue.

Although many of the things reported by the witnesses could never be confirmed by the NIDS team, there were some spectacular events that clearly validated the ranch as a place where very unusual phenomena occurred. For example, the witness once tagged a calf, went just a short distance away for only about forty minutes, and when he returned—in broad daylight—the calf had been horribly mutilated. Five hours later, thanks to the private jet, Kelleher and the NIDS team were on the site. This was no minor mutilation. All the insides were missing, and a leg was torn off at the knee. The ear with its yellow tag had been surgically removed. As usual, there were no signs of blood in the area—or anywhere else. A snarling dog had brought the witness back to the calf, but the dog then ran off, never to be seen again. The group went out before darkness set in to see if they could find any trace of whatever had caused the mutilation. They did not. Later, three dogs in a kennel began howling, and the group ran out and jumped in a truck to see what was going on. There were two spots of yellow light coming from a tree. Way up in the tree was a very large black shape. The witness shot it with his rifle, and it fell to the ground, but when the team got to the spot, nothing could be found. The witness spotted another animal shape and put two bullets into it from about forty feet away—but no body was found. Nor could any signs of blood be found.

One of the most memorable events in *Skinwalker* involved four large bulls. The witness's wife (who seldom came to the ranch) and the witness were driving in broad daylight toward the west boundary as they passed an enclosure with the four very special and very expensive bulls. Forty-five minutes later as they drove back, the bulls were missing, although the gates were tightly locked. *Skinwalker* says there was an old trailer at the back of the corral that had not been opened in years. The four bulls were crammed into the small space of the trailer in a seemingly hypnotic state! The witness pounded on the side of the trailer, and the bulls went into a bellowing panic, eventually kicking out a metal door and stampeding off! How could they have gotten into the locked trailer in forty-five minutes? The NIDS team arrived the day of the event but missed it by a couple of hours. Junior Hicks soon visited the small shed (not a trailer) where the bulls had been and confirmed the condition of the shed—as did the witness in one of our conversations.

The next day, while NIDS was investigating the corral where the bulls were, they found that the iron fence near the trailer was strongly magnetized. In the mean time, the witnesses were at the west end of the ranch where they witnessed a herd of cows splitting into two groups and stampeding in opposite directions as if some invisible presence seemed to move into the herd. The witness pulled out his compass, and the needle seemed to follow whatever it was that was stampeding the cattle. Again, the scientific team missed the event itself. And except for the magnetic anomalies and some plaster casts of round impressions in the soil, they had little tangible evidence that could be scientifically investigated.

Colm Kelleher tells about some later sightings of moving lights and observations he made with night-vision binoculars, but again no tangible evidence was obtained. The witnesses had subsequent encounters with flying orbs, these ones being bright-red, golf-ball-sized spheres that again stampeded the cattle. Calls the next day brought the NIDS team back to the ranch, but nothing could be detected. Two NIDS investigators, sitting on a ridge through the middle of the night, observed the ranch below. They noticed a tiny yellow light that slowly enlarged. One of them, watching it through exceptionally fancy night-vision binoculars, described a yellowish "tunnel" about 150 feet below the ridge where they were, out of which a large, black humanoid emerged! By the time the other investigator got the binoculars, the "tunnel" had shrunk and disappeared. One photo seems to show a small light, but examination of the area revealed nothing. There was also no sign of the strange being.

The lack of data that "could be presented at a scientific meeting" was frustrating to the NIDS group, so during much of 1998 and 1999 they spent time in Dulce, New Mexico. The situation there was very similar to the Uintah Basin and the skinwalker ranch. A local policeman had collected accounts much as Junior Hicks had in Utah. There were a tremendous number and variety of sightings, including some hovering object that was a mile or more wide, almost spanning a canyon from one side to the other! The NIDS team clearly gained an even broader insight into the UFO phenomena, but again no hard data were obtained. Kelleher and Knapp also described some other UFO hot spots scattered around the west and around the world.

There were a few more instances of paranormal activity. NIDS had installed three surveillance cameras on each of three poles. The three cameras on each pole recorded everything going on within the 360° areas around each pole. On July 20, 1998, the wiring was forcibly ripped out of all three cameras on one pole. The video recordings from that pole showed that this occurred simultaneously for all three cameras at exactly 8:30 PM. A camera on another pole some distance away viewed the vandalized pole and should have shown what happened. Nothing appeared in the video, although it was possible to see the small red lights on the three vandalized cameras, and all went out at precisely 8:30 PM! Junior Hicks was called to see if he could repair the electrical damage. That was when he told them again that they were being far too obvious in their hunt for the skinwalker.

Then in April 1999, a large red beast with a huge bushy tail chased two of the witness's horses around in a corral as the witness and his wife drove up to check things out. The horses' legs were bleeding but the animals were otherwise okay. The witness pursued the beast as it exited the corral and loped smoothly up a slight incline—where, in full sight of the witness, it disappeared into thin air! Sounds like another skinwalker! In the following months, others reported seeing the beast—as well as strange red birds, unusually huge spiders, and a fast, running, manlike figure. Remember, skinwalkers can take any shape.

The witness has wondered (to me) if the "portal" to that "other dimension" allows all kinds of things to slip through, some good and some bad. Strange experiences on the ranch seemed to be clustered together in time, leading to these thoughts. Some of these things might be strange animals, even birds. He told me about an experience that his family had. One day in the spring the family woke up to see that a huge Chinese elm tree by their home was filled with yellow birds, thousands of them (well, maybe hundreds to begin with). They built sock-shaped nests, and within the expected time, little yellow birds were in the nests. Before long the young learned to fly. In the morning, these thousands of birds were very loud, almost ear-splitting! They were quiet at night and not as loud as the day wore on. One day, they were gone! The nests remained but disintegrated rather rapidly. The witness tried to identify what they were, but the closest the family could come was South American canaries.

Some of my browsing on the web turned up descriptions of yellow warblers and other yellow birds that do indeed congregate in huge flocks, building cuplike or even socklike nests. As far as I can learn, however, large flocks in a single tree are not common in Utah, but they are certainly possible.

I've talked with a couple of local bird experts, and they don't remember seeing such flocks of yellow birds. Although it is tempting to relate this experience to the phenomenon, proper skepticism indicates caution.

Some Conclusions

What do I make of all this? We concluded above that the answer to the first question posed near the beginning of this chapter was: No, the Myers Ranch was most likely not a center of UFO activity in the Uintah Basin since its earliest history. True, we can't prove that the Myers didn't secretly join up with the phenomenon, but that seems to be a very remote possibility. What about the second question: Does the UFO phenomenon in the Uintah Basin include what are called paranormal events such as the strange beasts, poltergeist phenomenon, and apparent passage into other "dimensions"? Until relatively recently, there have been very few reports of such things in Junior's files. But the events on the skinwalker ranch shout a resounding yes to this question. That's what this chapter is all about. Furthermore, the witness tells me that some neighbors had similar tales to tell him—but not to tell the world at large or even Junior Hicks. Interestingly enough, the witness's personal response to the phenomena was not always terror, but sometimes he was deeply moved spiritually in a positive way—or in other cases he was neither afraid nor did he have any special, positive feeling, just neutral curiosity.

For me, there is another tentative conclusion that comes out of the skinwalker story: It is interesting that only the witness and sometimes his wife were there to experience the truly bizarre events after NIDS moved in. Although the witness's wife rarely visited the Bigelow Ranch, she was there to witness the transport of the bulls, stampeding of the herd, and the red beast. The NIDS team only got the "leftovers." Yet the witness tells me that they did have some impressive experiences not recorded in *Skinwalker*.

So here is my just-suppose conspiracy theory: The UFO and apparently related phenomena are controlled by some kind of high intelligence—high enough to choose a single victim or victim family, which they then bombard with strange events that cause much confusion, if not terror, but also some positive reactions. *Skinwalker* may have embellished the witnesses' stories, but they are not simply fabrications. Things really did happen. Were the witnesses singled out by the phenomenon when they moved onto the ranch? Looks like it. And just enough activity might have been "leaked" by the phenomenon to the NIDS team to keep them interested for a few years—and frustrated! Thus, an important conclusion is that the phenomenon can be very personal, and this is supported by accounts from all over the world as well as in my conversations with the witness.

Nearby UFO Events

In my frustrated mind, struggling to keep my sanity, two items aside from my conversations with the witness fortify his stories: The first is Junior Hicks's witnessing of the aftermath of some of the witness's pre-NIDS experiences and other stories: a spinning compass needle, what was left of two (actually three) dogs and burned leaves, a couple of calf mutilations, round cookie-cutter plugs taken out of the grass, the ripped NIDS video-camera wiring, and the battered shed where the bulls were confined. The second is the fact that the witness's neighbors also had encounters with strangeness while the witness was having his and before. For the record, here are two condensed interviews.

Curious Cows: John Garcia's Basketball UFO. The first is from John Garcia (Fig. 8-1; Mr. Gonzales in *Skinwalker*), who has owned the ranch east of the Myers/*Skinwalker*/Bigelow ranch since the 1970s.[7] He told us several stories, and some of these are related in *Skinwalker*. This story, which impressed me the most, confirms that there was activity while the Myers still lived there—but not that the Myers were aware of it:

> **John Garcia:** The one that I really liked was an object that I seen

Fig. 8-1 *Junior Hicks (left) talking with John Garcia by Garcia's home (2009).*

right here. One March, I was feeding cows, and the cows were right there waiting for me. And I got up early in the morning, and then I was coming to go get on my tractor to feed hay. I looked at the cows, and they was lookin' at something over that way, you know, and right there by the fence there was a big old object. It was larger than this house—big, you know. And that thing had stripes like a basketball. And it was reddish orange. And it had no lights or nothing cause it was early in the morning; I didn't see no lights! I got about halfway, about here when I seen it, and I run back to that window, and I knocked on the window, and I told my wife to come out here and look at this. I wanted her to see it. She was still in bed and watched through the front door and looked at it but just barely got a glimpse of it, and it just floated up like this, and once it got up so high—just zoom! We seen it, but when it was up, by the time she got around here, it was far away.

FBS: Bigelow owned the ranch by then?

John: No, it was still owned by Mrs. Myers. She lived there for a few years by herself. [We gave him dates of Kenneth and Edith Myers' deaths.] We used to go around there and check on her all the time; me and my daughter went around there on the tractor one time—and good thing we did because she had broken her hip and fallen out there just a little ways from her doorway on the sidewalk, and she couldn't get up. And my daughter said, "Look what's laying there." And I got off and I went to see, and it was Mrs. Myers. She was okay, but she had broken her hip, and she couldn't get up. So I just picked her up like a dog and took her in the house and laid her in bed and called Jessie Pickup.[8] She was taking care of her. She would come and go. So I called her and took her to the hospital, and I think right after that time they put her in a rest home. And then that [witness] appeared.

Junior Hicks: So when you saw the UFO thing, a basketball thing, that was the time when Mrs Myers was there?

John: Yeah, she was still there. Because I remember there was no padlocked gate there.

FBS: Well, if you were in contact with Mrs Myers, did she ever tell you anything about anything [UFO activity] like that?

John: No, she never did.

Attack by a Ball of Intense Light. My recording of the interview with Charles Winn (Fig. 8-2) lasted over 45 minutes. A grown grandson, Chance Sanborn, was present and had his own stories to tell, and the conversation led to several other secondhand stories—all quite interesting. Charles's ranch adjoins the skinwalker ranch on the west and some elevated ground

Fig. 8-2 *Charles Winn (right) and Chance Sanborn during their interview (2009).*

to the north. Here is the first and main story, told by Charles himself. The event took place about 1997, and it is one of the most frightening stories I've heard.

> **Charles Winn:** And it was an evening similar to this one. I'd been up and took a big slug of water, on the field down here. I change it every two hours so I get the good out of it, and so it was around probably two o'clock in the morning. I had my dams all set up; it don't take me any time at all, I just pull one out and it goes to the next one, you know. So I don't lose too much sleep. I went down there, and I just stepped over the fence to pull the dam out—as that main road turns to go over that sand hill—and thought, well, they're checking that power line with a helicopter because a light come just so bright, and it was quite a ways away then. The closer it got to me, the brighter it got, white colored. I want to describe it as an arc-welder light. And it was inevitably coming right toward me; it wasn't changing its course. So I dropped down in that ditch full of water, and just kind of buried my head so I could breath, you know, and my arms over my head like that. And that's the only way I could survive the light. It wasn't hot. It was coming right at me. I figured it was over cause it was just that close, it seemed like—on

me. And I didn't hear any noise or anything, and about as quick as I seen it coming, why that light kind of faded away out of my peripheral vision where I could look up again. And it turned and went into that hill, and I said, "Man, we're going to hear a crash here in a minute." There was no crash. I've had a lot of people tell me—you know how they do them holograms. They can show a picture on a rock or a hill or something, and they said the Air Force has got a lot of that stuff, but I didn't know the Air Force was down here that night with me, but anyway the light was as bright on the hill as it was on me: illuminated everything. I never seen the hill open, but of course the light was so bright that I don't know if I ever would or not.[9]

FBS: But it was headed right for the cliff and then it was gone?

Charles: Yeah. I was just looking for an explosion or a wreck any minute. If it was a flying object it would have hit them rocks solid! Then I got to thinking, it does come out as a point and maybe it would have gone around there. But I didn't see it do that.

FBS: But you were thinking, common sense says it must.

Charles: Common sense says it didn't have time to go around there, and I didn't see it go around. It disappeared. Just like you shut it off. Before that and after that, I haven't seen anything, and I've looked; I made it a point to look . . .

In answer to our questions, Charles said he couldn't see sharp edges to the light—it was too bright. Maybe, he thought, it was three or four feet in diameter. He mentioned looking into an arc-welder as have other witnesses. He estimated that he was about two hundred yards from the power line. There was no noise.

At this point, we went into some depth about activity on the Bigelow Ranch. Charles said that for a long time he denied any special activity there, but now he had become convinced, mostly on the basis of stories he had heard. He said Kenneth Myers was "very, very fussy about where the ditch company dug a hole or you done any excavation very deep, cause he said bad things will happen. So I don't know whether there was a portal there at that time or not." Charles's brother-in-law once did some digging for Myers and was told, "You can dig here, but you can't dig here at all." According to Charles, Myers also "had locks on his cupboards to keep these little white-blue balls from getting into his cupboards."

These ideas certainly support early activity, but it is hard to know how much Charles knew by personal witness or how much he had heard. He had clearly read *Hunt for the Skinwalker*. "We knew him quite well, but he wouldn't mention why [there was to be no digging]. No answers. He never told us about any cattle mutilations that happened to him, anyway." Charles says Myers never mentioned UFO activity. "Whether he was sworn to secrecy or scared to tell it . . . you know back then and even now, you're smoking the wrong weed, you know, if you tell somebody this. . . . I've talked with Junior and a lot of other guys that's been out in the wilds a lot, and the stories they tell . . . so I know there is something a little bit different . . . . I have people from Wisconsin wanting to buy twenty acres of my land over there that joins the ranch. They come in [last summer—2009] with a bunch of satellite dishes and lights and sound equipment, and they said "we need that piece of property." They stayed a couple of nights, but Charles hasn't sold them any property yet at this writing. We mentioned that many people were interested because of the *Skinwalker* book.

Charles asked if we thought there was a portal on the ranch. I immediately said, "Oh no!" Junior said, "I do!" We disclosed our feelings way too quickly! James Carrion said he didn't know because they wouldn't let us onto the ranch. I said we probably couldn't tell anything if they did. James agreed. Charles told us how kids sneak onto the ranch, hoping to get a thrill. He sometimes has to lock his gates to keep them out. But the guard dogs alert the guards.

Then Chance Sanborn told us about his experience with an orb.

> **Chance Sanborn:** I got just right here where this end of this camper is, and I saw this little—it looked almost as if someone had lit one of those bottle rockets. But it had blue on the outside and orange on the inside, and it was probably about that big around [a little bigger than a tennis ball, he said later], and it was letting sparks off. . . . It was like a firework but a lot slower. It took probably fifteen seconds to make it from there to . . . down among the trees and just died off. . . . No noise. When I seen it, I couldn't move. My feet was stuck to the ground just lookin' at it.
>
> **Charles:** But we have a lot of people in this area have more sightings of this ball than they do of any large object. So what are they? Phenomena? Orbs is a good word.

Junior then told how the skinwalker ranch witness had described the blue orb that finally incinerated his dogs, as related above. Junior saw the evidence—and even told me about it during our 1997 evening in Columbus, Ohio! Charles then told about a neighbor. The little orbs would go through one screen in her bedroom and out through the wire screen on the other side of the room!

Junior told about some kids who went to the gate of the skinwalker ranch about two in the morning—boys and girls in a car, looking for a thrill. In their headlights, they saw what looked like a big gray wolf running on its hind legs! A skinwalker! A cell phone video got some blurry shots of the apparition.

Chance told about driving with a friend to the ranch in the dark of early morning. They saw what looked like a donkey, with a head that turned into a human! As they raced away, the donkey followed them for the mile or so to the paved road—keeping up as they went at least forty miles per hour on the dirt road.

So there is a taste of the kind of stories told in the Uintah Basin. It wouldn't be difficult to talk your way out of these last ones. If the Virginias (Chapter 6) could see a big black object that probably wasn't there, imagine what a bunch of kids out for a thrill in the dark of early morning might conjure up in their excitement!

Before closing this chapter, I want to emphasize that much of *Hunt for the Skinwalker* is truly excellent. In this chapter, I've argued with the authors' pre-witness history because it gives a certain perspective to the Basin UFOs that is not supported by Garth Myers' version—and I've related that the witness sees many inaccuracies in the book's record of his experiences, although he confirms that the events did take place. But as I read the final chapters in *Skinwalker*, I was deeply impressed with the extent of the NIDS's research and the depth of thought Kelleher and Knapp put into their scientific research into what appear to be non-scientific topics. They present and discuss, with pros and cons, the various hypotheses that have been put forth to explain the UFO phenomenon. They clearly lean toward the multi-dimension, parallel universe, wormhole/portal idea. And at this point, so do I, as I'll explain further in the Epilogue.

Notes

1. Here is an example of how well known the ranch became after Bigelow bought it. Russ Perry in Vernal (Chapter 7) said his son-in-law talked about the UFO ranch over near Fort Duchesne and one time he said, "Let's go take a look. We figure out where the ranch is [and] we end up on the road that goes on the back side of Bottle Hollow." It was a little power line road. They jumped a fence into the ranch, looked at the towers built by NIDS—and saw a coyote. But they didn't see anything special. Then they decide,

We need to go out there at night. So we do, hike up to the top of the hill and stay for two or three hours. Kenny's cell phone rings. It's a text from his wife: "Are you okay?" "Yes." About five minutes later, here come the cowboys! They picked up that cell phone call. We watch with binoculars. "They know we're here. Let's get out of here!" We drove out in the moonlight with no lights on. Those guys were good! I underestimated their technology, but if they're going to catch inter-dimensional beings they've got to get up earlier in the morning because they couldn't even catch us!

James Carrion asked Russ if he had heard about the ranch before the book came out. He wasn't sure, but he didn't think so. Russ then mentions the possibility that the ranch is a portal to a different dimension—an idea that everybody in the Basin seems to know about.

2. I have thought about how much trouble it would have been to try to find the person who negotiated those sales. I would have started in Roosevelt and probably have been told that the previous owners lived in Salt Lake City. With some effort I might have found Garth Myers. As it was, my wife and I were just doing one of our church duties when we got to talking about my interest in the Uintah Basin UFOs with a couple named Suzanne and Richard Hammond. Suzanne said, "Oh yes. My uncle owned a ranch over there that later became well known for UFO activity." Her father was Garth Myers, whose brother Kenneth Myers had owned the ranch! As I got to know Garth, it turned out that his son had had a date with my wife's daughter, Helen, when they were in high school. It's a small world.

3. As far as I can tell from my own knowledge of the history of the Uintah Basin, and always with Junior Hicks as my consultant, *The Hunt for the Skinwalker* does an excellent job of reviewing that general history and many of the UFO-related events that have taken place there.

4. For example, *Skinwalker* makes a point of how the witnesses had owned a ranch in New Mexico. The witness tells me that this is simply not true, but he speculates that some of the discrepancies in *Skinwalker* were distortions included by the authors to protect the witness's privacy.

Frankly, it scares me to death when I'm writing a book like this one to realize just how extensive my research should be—and how little time and resources there are to support that research! I was embarrassed when I realized that I was writing a chapter about the witnesses' experiences only from a second hand source, the *Skinwalker* book, which is itself also a secondhand account!

5. Because of *The Utah UFO Display*, which is nicely acknowledged in *Skinwalker*, I was also flown to Las Vegas in September 2001 to consult with Bigelow, Colm Kelleher, Eric Davis, and others, but it was clear to them that I was long out of the UFO business, and they justifiably didn't consult with me again. I was so little interested that I have trouble remembering the trip, although I was impressed by Bigelow's empire—he was and is building conventional spacecraft that might one day take tourists into space.

6. In September, 2009, I wanted to visit the ranch, but I was told by Colm Kelleher, who was again working for Mr. Bigelow, that "it was an unfortunate time." He wouldn't even tell me where the ranch was located so I could drive by! As noted, I was accompanied on my visit to the Basin by James Carrion, director of MUFON. MUFON had a contract with Bigelow to investigate any good UFO sightings, with Bigelow paying expenses. Hence, we thought that Kelleher would allow Carrion to visit the ranch, but not so. "We want to keep a low profile," was the answer we received. After my phone conversation with Kelleher, I met Garth Myers who told me the location of the ranch (which was well known to virtually everybody in the Basin anyway), so we drove to the gate a couple of times to photograph the many KEEP OUT and NO TRESPASSING signs hanging on the tightly locked gate (blocking a county road, incidently). The rumor was that NIDS was no longer active at the ranch, but these experiences suggest otherwise. Recently (spring 2010) Junior told me that he is no longer welcome on the ranch—after all these years!

7. John Garcia, from Mexico, married a Native American woman, which gave him the opportunity to purchase his ranch east of the Myers ranch.

8. Jessie Pickup had a sighting that was mentioned near the end of Chapter 1 (pp. 67–68). Some strange lights followed her along the road about where Joe Ann Harris and her Native American girls had their spectacular experience.

9. The late Philip Klass, the king of the UFO debunkers, tried for awhile to explain most good UFO cases as ball lightning, a little-known weather phenomenon. He probably would have had a field day with Charles Winn's story because the bright, moving light does, in some ways, resemble ball lightning. For example, ball lightning often originates near power lines, and the sudden disappearance when it hit the cliff would be expected of ball lightning. Wikipedia has a long article on the phenomenon. For the most part, there are few similarities with Charles Winn's experience. Yet, combining some of the most bizarre observations in the article, ball lightning cannot be completely excluded as an explanation for Winn's terrifying experience. But I didn't see any examples in Wikipedia of ball lightning being large, bright, and aiming for an individual!

Epilogue

What Is the Meaning of It All?

In collaboration with Joseph Junior Hicks, I have now presented the Utah UFO display based on Junior's files, as well as *The Hunt for the Skinwalker* (Kelleher & Knapp, 2005) and even a few Basin accounts that I stumbled on without Junior's help. For good measure, I've added several classic cases. Now it is time to summarize my wonderment and speculate a bit about what it all means. First we'll look back and review the basic hypotheses but with a little different angle. Then I will present my own just-suppose stories (which I began to polish for a talk at the 2009 MUFON Symposium in Denver, Colorado; see Salisbury, 2009). But let's get it straight right from the beginning: There are no real answers that can be tested by philosophical or scientific methods. However, a little deep cogitation won't hurt us.

Based on the first edition of this book, we discussed five hypotheses, each with its own chapter (Chapters 3 to 7). In this edition, I have been unable to avoid mentioning the multi-dimension or wormhole hypothesis several times, but now it is time give it some closer thought.

Three Hypotheses

Including the multi-dimension idea, I think I can put the suggested explanations of the UFO phenomenon under just three hypotheses. (Do you have others?)

Hypothesis #1—the Debunker Hypothesis: Any UFO sighting, no matter how spectacular, can be understood if enough data can (or could) be assembled.

The debunkers have several ways to apply this hypothesis. There are natural phenomena (meteors, stars or planets, ball lightning, and reflections); human constructions (weather balloons, rockets, and airplanes); government developments (sometimes secret, sometimes not); psychological phenomena (hallucinations and misinterpretations of what is seen); and lies or hoaxes.

The problem is, except for simple sightings such as the planet Venus, it is typically impossible to gather sufficient data to arrive at a satisfactory conclusion, simply because the UFO experience cannot be repeated. Virtually everything depends on witness accounts. The debunker then invents explanations based on "probable" circumstances and psychology. Sometimes these just-suppose stories can be quite convincing—and might even be true—but other times they sound like wild speculations that strongly contradict the witness account. Because of the limitations of data collection, there is no way to be sure about the proposed explanation—it must be accepted or rejected on faith. Or ignored. A last resort of the debunker is to suggest that the sighting never occurred: The witness lied or it was a deliberate hoax. The debunker searches deeply for a motivation that might lead to a hoax, and it isn't hard to invent one if a real one can't be found. Again, this explanation must usually be accepted or rejected on faith— unless the hoaxer or liar admits the hoax or lie.

To the best of my knowledge, the debunkers never considered the Uintah Basin sightings. Some of them (e.g., the late Philip Klass) are very clever, but I can't imagine how they could explain the reported close encounters, movements, and so forth that are reported in Junior's files, let alone those reported in *Skinwalker*. Nor can I accept the idea that the numerous witnesses, often more than a single witness to a sighting, could all be hallucinating, dreaming, or (especially!) conspiring to carry out a hoax! It just doesn't make sense, although I'll admit that my conclusion must be mostly a matter of faith in my ideas about how the situation looks.

Nevertheless, most of today's educated skeptics accept this hypothesis—but probably know little about the sightings. This is the "acceptable" hypothesis for scientists and well-educated people, whose philosophy is mechanism: a universe understandable in terms of known (plus soon to be discovered) physical laws. But most of us closer to the UFO field can't accept this hypothesis. There is too much evidence. It is probably a vain hope, but just maybe this book will catch the attention of some of those scientists who presently know little about the phenomenon.

Hypothesis #2—the Nuts-and-Bolts Hypothesis: UFOs are highly advanced machines traveling through space from civilizations on planets in other solar systems (the ET hypothesis).

This basically means travel within our known universe by technologies that are extensions of our own current technologies, but of course based on things that we have yet to discover or develop. Often, those who tentatively accept this idea talk about exploration of our planet being a prime motive of our visitors—or perhaps they are monitoring us to keep us in line with the laws of the galaxy; maybe even to stop us before we destroy ourselves and our planet. (Of course, these motives could apply to the next hypothesis as well.)

Many if not most non-debunker UFO investigators probably accept this hypothesis. Usually, this is the idea that comes to the public mind when UFOs are mentioned. Several investigators (see references in Chapter 7: Stan Friedman, others) have made very strong cases for it—providing plausible just-suppose stories that might answer most of the arguments that have been raised. As far as I can see, the arguments against the ET hypothesis fall into two broad categories:

1. Physical law (special relativity as well as energy requirements) prevents interstellar travel in reasonable times. The simple, philosophical answer to this is that we just do not know all there is to know about physical law. More complex answers have also been proposed by capable investigators—speculations about time dilation and gravity propulsion systems, for example. But these are just-suppose stories. Their suggestions may sound highly reasonable, but they are seldom, if ever, founded on experimental data.

2. The UFOs don't act like space explorers who have found a new world. For example, why have they made no official contact? The simple, philosophical answer again is that we might well be unable to discern or to understand the motives and actions of an extraterrestrial intelligence. All this was discussed in Chapter 7, as well as in the skinwalker examples in Chapter 8.

In spite of the suggestions of UFO investigators for whom I have much respect, I am very uncomfortable with the nuts-and-bolts hypothesis. The physical problems really are serious. Yes, thanks to time dilation, occupants in a vehicle traveling at near light speed from a planet light-years away would feel like the time was much shorter, but if they returned to their planet, a whole new generation might welcome them. (If their life cycles are like ours.)

In addition to the problems of physical laws, I am also troubled by the sheer numbers of UFOs, counting only the good accounts, and by the variety of shapes of their reported vehicles, not to mention the purported millennia that they have been visiting us. Why would one or more civilizations of some star system or systems light-years away expend so many resources to visit us for so many years, only to do the strange things that witnesses say they do?

For me, that is the really important question. The reported activities just don't seem to fit the explorers-from-another-world hypothesis. True, I'm going on my gut feelings alone, but doesn't that question bother you a bit also? Sometimes they are interrupted while taking their samples, but they've had plenty of time to do that if they go as far back in history as seems to be the case. And the reported contacts seldom make any real sense—even if you discount a few thousand "abduction cases" as false memories formed in response to hypnotic probing (and I do tend to so discount them—except for a very few that were reported immediately after they occurred and did not depend on hypnotic regression). Even if we forget the recovered "memories" of egg and sperm removal, hybridization with the aliens, and so on, the UFOs' activities in the very best of cases are often bizarre. The Pascagoula, Mississippi, case was reported immediately and has other features that make it impressive to me, but it has very little in common with the repressed-memory cases. The Travis Walton case also impressed me, although there are some reasons to call it a hoax. And it is difficult to discount the idea that Marjorie Beal and Rebecca Crandall were abducted. (These cases are presented in Chapter 6.)

Hypothesis #3—the Star Gate Hypothesis: UFOs (and possibly many other paranormal phenomena) represent beings and their technology from some nearby parallel universe or other dimension—or some wormhole transport from distant parts of our universe.

This idea could easily be separated into two or three separate hypotheses: the extra-dimension hypothesis, the parallel-universe hypothesis, or the wormhole-from-distant-parts-of-our-universe hypothesis. Since I have no idea of how we might tell the difference based on the UFO data known to us, I'll lump them together. This hypothesis implies that there is some kind of portal to allow passage between the other reality and our own.

Although the possibility of such parallel universes, as well as "wormholes" or "portals" to allow passage between them and/or other parts of our universe, is being discussed by some top physicists, such things are not part of the standard physics accepted by educated people today. But if this hypothesis turns out to be a statement of reality, it could surely account for the strange UFO and related phenomena. Later, I'll make the case as best I can, but first, let me consider some more background.

Why Do I Think the Phenomenon Is Real?

I've said it before and I'll say it again: The Uintah Basin witnesses, along with many other well-documented cases in the UFO literature, report in all seriousness events and observations that plainly do not fit the debunker hypothesis but just might fit the other two. I know the events cannot be repeated and thus studied in ways that most scientists are accustomed to, so in one sense I'm left with only my gut feelings. Yet there are many accounts from ordinary people from all walks of life—people just like you and me—that involve truly strange events. I simply cannot call these people liars or hoaxers, nor can I believe that they were hallucinating or under the effects of mass hypnosis. (Mass hypnotism is about as far out as the nuts-and-bolts hypothesis, anyway.) Okay, I'll grant that some of the best cases (e.g., Virginia and Virginia in Chapter 6) might end up fitting the natural-or-man-made hypothesis, and I guess some might even turn out to be hallucinations. But after reading the many accounts presented in this book, do you think they will—or could—eventually be explained? I can't bring myself to think that. The phenomenon is real, but we just don't understand it. I am not persuaded by the debunkers.

Why Do So Many People Distrust Science?

On July 29, 2009, Mary and I attended the annual banquet of the Botanical Society of America, held at Snowbird, Utah. The speaker, Dr. Kent Holsinger, was the president-elect of the society, and he gave an excellent talk. Among other things he bemoaned the dismal degree of scientific understanding by the general public. He quoted statistics that showed that well over half of the population rejects evolutionary theory, and well over half accepts the reality of UFOs! That's how uneducated and stupid the general public is!

As Mary and I walked back to our condo after the fine talk, it occurred to me that those statistics might themselves provide some insight into the questions that he raised. It seems clear enough that the public is most happy to apply the findings of science, in say medical care or cell phone production, but that there is indeed a distrust of science as an institution, and by extension, the things that science tries to tell us. For one thing, scientists have developed weapons of mass destruction. And they often argue among themselves (as they should), such as in the current controversy over global warming. But for another thing, science in general and some scientists in particular try to tell us things that we simply cannot accept. The evidence is everywhere for UFOs, and most people know it—especially if they live in the Uintah Basin. True, the phenomenon can't be confirmed by the usual scientific procedures, as we've discussed at length. Yet those of us who are familiar with the witness accounts can't help thinking that the phenomenon is real. We just can't bring ourselves to reject it—there is too much witness evidence—but scientists say it is not real, so scientists must be nuts! Is that how many people react? I'm not sure, but it makes sense to me.

It may not belong here, but since Kent Holsinger brought up evolution, I must note that the same kind of thing applies to this issue. Some of the public is not knowledgeable about the vast evidence for the reality of evolution, and those people may reject it simply because what scientists tell us clearly seems to conflict with the Biblical Creation story. Others, like myself, may be aware of the evidence that evolution happened and are happy enough to accept the reality of that process and to find other interpretations for the biblical accounts. But we remain uncomfortable with the mechanism that is said to be at the heart of the evolutionary process. We just can't see the source of variety for natural selection to act upon (Salisbury, 2006). Nor do we think that evolutionary science has logically rejected the existence of God, as some scientists claim (e.g., Dawkins, 2006). Much of the population sees evidence for God's existence, much as they see evidence for UFOs. The result: much of the population rejects science and what it teaches. As a scientist, I certainly don't reject science. Instead, I do what scientists are supposed to do—I question some of the positions that other scientists take. For me the evidence is overwhelming that the UFO phenomenon itself is real, whatever the UFOs turn out to be.

And at a certain level, I also see evidence that natural selection of random mutations doesn't make sense.[1]

Back to the Display and Its Effects

I've said it over and over again, but it is so important that I must say it again in this concluding epilogue: The UFOs in the Uintah Basin wanted to be seen. They performed for their witnesses. They put on a display. I am hard pressed to discover any other reason for many of the antics of the UFOs and other strange phenomena in the Uintah Basin. Jacques Vallée (2008) has been saying this for many years in relation to witness accounts from all over the world, but he didn't have to tell me. The Uintah Basin sightings shouted it to me and Junior—which is why I titled my 1974 book, as well as this one, *The Utah UFO Display.*

So they want us to know they are there and that they are extremely intelligent and powerful—but evidently they don't want us to know officially. Their purpose seems to be to confuse and test the sanity of a significant portion of the population, delicately changing our outlook on our universe. But by no means do they want it to become official, scientific knowledge that they are here—and there is plenty of deception going on to hold reasonable scientists at bay! Otherwise-intelligent men and women have been caught up in wild tales about saucers secreted beneath the earth in Area 51, for example (Chapter 5). A superficial knowledge of the phenomenon, including such wild tales, is all that is necessary to convince a scientist that it is all a bunch of baloney (to quote Garth Myers). Hence, most scientists think that they know the answers without wasting time to learn what is really going on.

Contrary to some other hot areas of UFO activity around the world, most of the Uintah Basin sightings seem to support the ET hypothesis, the idea of space machines coming to visit us and explore the Basin—or maybe even working from a secret base located there. The skinwalker ranch seems to be an exception to this generalization. Many of the strange things that were reported just don't fit the nuts-and-bolts hypothesis. If the Basin sightings not associated with the ranch were designed to condition the residents into waiting for the friendly visitors from another solar system, could the strange skinwalkers and orange portals on the ranch be meant to condition their witnesses—and NIDS—to accept the alternative reality hypothesis? If all those things really happened, and I think they did, they certainly convince me! But what is the goal of manipulating our thinking in this way?

When the Oscar-winning movie *Close Encounters of the Third Kind* appeared in 1977, I wanted to see what Hollywood had to say about the UFO phenomenon, and I wanted to see it in a big-screen theater, which we didn't have in North Logan, Utah. So I drove alone down to Salt Lake City to an upscale theater to see the movie. It seemed to tell the story in a very straightforward way, and it included most of the phenomena that I knew about. I had expected that it would, since J. Allen Hynek was the consultant to Steven Spielberg for the movie and had coined the phrase that became its title. Jacques Vallée was the model for a French scientist in the movie, although he tells us that he had little to do with the actual movie.

In addition to the usual UFO sightings, there were poltergeist phenomena, which were not that well known in relation to UFOs back then, although I had personally talked with witnesses who reported such things. As Richard Dreyfuss was driven to build his models of Devils Tower in Wyoming, I was reminded of how subtle mind control had apparently been inflicted on some of the witnesses I had interviewed—not to mention the frequent telepathic conversations mentioned in contactee stories. I was deeply impressed with the authenticity of the movie and sat spellbound during the last scenes when the huge UFO arrives at Devils Tower in front of numerous witnesses (including J. Allen Hynek in the bleachers!). At last, the aliens made themselves known in a very public way!

Then, as I drove the hundred miles back to my home in North Logan, I began to see that here was an alternative story to what Christians believe. They look forward to the eventual return of Christ. The prophecies are clearly stated in scriptures. But the whole UFO display has been forming a modern myth, a legend that becomes a religion for some groups, such as the Raëlians and the followers of Billy Meier. Based on my very limited study, both of these groups emphasize alternative explanations for the Bible stories. Whether the UFO occupants are deliberately attempting to destroy Christianity or not, it is clear enough that they are providing powerful alternatives—and many of the "elect" seem to be caught up in these ideas. Certainly, there are "great signs and wonders; insomuch that, if it were possible, they shall deceive even the elect" (Matthew 24:24).

Actually, the UFO display might influence virtually any philosophy or belief. It has certainly influenced popular concepts of cosmology and even reality.

Science, Sanity, and the Phenomenon

I've done some writing and some preaching about magic: I reject it. (But I surely enjoyed the Harry Potter books!) Magic is when events occur without any possible causes. Physical law does not apply. Words might be spoken, but words by themselves are not physical causes. (In stage magic, of course, we know that somehow the magician is using physical laws to make things happen in such a way that we can't relate cause to effect— he fools us by concealing how physical laws are used.) My scientific faith rejects magic—and so does my theology. In LDS theology, even God acts within physical laws. God himself is restricted to doing that which is possible. (That's one of the things I like about LDS theology.)

When we examine UFO accounts, however, we encounter events that just don't seem to fit within our understanding of natural laws. Sometimes they look like magic. In the Uintah Basin alone there are plenty of goings-on that look like magic. We may imagine that UFOs are just ahead of us in their technology, but the sudden movements and especially the disappearances often look like magic.[2] The skinwalker disappearances must be better than any earthly magician could accomplish—for example, the red beast vanishing even as the witness watched. And it seems like it would take pure magic to get those four huge bulls into the small shed in such a short time. Or what happened to the black shapes that were shot out of the tree? Were these things really magic, or was there some unearthly magician who knew how to use physical laws far beyond our knowledge to pull off the stunts? Contemplating such things when we are so used to our "real world," and perhaps even falling back on magic as an explanation, certainly challenges our sanity.

If we reject magic in principle as I do, then we have to assume that the intelligence behind the UFO phenomenon must be applying physical laws that we don't know or at least can't detect. They are super stage magicians. Indeed, theologians of many faiths have suggested that even miracles do not contravene the sum of physical laws; it's just that we don't know those laws. The power of the divine is to know those laws. Retaining my faith in the idea that there is no such thing as magic and trying to hold on to my sanity, I have to take this approach with the UFOs—even those on the skinwalker ranch. There must be natural laws that allow intelligent beings who know those laws to pile four huge bulls into one small shed, incinerate dogs, and disappear into thin air! If there are portals or wormholes between alternate realities, all consistent with laws that we simply don't yet understand, it would explain many of the outlandish goings-on that so many have witnessed. This is the conclusion of Kelleher and Knapp in *Skinwalker*. It is presently my conclusion—although in the 1970s it led me away from a scientific approach and toward religious thinking.

In 1977, at the First International UFO Congress in Chicago, J. Allan Hynek presented his thoughts in a speech "What I really believe about UFOs." (See Hynek, 1980.) "I do believe," he said, "that the UFO phenomenon as a whole is real, but I do not mean necessarily that it's just one thing. We must ask whether the diversity of observed UFOs . . . all spring from the same basic source, as do weather phenomena, which all originate in the atmosphere" or whether they differ "as a rain shower differs from a meteor, which in turn differs from a cosmic-ray shower." We must not ask, Hynek said, what hypothesis can explain the most facts, but we must ask, which hypothesis can explain the most puzzling facts.

"There is sufficient evidence to defend both the ETI and the EDI hypothesis," Hynek continued. As evidence for the ETI (extraterrestrial intelligence) hypothesis he mentioned, as examples, the radar cases as good evidence of something solid, and the physical-trace cases. Then he turned to defending the EDI (extradimensional intelligence) hypothesis. Besides the aspect of materialization and dematerialization, he cited the "poltergeist" phenomena experienced by some people after a close encounter; the photographs of UFOs, sometimes on only one frame, not seen by the witnesses; the ability of some UFOs to change form right before the witnesses' eyes; the puzzling question of telepathic communication; the fact that in close encounters of the third kind, the creatures seem to be at home in earth's gravity and atmosphere; the sudden stillness in the presence of the craft; levitation of cars or persons; the fact that some witnesses develop psychic abilities after an encounter. "Do we have two aspects of one phenomenon or two different sets of phenomena?" Hynek asked.

Finally he introduced a third hypothesis.

> I hold it entirely possible that a technology exists that encompasses both the physical and the psychic, the material and the mental. There are stars that are millions of years older than the sun. There may be a civilization that is millions of years more advanced than man's. We have gone from Kitty Hawk to the moon in some seventy years, but it's possible that a million-year-old civilization may know something that we don't. . . . I hypothesize an "M&M" technology encompassing the

mental and material realms. The psychic realms, so mysterious to us today, may be an ordinary part of an advanced technology.[3]

Wormhole Portals

More and more, the UFO literature contains references to wormholes or portals that allow passage from our three dimensional world into some other dimension that must be very close but that we can't see. In other versions of the physics, wormholes allow instant passage between distant parts of the universe. Vallée (1988, 2008 a.) makes a strong case for this explanation of many UFO phenomena. Philip Imbrogno (2009) is also a strong convert to this approach—although he takes it so far (e.g., psychic phenomena, angels, jinn, and so on) that I had a rather negative response to his book.[4] Nevertheless, even if the only evidence for wormhole phenomena is the sudden appearance or disappearance of UFOs (or skinwalkers), those events strongly suggest that there might well be other nearby dimensions or wormholes. Abductee accounts of aliens passing unimpeded through solid walls are certainly of interest—although this is where I begin to wonder what really happened and what was part of a dream world.

The reporting of UFO disappearances or sudden appearances is such a wide-spread part of the phenomenon that we must surely take it seriously—and the skinwalker orange "sky portals" are most interesting. We've noted that some physicists are discussing the mathematics of other dimensions and wormholes into and out of them. Thus, I find it interesting that "mainstream scientists" tend to reject the UFO phenomena out of hand—and that without having really investigated the evidence, such as the accounts presented in this book. Here seems to be solidly witnessed evidence for those wormholes that physicists talk about, yet they want nothing to do with the phenomenon—perhaps because, if they do, they will be ridiculed by their fellow scientists. Furthermore, as noted, the fact that a high percentage of "common people" accept the reality of UFOs is a clear indication of how ignorant those folk are of modern science, those scientists say. I keep trying to understand just what it is about science that rejects UFO reality! We've seen that none of the usual arguments ("UFOs are impossible") hold up when considered fairly.

Imagine what would happen in our world if we unlocked the secret of the wormhole—the star gate! What if we could go where they come from? Suddenly all of our scientific, public philosophies would change! No wonder our visitors don't make formal contact. Yet they seem to want us to know. They put on their displays. Why?

Religious Traditions Help Us Understand

Here I am back where I was as the 1980s approached, developing religious thoughts. Now, however, I don't need specifically LDS scriptures and theology to make my points (although I like one LDS scripture so much I'll have to quote it). The point here is that witness accounts of events upon which religions are founded have much in common with the strange UFO phenomena that we have been wondering about. Witness accounts of the supernatural are, of course, subject to all the problems already discussed: imperfect memories, lies, difficult descriptive language (i.e., the Hebrew and Greek of the Bible), some of the witnessed events taking place hundreds to thousands of years ago, and (most of all) the non-repeatability of those events. Hence, religions have their detractors much like the UFO debunkers. Pointing out the problems just listed, these detractors reject the witness accounts in total—while often trying to retain the good moral teachings! Except for the long time interval, contemporary UFO accounts and religious events have much in common.

Yet direct familiarity with many of the UFO witnesses has led me to accept their accounts—while always remaining aware that there are probably distortions caused by those problems just listed. And probably for similar reasons, the early Christians accepted the founding testimonies (now scripture) of the early apostles. For example, consider Saul's (Paul's) vision of the resurrected Christ as he made his way to Damascus. Luke recorded the story as a secondhand account three times in the Book of Acts, and in one of Paul's earliest letters, he bears strong personal testimony that it really happened: "... and last of all, as one born out of due time, he was seen by me" (1 Corinthians 15:8).

Peter bears direct testimony that he (with James and John) was on the Mount of Transfiguration with Jesus when two beings appeared who said they were Moses and Elijah from ancient times. Peter says that he heard a voice from heaven proclaiming Christ's divinity (2 Peter 1:16–18; Matthew 16:13–18; 17:1–9). Of course, modern skeptics (debunkers) concoct just-suppose stories to refute the idea that specific books of scripture were really authored by these apostles, such as with Acts (Luke), Corinthians (Paul), and the two letters of Peter. But people of the time, both Greeks and Hebrews (Jews), accepted these testimonies by the thousands. Many knew the witnesses, and their testimonies rang true. (A majority of modern Biblical scholars do accept the letters to the Corinthians as authentic early documents written by Paul—and they were probably written within fifteen years of Christ's death and resurrection. Peter's letters are more difficult to verify but seem internally consistent.)

Speaking of wormholes, there are plenty of precedents in the New Testament for such events as sudden appearance and disappearance. Consider, for example, Christ's appearance among his ten disciples behind closed doors after his death and resurrection (John 20:19–20; see also Luke 27:36–49). Thomas was not present at the first appearance but was present when Jesus appeared within a room a second time, asking Thomas to feel his body, his corporeality, as the other disciples had already done (John 20:24–29). Where did Christ come from in that room? Traditionally, we have said heaven and some have spoken of hell as another place. Our space ventures have not found such places (as a Russian cosmonaut proudly bragged), but if these stories—and similar stories that are part of the phenomenon—are true, the only answer is the parallel universe or other dimension—or perhaps wormholes to distant parts of this universe.

How did Christ get in that closed room? We're back to portals or wormholes.

As you surely know, these are only a few of the many examples of wormhole events that could be offered from Christianity. Not to mention those from Judaism and Islam (e.g., Mohammad being taken into heaven).

Many ufologists have not overlooked the examples from the New and Old Testaments. Obviously, they have much in common with modern contactee stories. Certainly, they have provided precedent for many contactees. How do we distinguish between the values of the contactee stories and those of Christianity's founding events, for example? I'll come back to that question.

It occurred to me not long ago that the strangeness and the wormhole events of the UFO phenomenon have strengthened my faith in Christianity! The New Testament witnesses who actually left personal records of the founding events are rather few: the gospel writers (Mark, Matthew, Luke, and John), Paul, James, Peter, Jude, and perhaps an unknown author of the Epistle to the Hebrews (traditionally ascribed to Paul, but differing stylistically from Paul's other letters). But modern witnesses of similar "wormhole" events number in the thousands! They have led me to the other-dimensional hypothesis, which provides a way for me to imagine "heaven." Clearly there is plenty of biblical precedent for transport between dimensional realities.

But now come the key questions: Why should I (or you) believe in the revelations of Christianity and not believe the doctrines proclaimed by the contactees? Well, I'm afraid I can't answer that for you. The answer has to be a personal decision based hopefully on much study and even prayer. There is a key scripture that has helped me to make that decision: As Jesus finished the Sermon on the Mount, he said: "Ye shall know them by their fruits. . . . A good tree cannot bring forth evil fruit, neither can a corrupt tree bring forth good fruit" (Matthew 7:16–18).

The decision about which revelations to accept—Christianity or contactees—is not always easy, simply because there has been much corruption associated with Christianity (unholy crusades, inquisitions, and more). Yet if the basic messages of Christianity are applied in reasonable ways, the fruits will be (and have been) good. I'm not aware of any contactee cults that have exploded like Christianity did in the first century when its fruits were predominantly good. The Raëlians form the only contactee cult that I know anything about, and their fruits leave much to be desired. But what you might think is your decision, not mine to make for you.

We discussed the Fatima Sun in Chapter 7. The entire event took place in the context of the Catholicism of 1917 Portugal. Yet it is difficult to imagine a more impressive UFO display, and apparently many lives were made better by the emotion of the event. Does that mean that the UFOs are sometimes tied to religion? At Fatima, this surely seemed to be the case, but my theology is far from the theology of Catholicism (although I certainly admire their current good works). Fortunately, we have a Book of Mormon scripture that helps me to appreciate good-fruit revelation in any religion: "For behold, the Lord doth grant unto all nations, of their own nation and tongue, to teach his word, yea, in wisdom, all that he seeth fit that they should have: therefore we see that the Lord doth counsel in wisdom, according to that which is just and true" (Alma 29:8).

In the New Testament, there are plenty of accounts of evil beings or spirits that appeared to witnesses. Christ's temptation by Satan (Matthew 4:1–11) is one example—and in the first temptation, Satan apparently knew that Jesus possessed powers based on physical laws that we are far from understanding, powers that gave him the ability to transmute stones into bread! If Lucifer has been inhabiting that other dimension for some time, why wouldn't he and those with him know their part of the universe very well by now? They also apparently know how to enter our part! Could there be restrictions on what the evil ones can do, placed upon them by the more powerful good ones? My point is that those inhabitants of that "other dimension" can be good or evil—or perhaps various stages in between. So there is another precedent for UFO manifestations. The Fatima Sun apparently served a good purpose, but there was apparently much evil exhibited by some of the inter-dimensional beings that appeared at skinwalker ranch.

What About My Faith?

Much as I hate to move away from my objective approach to both the UFO phenomenon and religion, it would be disingenuous of me not to mention that the founding history of my own religion involves several portal events, often with more than one witness. If I describe these events, it will sound like I'm trying to convert you, but they have been well documented and discussed from many perspectives.[5]

One such event in Latter-day Saint theology is the appearance of Moroni to Joseph Smith Jr. in his bedroom on September 23, 1823. Here is a greatly shortened version of the account: When Joseph Smith was seventeen years old, he was praying in his room one night before going to bed. As he prayed, a prophet named Moroni appeared to him, claiming to be the historian who last had the plates on which the Book of Mormon was written. According to Moroni, this book was written in some kind of "reformed Egyptian"—in about 400 AD in the Western Hemisphere. Joseph recorded the event as follows: "when immediately a personage appeared at my bedside, standing in the air, for his feet did not touch the floor" (Pearl of Great Price, Joseph Smith—History 1:30). Moroni then instructed Joseph, providing directions that eventually led to the translation and publication of the Book of Mormon. At the end of the instruction, light gathered around Moroni, and Joseph saw "a conduit open right up into heaven, and he ascended till he entirely disappeared" (Pearl of Great Price, Joseph Smith—History 1:43). There's a portal to contemplate!

Two more times that night, Moroni appeared as before, giving the exact same instructions. Then it was morning and Joseph went to work in the fields, but Joseph was so weak that his father sent him home. On the way home, Moroni appeared to Joseph for a fourth time—again repeating the same instructions but telling Joseph to go to his father and relate the entire experience, which Joseph did. It seems significant that his father and indeed his large family accepted his story. Moroni then appeared each year for four years as he had promised he would, after which the plates were received and the Book of Mormon was translated and published. Moroni later showed the plates to three other witnesses, and, as instructed, Joseph showed the plates to eight others but without supernatural manifestation. (And there were other instances in which various witnesses besides Joseph Smith reported visions: portal events.)

As with the New Testament "contactee" accounts, ufologists have considered Moroni's visit to Joseph Smith to be a somewhat typical contactee story. Jacques Vallée (2008 a., pp. 210–214), for example, tells the story in more detail than I have here. He concludes: "It is futile to engage in a debate concerning the truth or falsity of the statements made by Joseph Smith." He notes that LDS people long considered the Book of Mormon to be a history of all the indigenous people of North and South America—a difficult idea to accept in view of modern ideas about the origins of Native Americans. Vallée asks, "Were such messages deliberately given to isolate the believers from the society around them?" I have certainly had that thought. But the story is not quite as cut and dried as Vallée presents it. Most Mormons no longer defend the idea that all Native Americans are descendants of Book of Mormon peoples—who might well have been a very small population restricted to Central America.[6]

Then there is the matter of "fruits." I have seen many good fruits brought forth by the Church since its organization in 1830. For one thing, the Church contributes much humanitarian help in the aftermath of disasters all over the world. It also provides welfare activities, mostly for its members, and even public works. Most members live productive, moral, happy lives. Of course there are exceptions as must be expected in a church that considers free will (agency) as a primary doctrine. An important point for me is that the Church presents a highly rational theology—if it is understood in the context of the multiverse, stargate concept!

So okay, I'm defending my own religious convictions. But of course I can't decide for you.

Notes

1. My doubts about evolution were generated originally, I suppose, by my belief in God. Now my doubts are much more scientific. Many proponents of evolutionary theory then and certainly now were and are convinced that the

theory of evolution by natural selection of random mutations (and other minor mechanisms) leads directly to a universe without a Creator. We can't directly test the role of a Creator, so it is proper science to try to understand nature on atheistic principles. But that doesn't mean that there is no Intelligent Creator. Nevertheless, some authors are concluding that evolutionary theory sufficiently accounts for the living organisms in our world so that there must be no God. My premise is that such a belief depends on a host of just-suppose stories. (For details, see Salisbury, 2006.)

Here's a brief but typical example of an evolutionary just-suppose story: On the Galapagos Islands, Charles Darwin collected thirteen species of birds which, after he returned to England, were classified as finches—now called Darwin's finches. Each one had (has) a beak that is highly specialized for the kind of food that it consumes, and most of the species are on all of the islands in the archipelago. Those are the facts. Now comes the question: How did these finches evolve? The answer is a classic example in evolutionary theory because it became so prominent in Darwin's thinking. And it may well be true or very close to the truth. But note that it is all "just suppose" and must essentially be accepted on faith:

Just suppose a pregnant finch made it across the hundreds of miles of water from Ecuador to the Galapagos (although finches normally do not cross open water). Just suppose that, as the centuries went by, mutations occurred in one member of a breeding group that changed its behavior (instincts) such that it gained its nutrition by sucking blood near the tail of large shore birds—and that genes controlling development of its or its offsprings' beaks also mutated so that the beak was adapted to sucking blood. Since no other finches were sucking blood, this individual had an advantage, and its offspring survived and multiplied until they became a species, spreading to all the islands. Just suppose another individual in a breeding group had mutations that changed its behavior to eating seeds and a beak that facilitated that way of feeding—and so on for the seed eater and the other eleven species. But how do you know what really happened?

How can you go beyond "just suppose"? Nucleotide sequences can be studied nowadays, and they might suggest the pathways in this evolution, but only tentatively. As with UFO accounts, history cannot be repeated. Furthermore, as to the origin of the necessary mutations, science simply cannot study the possibility that some kind of intelligence was involved in that creation. Science really can't, or it ceases to be science. Although the situation is closely similar, let's hope that science can find some way to study the UFO phenomenon. The parallel is that witness accounts (their existence, not necessarily their truth) are the "fossils" with which ufologists must work—plus a modicum of physical evidence.

2. In a series of DVD lectures by Jeanette Norden entitled "Understanding the Brain," made available by The Teaching Company, she discusses agnosias in which an individual with some injury or lesion to some part of the brain experiences a loss of some form of "knowledge" that depends upon that part of the brain.

In motion agnosia, the person with the disorder is unable to experience motion in the surrounding world. The person sees "frozen frames" of the world. For example, an approaching automobile might be seen as standing still down the road; a moment later the automobile is seen closer but again standing still. The automobile seems to jump from one spot to another. That sounds like several UFO accounts! A UFO seems to disappear from one spot and reappear instantly in another spot some distance away. What if the witness experienced a temporary shutting down of the appropriate part of the brain, a temporary motion agnosia? But will that work as an explanation in multiple-witness cases in which all the witnesses report the same observation of a "jumping" UFO? The obvious just-suppose story is that the UFO drivers not only have powers to influence witnesses' brains, but they can influence specifically the part of the brain that perceives time and thus motion, making the UFO appear to move instantly from one spot to another!

3. These paragraphs about Hynek's talk are from Wikipedia.

4. Imbrogno tries to be scientific and critical of some of his cases, but I kept wanting to argue with the validity of his evidence in other cases.

5. Following an enlightening phone conversation, Michael Scott Van Wagenen, a Latter-day Saint historian and folklorist from Brownsville, Texas, was kind enough to send me a preliminary manuscript of a chapter he is working on for a book coedited with W. Paul Reeve, to be published by Utah State University Press. The book is titled *Between Pulpit and Pew: The Supernatural World in Mormon Folklore*, and his chapter is titled "Singular Phenomenon: The Evolving Mormon Interpretation of Unidentified Flying Objects." The chapter is an excellent summary of Latter-day Saint beliefs and folklore on the topic of extraterrestrial life in general as well as UFOs. There are quotations from Church leaders as well as from far-out authors on the fringes of the Church—most of whom are no longer active Latter-day Saints. His conclusions are very close to my own.

6. In the late 1970s, it became very clear to me that the actual story in the book restricts the peoples to a small area, certainly no more than the size of a state such as Utah. For example, armies cross the Book of Mormon areas in just a few days. Since then, this localization of the Book of Mormon story has been pointed out by many LDS scholars and is the accepted version by Church authorities. It is also accepted that numerous Native Americans were already here when the Book of Mormon people arrived. I have no idea why it took so long for the Church as a whole to realize this, although surely many individuals had come to this conclusion from the beginning. That is another story, but it puts a different light on Vallée's understandable skepticism. Scholars have carefully examined the life of Joseph Smith (e.g., Bushman, 2006) as well as the Book of Mormon (e.g., Givens, 2002). They have answered many questions in ways that have satisfied me and other active members of the Church of Jesus Christ of Latter-day Saints.

Annotated Bibliography

Adamski, George. *Inside the Flying Saucers*. New York: Paperback Library, 1967. [This book tells of Adamski's "trip to the moon." It was first published in 1955.]

Asch, Solomon E. *Social Psychology*. Englewood Cliffs, New Jersey: Prentice-Hall, 1952.

Asch, Solomon E. in *Group Dynamics—Research and Theory*. Edited by D. Cartwright and A. Zander. Evanston and New York: Row, Peterson & Co, 1962.

Berlitz, Charles, and William Moore. *The Roswell Incident*. London: Granada, 1981.

Bloetcher, Ted. *Report on the UFO Wave of 1947*. Washington, D.C.: National Investigations Committee on Aerial Phenomena, 1967. [By researching newspapers, 853 cases were found. Most ufologists were aware of less than 50 for this period.]

Blumrich, Josef F. *The Spaceships of Ezekiel*. New York: Bantam, 1974. [An attempt by a NASA engineer to explain Ezekiel's visions in modern terms.]

Burt, Eugene H. *UFOs and Diamagnetism*. New York: Exposition Press, 1970. [A postulated UFO propulsion system.]

Bushman, Richard L. *Joseph Smith: Rough Stone Rolling*. New York: Alfred A. Knopf, 2006. [Bushman, then a historian at Columbia University, examines Joseph Smith and his times.]

Carrion, James. "New Avenues for UFO Research." *Dawn of a New Era in UFO Research: MUFON Symposium Proceedings,* August 6–9, 2009, 221–55. [For more information, please write to Mutual UFO Network, Inc., 2619 11th Street Rd., Suite 21, Greeley, CO 80634.]

Clancy, Susan A. *Abducted: How People Come to Believe They Were Kidnapped by Aliens.* Cambridge: Harvard University Press, 2005. [A UFO debunker book with much good information on the perils of hypnotic memory recovery.]

Condon, Edward U. *Scientific Study of Unidentified Flying Objects.* New York: Bantam Books, 1969. [The famous University of Colorado UFO report.]

Cramp, Leonard. *UFOs and Anti-Gravity: Piece for a Jig-Saw.* Kempton, Illinois: Adventures Unlimited Press, 1966.

Däniken, Erich von. *Gods from Outer Space: Return to the Stars or Evidence for the Impossible.* New York: Bantam Books, 1972. [There are several versions of Däniken's books; this happens to be the only one in Salisbury's library.]

Dawkins, Richard. *The God Delusion.* New York: Houghton Mifflin, 2006.

Dennis, Danniel S. *Horizons Beyond the Rim.* Roosevelt, Utah: self-published, 1991. [A wonderful memory of an earlier time in the Uintah Basin.]

Downing, Barry H. *The Bible and Flying Saucers.* New York: J. B. Lippincott, 1968. [An interesting attempt to relate the biblical miracles to the UFO phenomenon; Downing is a theologian.]

Friedman, Stanton, and Don Berliner. *Crash at Corona: The U.S. Military Retrieval and Cover-Up.* New York: Paragon, 1992.

Friedman, Stanton. *Flying Saucers and Science.* Franklin Lakes, New Jersey: Career Press, 2008. [A recent summary of ufology and argument for space ships.]

Friedman, Stanton. "Pseudoscience of Anti-ufology." *Dawn of a New Era in UFO Research: MUFON Symposium Proceedings,* August 6–9, 2009, 19–32. [For more information, please write to Mutual UFO Network, Inc., 2619 11th Street Rd., Suite 21, Greeley, CO 80634.]

Fuller, John G. *Incident at Exeter.* New York: Putnam & Sons, 1966. [A well-researched series of UFO sightings beginning at Exeter, New Hampshire.]

Fuller, John G. *The Interrupted Journey.* New York: Dial, 1966. [The famous Betty and Barney Hill case.]

Givens, Terryl L. *By the Hand of Mormon: The American Scripture That Launched a New World Religion.* New York: Oxford University Press, 2002. [Givens examines the Book of Mormon from several perspectives, all with scholarly skill.]

Harder, James A. in Roush, J. E. *Symposium on Unidentified Flying Objects.* Washington, D.C.: U. S. Government Printing office, 1968.

Hall, Richard S. *The UFO Evidence.* Washington, D.C.: National Investigations Committee on Aerial Phenomena, 1964. [An excellent compilation of information by NICAP but now very difficult to obtain.]

Hill, Paul R. *Unconventional Flying Objects: A Scientific Analysis.* Charlottesville, Virginia: Hampton Roads Publishing, 1995. [A postulated UFO propulsion system.]

Hopkins, Budd. *Intruders: The Incredible Visitations at Copley Woods.* New York: Random House, 1987.

Hynek, J. Allen. "UFOs Merit Scientific Study." *Science* 154, 1966, 329.

Hynek, J. Allen. *The UFO Experience—A Scientific Inquiry.* Chicago: Regnery, 1972.

Hynek, J. Allen, *Proceedings of the First International UFO Congress.* New York: Warner Books, 1980, 153–67.

Imbrogno, Philip. *Interdimensional Universe: The New Science of UFOs, Paranormal Phenomena & Otherdimensional Beings.* Woodbury, Minnesota: Llewellyn Publications, 2009.

Jessup, Morris K. *The Case for the UFO.* New York: Citadel, 1955. [The version annotated in the hoax by Carlos Allende was published by Varo Manufacturing Company of Garland, Texas.]

Jungk, Robert. *Brighter Than a Thousand Suns.* New York: Harcourt, Brace, and Company, 1958. [On development of the atomic bomb; contains a footnote suggesting that UFOs were secretly developed by German scientists during World War II.]

Kelleher, Colm A. and George Knapp. *Hunt for the Skinwalker: Science Confronts the Unexplained at a Remote Ranch in Utah.* New York: Paraview Pocket Books, 2005.

Klass, Philip J. *UFOs Identified.* New York: Random House, 1968. [In this book, Klass argues that most UFOs can be explained as plasmas—ball lightning.]

Klass, Philip J. *UFOs Explained*. New York: Random House, 1974. [Klass "explains" some of the best UFO cases.]

Lorenzen, Coral E. *The Great Flying Saucer Hoax*. New York: The William-Frederick Press, 1962. [Coral and Jim must have chosen the title to catch the eye of the public; claims that UFOs exist was no hoax, but government put-down of the phenomenon was the hoax.]

Lorenzen, Coral E. *Flying Saucers: The Startling Evidence of the Invasion from Outer Space*. New York: The New American Library, 1966. [An updated version of the 1962 book.]

Lorenzen, Coral E. and James A. Lorenzen. *Flying Saucer Occupants* Toronto: The New American Library, 1967. [A good summary of some UFO occupant cases up to that time. Salisbury wrote a foreword to this book.]

Lorenzen, Coral E. and James A. Lorenzen. *UFOs Over the Americas*. New York: The New American Library, 1968.

Markowitz, William. "The Physics and Metaphysics of Unidentified Flying Objects." *Science 157*, 1967, 1274. [A naive article on the impossibility of the UFO.]

Menzel, Donald H. and Lyle Boyd. *The World of Flying Saucers*. New York: Doubleday, 1963. [A sometimes impressive attempt to debunk (explain) a number of UFO cases.]

Menzel, Donald H. and Ernest H. Taves. *The UFO Enigma: The Definitive Explanation of the UFO Phenomenon*. Garden City, New York: Doubleday, 1977.

Michel, Aimé. *Flying Saucers and the Straight-Line Mystery*. New York: Criterion, 1958. [This is an important book on the wave of sightings in France during the autumn of 1954, including some of the most fascinating and well-described cases on record.]

Miller, George P. *Symposium on Unidentified Flying Objects: Hearings before the Committee on Science and Astronautics U.S. House of Representatives, Ninetieth Congress, Second Session*. Washington, D.C.: U.S. Government Printing Office, 1968. [This important document from the Chairman of the U.S. Congressional Committee on Science and Astronautics includes statements by J. Allen Hynek, James E. McDonald, Carl Sagan, Robert L. Hall, James A. Harder, and Robert M. L. Baker Jr. There are prepared papers by Donald Menzel, R. Leo Sprinkle, Garry C. Henderson, Stanton T. Friedman, Roger

N. Shepard, and Frank B. Salisbury. Salisbury's paper is a direct copy of his 1967 *BioScience* article.]

Nickell, Joe. "The Real Secrets of Fatima." *Skeptical Inquirer* vol. 33, no. 6, 2009, 14–17.

Pearse, Steve. "Update on Fish's Zeta Reticuli Theory." *MUFON UFO Journal*, no. 496, August 2009, 6–9.

Pennock, Robert T. *Tower of Babel: The Evidence against the New Creationism.* Cambridge: The MIT Press, 1999.

Phillips, Ted. "Physical Traces Associated with UFOs: Dramatic Changes Indicated." *Dawn of a New Era in UFO Research: MUFON Symposium Proceedings,* August 6–9, 2009, 80–91. [For more information, please write to Mutual UFO Network, Inc., 2619 11th Street Rd., Suite 21, Greeley, CO 80634.]

Pollard, Katherine S. "What makes us human?" *Scientific American 300*, no. 5, May 2009, 44–49.

Raël, Claude Vorilhon. "The Book Which Tells the Truth" from *The Message Given to Me by Extraterrestrials.* Tokyo: AOM Corp, 1986.

Randle, Kevin. "Bringing the Scientific Method to the Study of UFOs." *Dawn of a New Era in UFO Research: MUFON Symposium Proceedings,* August 6–9, 2009, 107–37. [For more information, please write to Mutual UFO Network, Inc., 2619 11th Street Rd., Suite 21, Greeley, CO 80634.]

Randle, Kevin, and Don Schmitt. *UFO Crash at Roswell.* New York: Avon Books, 1991.

Richardson, Robert S. *Exploring Mars.* New York: McGraw-Hill, 1954, 128–32.

Rock, Irwin and Lloyd Kaufman. "The Moon Illusion, Part 2." *Science 136*, 1962, 1023.

Rutkowski, Chris. *A World of UFOs.* Toronto: Dundurn Press, 2008.

Salisbury, Frank B. "Martian Biology: Accumulating Evidence Favors the Theory of Life on Mars, But We Can Expect Surprises." *Science 136*, April 1962, 17–26.

Salisbury, Frank B. "The scientist and the UFO." *BioScience 17*, 1967, 15–24.

Salisbury, Frank B. "Natural selection and the Complexity of the Gene." *Nature 224*, 1969, 342–43.

Salisbury, Frank B. *The Utah UFO Display: A Biologists Report.* Old Greenwich, Connecticut: Devin-Adair, 1974. [The first edition of this book.]

Salisbury, Frank B. "Recent Developments in the Scientific Study of UFOs." *BioScience 25*, 1975, 505–12.

Salisbury, Frank B. "Can Science Solve the UFO Mystery?" *Proceedings of the First International UFO Congress.* New York: Warner Books, 1980. [Followed by a paper by Stanton Friedman on UFO propulsion systems. Salibury also took part in symposia.]

Salisbury, Frank B. "Are UFOs from Outer Space?" *Proceedings of the First International UFO Congress.* New York: Warner Books, 1980.

Salisbury, Frank B. "Gravitropism: Changing Ideas. Horticultural Reviews." *Proceedings of the First International UFO Congress.* New York: Warner Books, 1980.

Salisbury, Frank B. *The Case for Divine Design.* Springville, Utah: Horizon, 2006.

Salisbury, Frank B. "Reflections of an Old UFO Chaser." *Dawn of a New Era in UFO Research: MUFON Symposium Proceedings*, August 6–9, 2009, 33–55. [For more information, please write to Mutual UFO Network, Inc., 2619 11th Street Rd., Suite 21, Greeley, CO 80634.]

Salisbury, Frank B. and Cleon W. Ross. *Plant Physiology, Fourth Edition.* Belmont, California: Wadsworth Publishing, 1992.

Sanderson, Ivan T. *Uninvited Visitors.* New York: Cowles Education, 1967. [An interpretation of UFOs by a zoologist and collector of unexplained phenomena.]

Schwarz, Berthold E. "UFOs in New Jersey." *Journal of the Medical Society of New Jersey* vol. 66, 1969, 460. [A search for UFO stories in mental patients.]

Shibutani, Tamotsu. *Improvised News.* New York: Bobbs-Merrill, 1966. [A sociological study of rumor formation.]

Steiger, Brad, with Joan Whritenour. *Allende Letters: New UFO Breakthrough.* New York: Award Books, 1968. [A rather superficial book suggesting that the UFOs are being produced on Earth by a secret organization with its roots in the alchemists of antiquity.]

Strieber, Whitley. *Communion: A True Story.* New York: Beech Tree Books, 1987. [Probably the first book to document nighttime abductions.]

Thompson, James L. *Aliens and UFOs: Messengers or Deceivers?* Bountiful, Utah: Horizon, 1993.

Trench, Brinsley LePoer. *The Flying Saucer Story*. New York: Ace Books, 1966. [Illustrating poor reporting combined with pseudoscience.]

"UFOs: An Earthly Debate between Believers and Skeptics on Flying Saucers, Extraterrestrial Visitors and Things That Go Flash in the Night." *Playboy*, January 1978, 67–98, 128–29, 249–50.

Vallée, Jacques. *Anatomy of a Phenomenon*. Chicago: NTC: Contemporary Publishing, 1965. [A penetrating scientific evaluation of the UFO enigma.]

Vallée, Jacques. *Passport to Magonia*. Chicago: McGraw Hill/Contemporary Publishing, 1969. [Vallée presents his comparison of UFO reports and the fairy faith, angels, and demons.]

Vallée, Jacques. *Dimensions: A Casebook of Alien Contact*. New York: Anomalist Books, 1988. [Vallée updates and expands his comparison of modern UFO reports with legends and historical events.]

Vallée, Jacques. *Confrontations: A Scientist's Search for Alien Contact*. New York: Anomalist Books, 1990. [Vallée presents about 100 cases that he has personally investigated, including some that led to the death of the UFO witness.]

Vallée, Jacques. *Revelations: Alien Contact and Human Deception*. New York: Anomalist Books, 1991. [Vallée presents evidence that well-constructed hoaxes and media manipulations have misled ufologists, diverting them from the UFO phenomenon.]

Vesco, R. in "The Truth About Flying Saucers," by John Ashton. *Argosy 369*, no. 2, August 21, 1969, 22. [A "secret-weapon" explanation for the UFOs.]

Walsh, William Thomas. *Our Lady of Fatima*. New York: Macmillan, 1947. [A review of the Fatima Sun incident by a Catholic historian.]

Walton, Travis. *Fire in the Sky: The Walton Experience*. New York: Marlowe, 1997. [This a third edition; previously published in 1978 and 1996.]

Warren, Donald I. "Status Inconsistency Theory and Flying Saucer Sightings." *Science 170*, 1970, 599–603.

Warren, Larry and Peter Robbins. *Left at East Gate*. New York: Marlowe, 1997.

Wittmann, Richard G. "Flying Saucers or Flying Shields." *The Classical Journal* vol. 63, 1968, 223. [UFOs among the Romans.]

Appendix

Table 1

UFO Cases in Joseph Junior Hicks's Files Prior to 1973

*Note that the data in this table sometimes disagree with data presented in the interviews in Chapter 1. The data in the table are from the files of Joseph Junior Hicks, usually prepared shortly after a sighting, and sometimes a witness presented a different version when interviewed months or years later.

**The plus sign (+) indicates windows. A zero (0) indicates no windows.

Table 1. Uintah Basin Sightings*

No.	Date	Event, Including Size and Shape	Name of one Witness and Location	Sound	Number of Witnesses	Shape**	Time	Day	Night	Estimated distance
1.	Summer, 1956	Orange ball, over hill, into river bottom, 100 ft. overhead, humming sound, fast.	Sandy Richman, east of Bridgeland	X	1	Ball 0	22:00		X	100 ft.
2.	Spring	Silver, dome, small-house size, hum; saw through scope on rifle, saw face in window: long skinny human face. Overhead, felt pressure. Moved, hovered.	Sam Brough, 3 miles east of Roosevelt	X	2	Disc/dome +	7:30	X		30 ft. overhead
3.	Summer, 1965	Silver, metallic, saucer, whirring, 40 ft. diameter, hovered at 30 ft., took off rapidly.	Carlos Reed, Arcadia, Utah	X	1	Double convex +	—		X	150 ft.
4.	June 14, 1965	Looked like a star; got close, but thought it was helicopter until later saw picture of UFO.	Brent D. Young, Dry Fork		5	Double convex +	—		X	2 miles
5.	July 20, 1956	Silver dome—great speed. Dark band around middle. Whistle—screeching.	Bill Locke, 72 miles west of Roosevelt	X	2	Double convex. Dark rim?	Midnight		X	20,000 ft. (?)

No.	Date	Event, Including Size and Shape	Name of one Witness and Location	Sound	Number of Witnesses	Shape**	Time	Day	Night	Estimated distance
6.	Aug. 9, 1965	Object on ground—standing up like rocket. Top was flat, row of windows below—room inside with bright lights. Rotating, flashing light on top. Flames on bottom, rose 30 ft, hovered—flame—up fast. No sound.	Kent Denver, South Myton Bench	0	3	Rocket, 40 ft. diameter	Midnight		X	100 yards (?)
7.	Early Sept. 1965	Cream colored, size of six cars, no sound, windows around edge.	Myra Cook, Airport Road to Shisler's field, 1 mile NE of Roosevelt	0	1	Double Convex +	22:30		X	0.5 mile
8.	March 2, 1966	Flashing light, stood still, 15 min, then up with high speed.	Norma Denver, east of Roosevelt (2 miles)		1	Light 0	19:00		X	—
9.	Aug, 1966	Silver saucer, larger than airplane—moved across the sky.	Hal McKee, Tridell (NE Roosevelt)		3	Double convex 0	12:00 noon	X		0.5 mile
10.	Aug. 20, 1966	Hovered, glowed orange, approached, red beam out bottom, children ran toward it, it left.	Gladys Cuch & husband, Randlett	0	ca. 12	Convex plane 0	Dusk		X	50 to 100 yards

No.	Date	Event, Including Size and Shape	Name of one Witness and Location	Sound	Number of Witnesses	Shape**	Time	Day	Night	Estimated distance
11.	Sept. 1, 1966	Reddish orange, round, slow. Several occasions, up in sky, then down.	Colin Murdock		6	Light	22:30		X	Close
12.	Sept. 5, 1966	Ten feet wide, height not known, colored light.	Elaine Cook		1	Double convex +	21:00		X	1.5 miles
13.	Sept. 7, 1966	Size of house, moved slowly, blueish white light in dome; landed on ground, pulsating red & yellow. (Bishop Garth Batty gave TV interviews about this sighting.)	Mr. & Mrs. Valda Massey, Maeser–NW of Vernal		3	Half sphere 0	23.25		X	1.5 miles
14.	Sept. 15, 1966	Silver disc.	Lynn Cuch (Native American), Lapoint	0	2	Double convex	Sundown	X		Long ways
15.	Sept. 15, 1966	Five feet off ground, 50–60' diameter—silver metal, encountered in the woods; took off vertically, spinning slowly—rapid as it rose.	James Cuch (cousin), White Rocks	0	1	Double convex	14:00	X		100 feet
16A	Sept. 20, 1966	Family watching TV, room lit up red, outside lighted, also humming sound, hovering over house (ran out), moved slowly, wobbled.	Priscilla Sireech (Native American), Randlett	X	8	Convex plane	20:30		X	30–40 feet above
16B	Sept. 20, 1966	Same as above; drawings very similar.	Boots Sireech (brother)		1					

No.	Date	Event, Including Size and Shape	Name of one Witness and Location	Sound	Number of Witnesses	Shape**	Time	Day	Night	Estimated distance
17.	Sept. 20, 1966	Band, transparent cone, pulsating red, blue, white. On edge, then dome down, then went up—went away with great speed, came back and hovered.	Garth P. Batty; Lapoint Road, west end of valley, NW of Vernal	0	1	Convex plane, on edge 0	20:45		X	2,000 feet
18.	Sept. 25, 1966	Large, red lights around edge, green on top, hovering, flashing, then straight up "like crazy."	Keith Haslem, Tridell, Utah		1	Convex plane 0	Sunday evening		X	~mile
19.	Sept. 26, 1966	Pulsating various colors: blue, green, orange, purple flames moving; cows bellowing (woke them up—looked out toward cows, saw object rise, saw through binoculars, hovered, took off.	Mrs. Ronald Batty, ~mile NE of Vernal			Double convex? +?	0:55		X	~mile
20A	Sept. 28, 1966	Watched half an hour. Appeared as big orange-red ball, but saw double convex shape.	Kent Denver; south of Fort Duchesne	0	3	Double convex, Red Ball	21:00		X	
20B	Sept. 28, 1966	Orange light above house, palpitating, moved to south as they approached, stopped again—sudden, no noise. Light off, changed colors, up suddenly away ("meteor in reverse").	Veri Haslem, east of Roosevelt	0	3	Orange ball			X	

No.	Date	Event, Including Size and Shape	Name of one Witness and Location	Sound	Number of Witnesses	Shape**	Time	Day	Night	Estimated distance
21A	Sept. 28, 1966	Slow, then fast, size of large airplane; taking four Native American girls home—came around bend, dome light came on, coming at them, light flashing! Another car came; she was trying to back up—girls on floor! Girls screaming and heart beating.	Joe Ann Harris, 0.5 mile south of Fort Duchesne	0	5	Convex plane 0	22:30		X	50 to 100 yards
21B	Sept. 28, 1966	Driving toward Vernal, saw object south of road, turning into driveway toward it—it took off. Had followed road 0.5 mile.	Estel Manwaring on road to Vernal	0	2	Convex plane 0	22:30		X	100 yards
22.	Sept. 30, 1966	Measured width 50–60 ft. rim 10 ft. silvery metallic, hovered at 50 ft., moved along wash at 30 mph for 100 ft.—then away like a jet! Wobbled when hovering. Witnesses were on tractor in field.	Curtis Ercanbrack, 0.5 mile NE of Roosevelt Airport		3	Double convex, extra thick rim 0	16:30	X		200 ft.
23.	Sept. 30, 1966	Bright (white—green on bottom), down to ground, disappeared!	Mrs. Weston Justice		1	Dome? 0	17:30	X		Unknown
24.	Oct. 6, 1966	Flashing red, white, and green, large oval—slow, then sped up. Two girls walking, called sister just before zoomed off.	Lynda Thompson, Fort Duchesne	0	2	Double convex +	20:30		X	"not far"

No.	Date	Event, Including Size and Shape	Name of one Witness and Location	Sound	Number of Witnesses	Shape**	Time	Day	Night	Estimated distance
25.	Oct. 9, 1966	Red light on edge—bigger than plane—body glowing yellow; walking, looked up "to see a UFO."	Susan Denver, Fort Duchesne		2	Double convex 0	19:20		X	2 miles
26.	Oct. 15, 1966	Silver colored, 30–40' diameter. Fast, low flying (300 ft. overhead), bluish light from windows.	Freddie Gruenwald, Fred Brown (KVEL in Vernal), Roosevelt	0	2	Double convex +	22:30		X	300 ft.
27.	Oct. 17, 1966	Silver—saw only a few seconds.	Arnold Clerico; Lapoint, Utah	0	1	Two lens shaped	Sunrise 5:45	X		Way up in sky
28.	Oct. 21, 1966	Whistling, buzzing—orange, red light on end, blue light top and bottom; jet coming, looked like they would collide. Disappeared "like it turned invisible." Orange "tail" 500 yds long (200 mph, he thinks).	Withheld name, Native American, Gusher, Utah	X	1	Double convex 0	19:30		X	500 yards up

No.	Date	Event, Including Size and Shape	Name of one Witness and Location	Sound	Number of Witnesses	Shape**	Time	Day	Night	Estimated distance
29.	Oct. 24, 1966	Two objects 150 feet above horizon in SE, brilliant blue-white like welding torch. Changing to yellowish and fading. One moved fast, then pulsated red and hovered—watched over an hour with binoculars.	Ute Tribal Police Officers, south of Fort Duchesne		2	Two lights 0	21:30		X	
30.	Nov. 1966	Flew alongside of car a few seconds, then took off!	Russell Squires, Halfway Hollow		1(?) (family?)	Double convex with windows +			X	50–100 ft
31.	Nov. 1, 1966	Orange—light out, could still see shape—moving south.	Arnold Clerico reported by daughter (Delores), Lapoint, UT, road to Highway 40	0	1	Double convex 0	6:45 Sunrise	X		1 mile
32.	Nov. 2, 1966	Blue white, large star, extra one in handle of Dipper! Then moved off, changed direction, finally disappeared.	Mr. & Mrs. Keith Bergquist, north of Neola		2	Light 0	18:30		X	Long ways away

No.	Date	Event, Including Size and Shape	Name of one Witness and Location	Sound	Number of Witnesses	Shape**	Time	Day	Night	Estimated distance
33.	Nov. 10, 1966	Silver, 2 objects. First sounded like busy signal on telephone. Second followed, same sound.	Thelma Lamb, Lapoint, UT	X	7	Double convex	18:00		X	1 mile
34.	Nov. 10, 1966	Object just above tree, size of moon, or larger—red, dimmed, then brightened. Never moved.	Becky Jenkins, south of her house, 1 mile E of Roosevelt		1	Round 0	22:00		X	1 mile
35.	Nov. 17, 1966	Bright silver, gleamed in the sun. Moving fast, very low, went behind trees.	Annette Cook, N of Hullingers and Hilltop		1	Double convex 0	11:30	X		3–4 miles
36.	Nov. 21, 1966	Moving very fast. Silver object—moved back and forth, then hovered, up and down.	Mr. & Mrs. John Clerico, NW of Lapoint	0	2	Fish shaped	6:45		X	Closer than stars
37.	Week of Nov. 21, 1966	Saw two cars parked, stopped, observed object on top of nearby hill; after a few moments, object took off!	Hiland Milk Driver, Badlands Highway to Bonanza		1+	Half dome (top of parachute)	7:30	X		50–100 yards
38.	Nov. 25, 1966	35 ft. diameter, moved slow, red color. Brother and friends saw it. Flew over town 5 minutes, then light out.	Lewis Horrocks, above Lapoint	0	2+	Dumb-bell 0	19:30		X	200+ feet

No.	Date	Event, Including Size and Shape	Name of one Witness and Location	Sound	Number of Witnesses	Shape**	Time	Day	Night	Estimated distance
39.	Nov. 26, 1966	Round, glowing green, then orange light. Wife woke, room green in color—went out, object maneuvering around house and field—few minutes, flew away.	Lairn Becksted, 2 miles N of Talmage, Utah	0	2	Round 0	2:00		X	100 yards (?)
40.	Jan. 15, 1967	Big, yellow glow from inside dome, hovered, moved slowly. Watched 10 min. with binoculars. Moved up, then stopped. Called Joe Reidhead; he and wife also saw.	Mr. & Mrs. Quivonton Lawson, (E end of Ben Dye Hill), N of Roosevelt 3 miles	0	4	Convex plane 0	18:00		X	2 miles
41A	Feb. 23, 1967	Children played with Ouija board, said to expect saucer at 8:00 PM over Roosevelt Hospital. Kids went out to look, came in screaming, she and husband saw orange-yellow light moving toward them—went out, came on bright and large, moving toward them, then went out. Full moon shape, S to N.	Mrs. Clyde McDonald, Roosevelt, Utah	0	5	Round 0	20:00		X	2,000 feet (?)

No.	Date	Event, Including Size and Shape	Name of one Witness and Location	Sound	Number of Witnesses	Shape**	Time	Day	Night	Estimated distance
41B		Car coming south to Roosevelt. Size of full moon—moved over them S to N.	Ken Vowers, BLM South Roosevelt (Burland man)	0	2	Round 0	20:00		X	Overhead
41C		Looking toward Roosevelt—saw it move S to N over town.	Leah & Veri Haslem, Montes Creek, NE Roosevelt, 5 miles	0	2	Round 0	20:00		X	5 miles
41D	Feb. 23, 1967	Driving truck from Currant Creek going E toward Roosevelt 60 miles away. He said moved N to S, same size and shape. Half mile ahead of truck.	Wesley Ercanbrack, Currant Creek	0	1	Round 0	20:00+		X	0.5
41E		Same size and shape—moving S to N over Roosevelt.	Julias Murray	0	2	Round 0	20:00		X	6+ miles
41F		Flew alongside car—orange light, followed for about a mile—stopped truck, turned off light—went straight up until smaller than star—10 min. Then down into south fast—out of sight.	Roy Marchant, Milk Driver, Boneta	0	1	Light	20:00		X	~mile

No.	Date	Event, Including Size and Shape	Name of one Witness and Location	Sound	Number of Witnesses	Shape**	Time	Day	Night	Estimated distance
41G		No details—heard he saw it.	Dave Roberts, Roosevelt Police							
42.	Feb. 27, 1967	At first glance, size of full moon, orange. Close look: 100 ft. in diameter, covered road, flames from fence to fence. Saw just behind hill, thought an airplane about to crash, followed along at the same speed slightly to right, sparkling bluish-white light at bottom. Dipped low, appeared to nearly crash into flume across road, followed clear to Roosevelt, 30 miles, going 55 to 60 mph. Went on west of town and disappeared over hill. Maybe 30 minutes.	Thyrena Daniels (Roosevelt, UT), west of Vernal, Highway 40	0	1	Dome 0	19:30		X	300 to 500 feet
43.	Mar. 12, 1967	Very fast—ground lit up around car; got out to see—saw "windows" lit up like a train—orange. Round at one end of row, square at other. Bluish-white light coming down from windows.	Mr. & Mrs Tony Zufelt, Hwy 40, half-way between Vernal & Roosevelt (Halfway Hollow)		2	Row of "windows" +	20:15		X	150 feet

No.	Date	Event, Including Size and Shape	Name of one Witness and Location	Sound	Number of Witnesses	Shape**	Time	Day	Night	Estimated distance
44.	Mar. 13, 1967	Followed in car by orange light. She sped up, so did it—stopped, it faded slowly away. Had a "door" brighter than rest of object—orange.	Sandra Murdock, daughter Mrs. Murdock and Children, between Lapoint & Fort Duchesne		6	Double convex +	20:30		X	
45A	Apr. 17, 1967	Pulsating light: red, blue, white. E to W.	Marvin Rawhouse, Roosevelt		1	Light 0	20:00		X	
45B		Binoculars: pulsating red, blue, white, E to W.	Val Anderson, Windy Ridge		1	Saturn 0	20:00		X	
45C		Pulsating light: red, blue, white, E to W	Sam Brough, Randlett		1	Light 0	20:00		X	
46.	Apr. 21, 1967	Nine silver, lens-shaped objects, violent maneuvers—no vapor trail, seen through binoculars. Hovered, no rudder or tail section. Could outmaneuver any craft he had seen.	David B. Hall, USAF (retired), Maeser to Vernal, Utah	0	1	Lens, 9 objects 0	22:50		X	20,000 feet

No.	Date	Event, Including Size and Shape	Sound	Name of one Witness and Location	Number of Witnesses	Shape**	Time	Day	Night	Estimated distance
47.	Apr. 22, 1967	Bright red, 50' diameter. Coming into driveway, dogs barking, saw red football-shaped object sitting on the ground. Turned off car lights—object rose and left rapidly.	0	Cliff Hackford family, Lapoint, Utah	4	Lens 0	Evening		X	0.5 mile
48.	May 12, 1967	Silver football or disc—45' long, 15' thick. No windows, bright distinct outline. Fast at first, then very slow. Came down fast, level with road, along it for a ways, almost stopped, tilted, slipped over crest of hill into valley and out of sight.	0	Richard Faucett, Charles Winn, 5 miles S of Neola on Highway 40	2	Oval 0	20:00 Sunset	X		1–2 miles
49.	May 22, 1967	Saw first as a star. Observed through telescope. [I don't understand the 100 yards.] Faster than airplane, slower than jet. Four lights, 2 orange, red, yellow mix, yellow-white centers, followed by 2 red lights.	0	Aaron Daniels, Lapoint, Utah	2?	Four lights 0	21:00		X	100 yards
50.	Aug. 15, 1957	Orange color becoming deep red, coming up canyon. On and off, stopped car and watched. When off, could see no object although full moon; 75 feet in length.	0	Jay Larsen, Hanna North—North Fork, Duchesne River	1	Light 0	01:00		X	1–2 miles

No.	Date	Event, Including Size and Shape	Name of one Witness and Location	Sound	Number of Witnesses	Shape**	Time	Day	Night	Estimated distance
51.	Sept. 1967	Flash of light to the west. White dome on top, very bright to begin with, then blue lights on each end. Went straight up, disappeared in SE.	Name withheld; Ioka, Utah	0	2	Cigar 0	20:00		X	~1 mile
52.	Oct. 14, 1967	Orange, red, huge, incredible speed. Noticed "fire" on road to Ouray, into draw, lost sight, then saw again. Object rose toward full moon—made loop around the moon, went in front of face, blotted out a fraction of a second. Kept flat side down. Disappeared in the NW.	Orvil Rudy, Czar Rudy (father). Halfway Hollow, junction of Ouray Road with Highway 40	0	2	Half dome 0	19:45		X	~mile
53.	Oct. 11, 1967	Pulsating red, green, yellow lights, flat bottom, dome shape, large size—all descriptions below essentially the same.	Gerald Nebeker, Mrs. Nebeker, older brother (from Ft. Duchesne), store on Hwy. 40, 1 mile N of Fort Duchesne	0	3	Dome	20:30 to 21:00		X	

No.	Date	Event, Including Size and Shape	Name of one Witness and Location	Sound	Number of Witnesses	Shape**	Time	Day	Night	Estimated distance
		Home teaching in Avalon with companion. Saw it to the W over Leland Bench way in S. North over Fort Duchesne.	Edwards Betts, Avalon	0	2					
		Orange-red ball, S to N.	Jerry Goodrich, Tridell— Norman Winn, Leland Bench	0	6					
		Saw object moving W of them, S to N, orange-red, 45 degrees up.	Mr. & Mrs. Weston Justice, Lapoint Road, 2 miles N of them		4	Ball	20:30			
		Five miles north on White Rocks Road. Low to right, E of highway. Orange-red ball, S to N. Blinking on and off.	Gerald Bolton, Bennett	0	1	Ball				
		Orange-red ball. Came S over house. Saw it go up into Farm Creek.	Willis, Chivers, Farm Creek	0	4	Ball				
		Parked by road—saw orange-red ball go up into Farm Creek.	Mrs. Dick Hackford, children	0	4	Ball				
		Driving truck up road. Hovered over him.	Dick Hackford, Farm Creek	0	1	Round ball 0				

No.	Date	Event, Including Size and Shape	Name of one Witness and Location	Sound	Number of Witnesses	Shape**	Time	Day	Night	Estimated distance
		Saw light in SW. Hovered a moment and then flew rapidly up into sky. Daughter saw it on her way home.	David Rasmussen + 3 adults—all at phosphate plant, N of Vernal	0	4	Round or oval, "larger than any star"				
53A	Oct. 12, 1967	Luminous figure in home. Standing in doorway, metal suit, luminous glow, turned and walked out.	Jay Anderson, White Rocks		1		3:00		X	
54.	Oct. 17, 1967	Large orange ball hovered over corral. In a few minutes, joined by a second one. Left together to the east and out of sight.	Sandy and LaJean Richman, at home in Roosevelt	0	2	Ball of light 0	22:00		X	50 yards
55.	Oct. 18, 1967	Oval, shiny, silver. Large, no wings. Stopped truck for better look. Gone by the time he had the truck stopped.	Norman Shelley, Junction of White Rocks & Lapoint Road	0	1	Oval 0	17:20	X		3 miles

No.	Date	Event, Including Size and Shape	Name of one Witness and Location	Sound	Number of Witnesses	Shape**	Time	Day	Night	Estimated distance
56.	Oct. 18, 1967	Saw airplanes, then object coming toward them. Brother-in-law a ways away also saw. Was disc, turned so that they could see profile. Followed plane west into the sun—"just disappeared." Top looked like glass dome—both coming and in profile.	Lori Ann Gardner, ~mile W of West Junior High	0	3	Convex plane +	17:20 sunset	X		2 or 3 miles West
57.	Oct. 25, 1967	Orange, round, very large ball, moved east toward Vernal, very fast. Jet came in few minutes—could hear it although much higher.	Beth Reynolds, Roosevelt, Utah	0	1	Round 0	21:30		X	Low altitude
58.	Nov. 20, 1967	Pulsating, rotating lights: green, red, amber. Shadowy round area below lights. Slow, then very fast. Watched with night binoculars—could see no shape of plane. Made several maneuvers.	Dave Roberts, east side of Roosevelt	0	1	Round with lights 0	22:00		X	100 yards
59.	Jan. 23, 1968	Blue, slowly moving. Then red and very fast! Maneuvered over mountains.	Bonnie Chapman, 5 miles from White Rocks	0	1	Half dome? 0	ca. 22:00		X	Way far

No.	Date	Event, Including Size and Shape	Name of one Witness and Location	Sound	Number of Witnesses	Shape**	Time	Day	Night	Estimated distance
60.	Feb. 1, 1968	Ball of light, reddish-orange, much larger than biggest star. Moved rapidly, blinked on and off. Disappeared in the south.	Earl Allred, Jack Barton, 6 miles W of Vernal in the "twists"	0	2	Round 0	20:15		X	
61.	Feb. 12, 1968	Green then turned red, large. Near the ground, then left rapidly, maneuvered.	Selma Christiansen, Farm Creek Hill W of Ranger Station		1	Round 0	?		X	0.5 mile
62.	Mar. 1, 1968	Large, pulsating left to right, red, moving from Roosevelt rapidly	Kenneth Hardy and wife, NW area		2	Round 0	21:00		X	
63.	Mar. 2, 1968	Through binoculars, she and a group saw it maneuver—round and shiny silver object.	Sandra Wardle, Randlett	0	3+	Round 0	-	X		?
64.	Mar. 3, 1968	"Observed a UFO in the sky."	Mrs. Oberhausly reported: Gerald Mitchell, White Rocks	1	1	? 0	9:00	X		?

No.	Date	Event, Including Size and Shape	Name of one Witness and Location	Sound	Number of Witnesses	Shape**	Time	Day	Night	Estimated distance
65.	Mar. 4, 1968	On the ground, large (20'), reddish; watched for ~hour, light suddenly went out.	William Taylor, Lapoint		1	Round 0	19:30		X	~mile
66.	Mar. 21, 1968	Hovered over house in White Rocks for a few minutes.	Henry Wopsock, White Rocks		1	Half-dome 0			X	?
67.	May 21, 1968	Oval, quite large, shining silver, changed speed. Maneuvered, hovered, dropped near the ground. Students had just come into English class, one noticed it out window—others and teacher came and watched 7–8 minutes.	Carma Winterton and 21 Union High School students, east Roosevelt—toward Roosevelt hilltop		22	Oval 0	8:50	X		2–3 miles
68.	Sep 23, 1968	In bed, looking out window. Steady red light, moved at speed of plane.	Vern Ballease, 6 miles east of Roosevelt, highway	Hum	1	Double convex, flatter on bottom. Red lights on top. 0	22:00		X	In sky, 30 degrees

No.	Date	Event, Including Size and Shape	Name of one Witness and Location	Sound	Number of Witnesses	Shape**	Time	Day	Night	Estimated distance
69.	Oct. 15, 1968	Out to check on an animal, saw object coming down to land in the south. Saw for five minutes. Size of school bus. White light on top, green and purple, round edges.	Steve Sisson, Pelican Lake	0	1	Double convex 0	20:45		X	1.5 miles
70A	Oct. 16, 1968	Family watched silver UFO with red dots out window; observed with field glasses, moved to southwest.	Becky Dow, Randlett	0	4	Oval, round 0	8:00	X		0.5 mile
70B	Oct. 16, 1968	Getting out of car to go to school, saw yellow, silver, shiny object in sky.	Independence			Convex 0	8:00	X		1–1.5 mile
70C	Oct. 16, 1968	Saw a silver UFO.	Roger Betts, Independence	0	1	Round 0	8:00	X		7 miles
70D	Oct. 16, 1968	Saw a silver UFO on way to school.	JoAnn Sixkiller, south of Todd School	0	1	Cigar-shaped 0	8:05	X		
70E	Oct. 16, 1968	Saw a silver UFO on way to school.	Donna Davis, west of West Jr. High	0	1	Oval 0	8:25	X		5 miles

No.	Date	Event, Including Size and Shape	Name of one Witness and Location	Sound	Number of Witnesses	Shape**	Time	Day	Night	Estimated distance
71.	Nov. 14, 1968	Hunting geese, thought saw weather balloon with "string" hanging below—thought it was close and drove to go get it. Stopped often to observe with binoculars. When got close, hanging "tube" appeared much thicker—3 to 4 ft. diameter all the way up. Silver at first, then became dark. Had light on top and bottom (white to yellowish). Tube seemed to be spinning, swirl of dust at bottom. Sucked up tube rapidly, then "disappeared." Hanging tube was arched.	Morlin Buchanan, Richard Faucett, Pelican Lake to Randlett	0	2	Spherical, hanging "tube" 0	16:30 to 17:00		X	4 miles to 200 yards.
72.	Nov. 29, 1968	Driving home from Vernal, saw 3 objects, silver colored. Three more came. One moved, flashed red light, disappeared. Two came and joined the formation, and then another. Two flashed red lights. One flashed red and disappeared. Dark ones were convex plane; bright one appeared as ball of light.	Renae Chasel, and Paula Bell, Halfway Hollow	0	2	Convex plane 0 Ball of light also	Sundown	X		~mile

No.	Date	Event, Including Size and Shape	Name of one Witness and Location	Sound	Number of Witnesses	Shape**	Time	Day	Night	Estimated distance
73.	Dec. 2, 1968	Driving home, turned north toward White Rocks. Saw large red, blinking light on ground near river. Suddenly took off in a red blue, like a falling star in reverse—very fast. Made an arc and stopped above witnesses, blinking its light. Looked at horses crossing road, when looked back, object was gone.	Ann Bolton Zufelt, and Janet Hunt, Uintah River bottom, north of Fort Duchesne	0	2	0	22:30		X	1 or 2 miles
74.	About June 7, 1970	Driving around a sharp curve when UFO came across lake and almost collided with car—veered away sharply. Many colors, mostly green. Moving with apex of triangle to front, two "exhaust" jets out back. Points rounded, base cordate.	Earl Manning and 3 boys, Towarie Reservoir (42 miles south of Ouray)	Beep	4	Triangular 0	Midnight		X	20 yards

No.	Date	Event, Including Size and Shape	Name of one Witness and Location	Sound	Number of Witnesses	Shape**	Time	Day	Night	Estimated distance
75.	Sept. 4, 1970	Riding horses—saw object in the hills to the west. It was red, egg-shaped, distinct edges but soft halo of light (indistinct dome of light) above. Lit up sky and ground for half mile on each side (trees as easy to see as in daylight). Fan arrangement of red rays came out of bottom—much brighter than object. Where rays struck ground, caused great clouds of dust or smoke to boil up almost halfway to object. Ran horses home; object disappeared as it was out of sight behind trees, but halo, rays, and dust remained. Halo dropped to ground, became smaller, finally dimmed out. Saw a car—people saw halo but not the object. (Dee Hullinger and wife) saw halo but not the object.	Leland Mecham and son, 2 miles west of Roosevelt	0	2	Egg-shaped 0	22:00		X	1–1.5 miles
76.	Sept. 14–15, 1970	In bed, saw light flashing different colors out window. Saw object approaching, got fairly close, then went up with great speed. Red on top, blue, orange, green around bottom rim.	Earl Miller and two foster brothers, Native American Bench	Hum	3	Half-dome, flat rim on bottom (convex plane) 0	23:30 to midnight		X	3 or 4 blocks

No.	Date	Event, Including Size and Shape	Name of one Witness and Location	Sound	Number of Witnesses	Shape**	Time	Day	Night	Estimated distance
77.	Dec. 5, 1970	Sent seven-year-old boy out to shut gate—ran in telling of flying saucer. Saw two objects to east over tower, one closer. Watched with binoculars. Silver dome, colored lights around rim of flat bottom. Both maneuvered for an hour—flat part was horizontal, then vertical—sometimes facing them so it looked round. Finally climbed vertically until they looked like stars—then disappeared.	Lynn Hall family and neighbors, Fort Duchesne	0	15	Convex plane 0	19:00 to 20:00		X	ca. 2 miles
78.	Christmastime, 1970	Watched "star" for a while; it approached rapidly, resolved into a red, green, and white light. Followed home, including two sharp turns. Witnessed by parents (white light only).	David Martin, Ruth Martin, Walter J. Martin, Crescent Road	0	3	Convex plane (tri-angular) 0	1:30		X	200 yards
79.	Sept. 20, 1971	Two boys saw UFO with dome, green, red, and blue lights around bottom edge. Large object.	Michael Wardle, Fort Duchesne, Funny sounds		2	Convex plane 0	21:00		X	900 feet

No.	Date	Event, Including Size and Shape	Name of one Witness and Location	Sound	Number of Witnesses	Shape**	Time	Day	Night	Estimated distance
80.	Feb. 10, 1972	Saw object moving from north to south, passing overhead. Hovered over field, tried to call Junior Hicks (not home). Object remained 10–15 minutes then moved north again.	Allan Clanton, Mary Carol Murray, Connie LaRose, West Junior High, Fort Duchesne	0	3	Dome 0	19:30 or 20:00		X	1000 feet to 1 mile

About the Author

Frank Boyer Salisbury grew up in Springville and Salt Lake City, Utah. After a year in the Army Air Force, he served as a missionary in Switzerland. As a teenager, he led hikes and taught nature and crafts at two scout camps, where he began a lifelong fascination with biology in general and botany in particular—as well as with all the physical sciences.

After earning bachelor's and master's degrees in botany and biochemistry at the University of Utah, he earned his doctorate in plant physiology and geochemistry in 1955 at the California Institute of Technology. After teaching ecology, general biology, and other subjects at Pomona College for one year, he spent eleven years at Colorado State University before moving in 1966 to Utah State University to become the department head of the newly organized Plant Science Department in the College of Agriculture. He resigned as department head after four years to spend more time writing, continuing at Utah State for a total of thirty-one years.

He has written or cowritten sixteen books, including a basic textbook in plant physiology that went through four editions and was translated into several languages. His research projects have involved the physiology of flowering, plant growth under snow, plant growth in controlled environments (to provide food and oxygen for astronauts), and plant responses to gravity. He led a project that grew wheat in the Russian space station Mir. He spent sabbaticals in Germany, Austria, and Israel (at the Hebrew University of Jerusalem). He also took a leave of absence for a year with the Atomic Energy Commission (now the Department of Energy).

Frank retired in 1997, and with his present wife, Mary Thorpe, served in the Ohio Columbus Mission for the Church of Jesus Christ of Latter-day Saints. The couple then returned to live in Salt Lake City, where Frank has since been working on writing projects. He and his former wife, L. Marilyn Olson, are the parents of seven children.

CPSIA information can be obtained
at www.ICGtesting.com
Printed in the USA
BVHW060044260321
603416BV00002B/102